Advertising
Pure and Simple

THE NEW EDITION

Advertising Pure and Simple

THE NEW EDITION

Hank Seiden

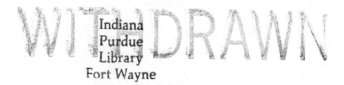

AMERICAN MANAGEMENT ASSOCIATION

This publication is designed to provide accurate and authoritative information in regard to the subject matter covered. It is sold with the understanding that the publisher is not engaged in rendering legal, accounting, or other professional service. If legal advice or other expert assistance is required, the services of a competent professional person should be sought.

Library of Congress Cataloging-in-Publication Data

Seiden, Hank.
 Advertising pure and simple / Hank Seiden. —New ed.
  p. cm.
 Includes index.
 ISBN 0–8144–5981–1
 1. Advertising. 2. Television advertising. I. Title.
HF5823.S42 1990
659.1—dc20
               90–55209
                CIP

Printing number

10 9 8 7 6 5 4 3 2 1

To **Helen**

with a promise to make up for
all the evenings and weekends and movies and
shows and dinners and talks we
missed while I was writing this book.

To **Deborah L. Jacobs**

a wonderful collaborator
a wonderful organizer
a wonderful writer
a wonderful person
who worked with me from the very beginning
of this book and without whom it would
never have been completed.

Contents

Foreword

Hank Seiden has done it again. The first edition of *Advertising Pure and Simple* was acclaimed as one of the most straightforward and demythologizing treatises ever published on advertising. Al Hampel, then Director of Creative Services for Benton & Bowles, said, "It is a book I wish I had when I was getting started. A place to learn what advertising is, and maybe even more importantly, what it isn't."

The business and the practice of advertising have seen dramatic changes since then. This new, improved version of Seiden's book recognizes these changes but, more importantly, celebrates the eternal verities of our craft.

Seiden still believes, for instance, that the product is invariably the hero in great advertising. That's one reason he speaks so persuasively on the power of demonstration.

Can you imagine? Seiden believes that the advertisement should sell, not just titillate. That if it isn't designed to kill the competition, it's not really advertising. He believes in advertising pure and simple, not in show biz, not in obfuscation, not in tricks, mirrors, smoke, and extravagance. Above all, not in extravagance.

It is difficult for me not to think of this book as *the* basic advertising text. It is almost painfully basic. But isn't that how we'd like tomorrow's practitioners to learn? Isn't that what we'd like more of today's award seekers to think of occasionally? His reasoning is so pure, so fundamentally rooted in human nature and behavior, that it is almost impossible to put down (as is the book).

Hank Seiden believes in advertising as cabinetmakers believe in walnut. He loves it, respects it, and hates to see it abused. Like

Bill Bernbach, he believes that the surest way to bring down a bad product is to advertise it well. Like Rosser Reeves, he believes that an advertisement without a central, clear, and winning proposition is lost effort and wasted client money.

Hank does yank us back to the verities: that advertising should respect the people it addresses; that advertising doesn't make customers . . . only the product does. He believes infinitely in the ability of creative imagination to light up an advertisement and to take a good product to greatness. But he believes equally in creative discipline and the importance of strategy.

Perhaps the highlight of this new version of *Advertising Pure and Simple* is the chapter on Seiden's brainchild, The Spectrum Analysis. Like all worthy creations, its beauty is its utter simplicity. Upon a platform of three little words—Who, What, and How—Seiden describes and diagrams a simple, foolproof methodology to assure that the strategy is fundamentally right, that the target is properly defined, and that the executional possibilities to be considered or imagined fit the product and the audience. This chapter alone justifies the book's existence.

No one will agree with everything Hank Seiden says, including me. But how refreshing it is for a true professional to put forth his convictions without shading, blunting, or mincing. We need more of this.

Some will say Seiden's book is old-fashioned. They are wrong, unequivocally wrong. This is a book about the permanent truths of our business, and it will be sage and sensible and right in the waning years of the twenty-first century, too.

William H. Genge
Chairman and Chief Executive Officer
Ketchum Communications, Inc.

Acknowledgments

There's more to putting a book like this together than meets the eye. There are more people who helped put it together than I can ever repay. First of all, every book needs an advocate—someone, the only one, who knows where every part of it is every step of the way and somehow miraculously pulls it all together at the end. I owe much to Karen Welsh for being this book's staunch advocate; I will feel indebted to her until the last copy of this book disappears forever.

The single biggest task that had to be completed before anything else could be done was the mammoth job of collecting the hundreds of commercials and print ads to be used as examples throughout the book. It took months of watching TV and taking notes. It took thumbing through hundreds of magazines and clipping ads. It took sorting, cataloguing, and classifying the advertisements into categories. I am grateful for the help of the following people in providing the raw material for this book: From Ketchum, New York—Jean Bass, Leslie Bock, Frank Carbone, Melanie Lester, Hilary Snell. From Ketchum, Philadelphia—Becky Burek, Lucy Erdelac, Susan McKenna. From Ketchum, Pittsburgh—Lynn Charles Bunting. From Ketchum, San Francisco—Dianne Snedaker, John Faville, Dorothy Kaiser, Kelley McGrath, Greg Montana.

After the selections were made, the actual commercials had to be viewed for accurate reviewing. I thank DeWitt Mallary of Video Monitoring Services (VMS) of America and his staff, Harriet McIntosh, Steve Shorten, and Edie Thomas, for supplying photoboards and cassettes of everything we needed—and for doing it pro bono as a contribution to the industry. I will never forget their generosity. And thanks to Margaret Shiverick and the AdBank research staff, whose vast knowledge of TV commercials helped us select additional commercials for review.

My thanks to the following people at rival, but friendly, agencies who were so cooperative in supplying us with commercials and print ads from their agencies: Sandy Birko and William Mattes (DDB Needham Worldwide), Kim Trimmer (Jordan, McGrath, Case & Taylor), Ernie Roth (Furman Roth), Ole Riise (Ogilvy & Mather), Joseph Rodriguez (Dailey & Associates), Susan Swartz (Leo Burnett Co.), Bill Keeshon and Donna Loitus (Della Femina, McNamee WCRS), Kim Shroyer (N. W. Ayer), Michael O'Bren (DMB&B), Nancy Budd (Chiat/Day, Los Angeles).

Special thanks to Jim McHugh and Peter Cascone, both of Ketchum, New York, for their help with the print and TV production chapters respectively. Thanks also to Karen McIver, Judy Lotas, and Joanna Patton, all of Lotas, Minard, Patton and McIver, as well as to Joy Golden of Joy Radio for their suggestions on the woman's chapter. Also to Gerry Shoenfeld of Shoenfeld, Chapman & Pearl for his contribution to the chapter on introducing a new product. My gratitude to Dick Guiterman for volunteering his masterful command of the English language and his valuable time to read the manuscript and to make invaluable suggestions. And to Tim Campbell of Ketchum, New York, for his creative contributions to the book jacket.

For their help with the word processing, I thank Jennifer Bancks, DeLisle Callender, and Stephanie Karayeanes. And, for the thankless job of proofreading, I primarily thank Ann Perez, and, in addition, Stephanie Karayeanes, Brooke LeBaron, Karen O'Brien, Rosemary O'Toole, Ruby Tam, and Helen Seiden.

And, lastly, my thanks to Adrienne Hickey, my editor at AMACOM, who made very few suggestions, but each one made this a better book, and for her original suggestion that I do this book in the first place.

Advertising
Pure and Simple

THE NEW EDITION

Introduction

"When you take away the exposés, the psychology, the personalities, the textbooks, and the rules, what have you got left? This book!"

I wrote the words above in the last chapter of the first edition of *Advertising Pure and Simple,* published in 1976. I wrote them in good conscience, thinking I had just rid the world of lousy advertising. I felt that everybody who read the book would know everything there was to know about creating good advertising and that bad advertising would be banished from the face of the earth forever. Was I mistaken!

Just recently, for example, twenty devastating events scared the heck out of me and convinced me to write a new edition of the book. I'll begin this new edition with the events that caused me to write it:

• *Event 1:* A prospective client insisted that the answer to all his marketing woes was funny and/or musical radio commercials. I tried to explain that although radio was a perfectly good medium (though admittedly not my favorite), it was wrong for him because his product was relatively new and unknown, and it would be nice if the consumer knew what package to look for in the supermarket.

1

Also, his product was one of those rare few with a visual demonstrable difference, and not to show it would be a crime. For these reasons, I pleaded, he really should be on television.

I also told him that humor and music would be incompatible with the nature of his product difference and in conflict with the seriousness of his message, which concerns health and nutrition. In addition, his giant competitor was using musical radio spots.

I closed the meeting by digging in my heels and insisting that under no circumstances would I give him funny or musical radio commercials.

I didn't get the business. What scares me is that some other agency did.

What scares me even more is that I've just heard his musical radio spots.

- *Event 2:* A "famous" adman in a *Wall Street Journal* ad featuring him is quoted as saying, "The idea is to create ads that make people say, 'Wow, I love that ad!' "

Well, Mr. Famous Adman, I've got news for you. The idea is *not* to create ads that make people say, "Wow, I love that *ad!*" The idea is to make people say, "Wow, I love that *product!*"

The adman goes on a little further regarding the effectiveness of an ad: "Just ask these questions: Does the ad ring true? Does it break through? Will it make someone like you?"

There's just one little, unimportant question he neglected to ask: Will it sell the product?

Articles like these from self-proclaimed experts in the field scare me.

- *Event 3:* An associate of mine in account service told me about the great new commercial he had just seen for a traveler's check (interesting that he couldn't recall which one, except that it wasn't American Express) featuring a white horse galloping along a beach.

I asked him what a horse had to do with traveler's checks, and he couldn't tell me. I asked him what unique advantage these traveler's checks had over all others, and he couldn't tell me. I asked him what reason they gave him for switching from American Express Cheques (the kind he usually bought) to theirs, and he couldn't tell me. Finally, I asked him if he would buy these traveler's checks the next time he traveled, and this he *could* finally tell me. His answer was "no."

Yet he, a professional, still thinks it was a terrific commercial. That scares me.

• *Event 4:* A young product manager I work with lauded a commercial (not one of mine) for its "production values" but never once noticed that it had absolutely no redeeming "idea value" at all.

How anyone can reach that level of approving advertising and not yet understand that ideas, not production values, sell products scares me.

• *Event 5:* An older, more experienced client (someone else's, thank goodness) told me that all advertising is the same and what he looked for primarily in his advertising were executional devices that "break the clutter." How can a man spend so many years in the business without understanding that the best clutter breaker of all is a unique promise that fulfills an unfulfilled human need?

The use of devices instead of consumer needs to break clutter scares me.

• *Event 6:* The president of a medium-size advertising agency told me that all products are the same and the only way a consumer can distinguish one from the other is by the uniqueness of their advertising executions.

I still maintain there are fewer parity products than there are parity advertising agencies. Every product is created different from every other product, just as God created every human being different from every other human being, which we would readily discover if we took the time and effort to get to know them.

That "parity products" have become the biggest cop-out for parity advertising scares me.

• *Event 7:* A well-known marketing professor in a well-known graduate school of business asked me at a lecture if I believed in competitive advertising. To me, that's a redundancy.

All advertising must be competitive by my definition. All products exist in a competitive environment and are competing for conquest sales. The more competitive/comparative the advertising, the more successful it will be. If it's not competitive, it's not advertising.

The fact that this question has become the most frequently asked of me by teachers and students of advertising scares me.

• *Event 8:* The second most frequently asked question is what do I think about the "slice-of-life" format long associated with the success of Procter & Gamble advertising.

An executive vice-president of marketing of a large advertiser told me that he would never approve a commercial that wasn't slice-of-life, and an art director in my own agency told me he would rather quit than do one.

They're both wrong because neither understands "slice-of-life." To me, "slice-of-life" is irrelevant—it's just another executional format. It receives more credit—and blame—than it deserves.

It isn't "slice-of-life" that makes P&G advertising so successful; it's the comparative side-by-side demonstrations that are included within the format. Any format, so long as it does not detract from the believability of the demonstration, would do as well.

That professionals—clients and agency people alike—can't see the forest for the trees scares me.

• *Events 9, 10, and 11:* The presenter for a leading copy-testing research company told us and our client not to run a particular commercial because it scored below his norms, when unbeknownst to him the commercial had been running in four test markets and was breaking the bank.

Another copy-testing company not only told us our commercial was terrible but had the arrogance to show someone else's commercial to us and our client to demonstrate how it should have been done (*it* was an awful commercial).

A new client introducing a new product abandoned a superb introductory commercial in favor of a more pedestrian "real people, hidden camera" one based on the crude, inconclusive, nonprojectable results of a test that could not be duplicated. There were ideal quotes written into the test version that would never be uttered in a real-life filming situation.

Copy-testing research companies scare me. Clients who accept their scores as absolute gospel scare me even more.

• *Events 12 and 13:* A client researched and introduced a new product that the agency warned had no reason for being. It failed. The client blamed the advertising for the failure.

Another client ran a commercial that tested better than the agency's recommended commercial. It too failed. The client blamed the agency for the failure.

Clients who don't take their agencies' advice and then blame the agencies for their own failures scare me.

• *Event 14:* A cosmetics company with a unique product, unique positioning, unique copy, and a unique look recently switched to another agency that would make its advertising look more like cosmetics advertising.

Advertisers with unique products who are uncomfortable with their uniqueness scare me.

• *Events 15 and 16:* The reason given for two recent huge account switches was personal friendship. In both cases the losing agencies had done magnificent advertising.

The resurgence of cronyism scares me.

• *Event 17:* As I listen to radio commercials, I'm struck by their similarities. It seems the same comedy teams (or comedy writers), using the same format, are writing all the commercials.

Agencies who allow comedians or comedy writers to write their commercials scare me.

• *Event 18:* I asked a young copywriter if he knew who Rosser Reeves was and what he stood for . . . and he couldn't tell me.

• *Event 19:* The British are buying up our ad agencies. (Among the most important to fall were the highest and mightiest of them all, J. Walter Thompson and Ogilvy & Mather, both gobbled up by a fly-by-night British shell company barely one-tenth their size with the inelegant monicker of Worldwide Plastic Products—WPP.) What worries me is the implication that somehow the English conquest of American agencies was a result of superior advertising. The English takeover has nothing whatsoever to do with advertising. It has to do with money. The British are coming for two simple reasons: The London Stock Exchange values ad agencies at a three times higher multiple than do ours, and British tax law, unlike ours, allows acquirers to write off goodwill. But good multiples and goodwill do not necessarily make for good advertising.

▪ *Event 20:* American advertising is emulating British advertising. The British, self-admittedly, don't believe in the power of advertising. They believe in the power of the pun. Most British advertising is merely a platform for puns and production technique. "If it ain't clever or funny, it ain't good" seems to be their credo. I don't find that either funny *or* good. I find that to be the scariest event of them all.

For all these reasons, I wrote this new edition of *Advertising Pure and Simple.*

I wrote it as a matter of conscience.

I wrote it to honor those who went before us in advertising and blazed the trail for us to follow.

I wrote it to encourage those in advertising today who are making the trail even clearer.

I wrote it to inspire those who will follow us into advertising and blaze new trails from the old.

I wrote it to enlighten teachers of advertising who will lead a bright new generation to where the trail begins.

I wrote it to guide those poor souls who have lost their way in advertising back onto the straight and narrow.

I wrote it to embolden clients, big and small, charged with the responsibility of advertising approval, to reject what's bad, demand what's good, and defend the difference between the two.

I wrote it to open the minds of those who have a negative impression of advertising as a result of misinformation.

I wrote it to clarify what the business is all about to people who have no connection with advertising except as interested targets of it.

But mostly I wrote it because I care deeply about this business and want to see the kind of advertising that makes me feel proud I chose to spend my life in it. In this selfish pursuit I will speak my mind about ads and commercials, separate the good from the bad, the silly from the valid, and let the chips fall where they may.

1

The Pure and Simple
School of Advertising

For my money, the only school of advertising worth the price of tuition is the Pure and Simple school. Admittedly, it's not very fashionable. It's not terribly chic to admit you're a graduate. Its alumni aren't famous enough to be invited to the industry's better social gatherings or awards dinners. But I'm a believer, and I just couldn't feel at home in the fancier, snobbier, more sophisticated schools. They're not my style. And I suspect they're not even very good.

The essential lesson taught by the Pure and Simple school is that advertising must have something to say. Beyond that, what it has to say is all-important. Finally, advertising should say it straight, plain, and simple. It's a straightforward credo and one that's particularly applicable to the medium of television, where so many temptations are available to distract from the message.

I love to see one simple objective for a campaign established, and I like to see it tackled head-on. I have no patience for subtlety, finesse, deviousness, velvet gloves, and syrupy tongues. I hate hidden meanings. (I never understand them anyway. In movies or plays or books, my wife has to explain all the hidden meanings to me later.) Like most people, I take everything at face value because I don't like to spend time and effort figuring out what some-

7

body really meant. Why not just say it? Life is too short and time too precious—especially TV time—for advertisers to beat around the bush.

So I'm generally against any kind of advertising that relegates the product to a secondary position or treats it as anything less than the hero of the commercial.

"But how can the product be the hero of the commercial? Most products today are parity products, so the difference has to be in the advertising." How many times have you heard that? Every time I hear it I shake with rage. People who believe that don't know the first thing about advertising or what it's supposed to do in a competitive environment.

Clients come to agencies to "un-parity" their products—to convince people who are now using a competitive brand to switch to theirs. That's what advertising is all about. That's supposed to be what we get paid to do. And I don't mean to convince people with a silly, superficial, meaningless feature. I have too much respect for the buying intelligence of consumers for that.

I'm talking about finding a meaningful, inherent, or preemptive unique benefit that fulfills a consumer need. It can be in the product, in the dispenser, in the packaging, in the distribution, in the positioning, in the name, in the guarantee, in the company, in the price.

It's out there somewhere, and it's your job to find it. It may not be easy. You'll have to dig for it—at the factory, from the consumer, within yourself. But it's critical that you find it because what you're looking for is the product's very reason for being.

If *you* don't know why there's a need for the product, how can you convince others to buy it? And the reason to buy it cannot be the advertising. People don't buy advertising, they buy products. If you don't believe it, then the role of advertising is reduced to merely execution, and Hollywood executioners are better at it than we are.

If all products were born with breakthrough differences, there would be no need for advertising agencies. Fortunately, most products appear to be created equal, and agencies are needed to find the differences.

The day I believe that the difference in products is in their advertising is the day that I leave advertising. I believe instead that there's no such thing as a parity product, only parity advertising agencies and parity adpeople.

These are the teachings of the Pure and Simple school, and I believe them even more today than I did when I wrote the first edition of this book. I will always believe them because the principles of advertising will never change so long as human nature never changes, and human nature never does change. People's basic needs, wants, and desires will remain the same as long as there are people. Only the trappings, the superficial things of life are constantly changing: music, art, language, food, fashion, style, entertainment, life-style.

So I have changed the trappings for the new edition of this book, incorporating more modern examples of the best and worst commercials I see nightly on TV. I have included a chapter on selling to a mature audience, because today people over 50 are a fast-growing segment of the population. I have included a chapter on The Spectrum Analysis®, a strategic methodology I have developed over many years and proven since the first book. The Spectrum Analysis has helped me solve difficult marketing problems by forcing me back to basics. I hope it helps you as much as it has me.

———

Many people, laymen as well as a surprising number of professionals, get their information about advertising largely from books. Some of the books are good. Some bad. Some are useful. Some entertaining. Some misleading. Some even distorting. Many thoughtful books have been written on the subject, each colored, of course, by the author's field of expertise, experience, and point of view, just as this book is. I agree with some and disagree with others. Here are the books I most agree with:

The best book I have ever read on advertising, and the one that has had the greatest influence on me, is Rosser Reeves's book, *Reality in Advertising*, published in 1961. Perhaps the most pragmatic advertising thinker of our time, Reeves objected to advertising that placed undue emphasis on execution and winning awards to the exclusion of concept. He was known somewhat derogatorily and very unfairly on Madison Avenue as a stifler of creativity and the father of the hard sell. In fact, Reeves was the father of the *smart* sell. His Unique Selling Proposition (USP) theory is the basis for all smart advertising, hard or soft. With it you can't possibly have a dumb ad, no matter how poorly executed. Without it you can't possibly have a smart one, no matter how creative. Contrary to popular belief, the USP and a creative execution are not mutually exclusive. On the contrary, an arresting execution can enhance the communication of the USP. Together, they can make a great ad.

If I were asked to recommend only one book on advertising, *Reality in Advertising* would be the one.

After the first edition of *Advertising Pure and Simple* appeared, I got a phone call from Rosser Reeves. He told me how much he admired my book and invited me to lunch. I had seen him only once in my life, many years before, but he looked the way I remembered him. Heavy of jowls, heavily bearded with a five o'clock shadow that hung around all day, Reeves was heavily built, with a gravelly voice from a lifetime of heavy cigarette smoking. Nothing about Rosser Reeves was subtle. Not his face. Not his size. Not his sound. Not his presence. Not his manner. And certainly not his advertising.

Many years earlier when I was a bright-eyed young creative just entering advertising, my heroes were Bill Bernbach and David Ogilvy, of course. The archenemy of all creatives was Rosser Reeves. I abhorred what he preached and ridiculed everything he stood for. I neither believed what he said, liked the advertising he was doing, nor even bothered to read his book, *Reality in Advertising,* for fear of contamination.

Over the years I formed my own theories about advertising. What surprised me when I met Reeves for lunch and we discussed our philosophies was that I had come to many of the same conclusions entirely independently. Rosser Reeves had been right all along. It took me a lifetime in advertising to realize that he preached the unpopular truth, that this much-maligned zealot understood the business right down to its roots, that I agreed with him much more than I did with the heroes of my youth, and that Rosser Reeves, not Bill Bernbach or David Ogilvy, for all their considerable talents, was the conceptual genius of the business.

At the end of our lunch, which extended into the evening, Rosser presented me with an autographed copy of *Reality in Advertising* with an inscription that I will always treasure. We developed a close professional friendship and had many subsequent, challenging lunches together until his death a few years later.

I also recommend *My Life in Advertising* (as well as its predecessor, *Scientific Advertising*) by the legendary Claude Hopkins. Although it was written in 1927, much of its theory is surprisingly relevant today. Hopkins was a brilliant, innovative copywriter, considered by many to be the father of copywriting. And he worked for the old Lord & Thomas advertising agency, considered by many to be the father of the modern advertising agency. I recommend this book to all who are deeply interested in advertising with two cautions: First, it is egotistically autobiographical. Nobody could ever accuse Mr. Hopkins of having been modest. Second, it is dated in practicality. The world has changed dramatically since Mr. Hopkins's day, most notably because of the bright new world of television, today's most potent medium for the delivery of an advertising message.

For a more up-to-date view of advertising, read David Ogilvy's *Ogilvy on Advertising*.

Although these are some of my favorites, I don't think much of most books about advertising. Unfortunately, the world has gotten its impressions of the advertising business and advertising people from these books, as well as from movies, television, and a few self-appointed experts in and out of the field. These impressions are probably all wrong.

———

The advertising business is a tough, demanding taskmaster. The people who labor in it are, for the most part, honest, hardworking, dedicated people who work longer hours under more pressure than almost any other group I know. They've got to be able to work hard because they're in a service business that can lay claim to no tangible product. No factories. No machines. No inventory. Someone once said that an ad agency's inventory goes up and down the elevators twice a day. All we have are people—and their ideas. The people (particularly the creative people) are un-usually socially conscious, and they take great pride in the quality of their work. Although the pressure and competition are killing, I have never in my career (contrary to popular belief) worked with an alcoholic. And, believe it or not, I know of no one suffer-ing from ulcers, although I know a few clients who do, which may or may not be coincidental.

The people who work in advertising represent the best from all sections of the country, from all countries of the world, from all schools, and from all social strata. Those from higher-income backgrounds, from the midwestern states, and from white Anglo-Saxon Protestant origins seem to wind up in account-handling capacities, while those from the inner-city minority groups find their way into the creative departments. That's a generalization, of course, but an interesting side note. To generalize still further, I find that advertising people—the good ones, anyway—have two traits in common. The first is their intelligence. The second is the unique way in which they approach a problem.

Advertising people tend to simplify problems. I'll prove that right now by stating that there are basically two kinds of people in the world: the Complicators and the Simplifiers. Complicators have wonderfully analytical minds. They're inquisitive. They see ramifications of problems that nobody else sees, endless variations on a single theme. To them, simple problems become, of neces-sity, complex. They make great scientists. And lousy advertising people. Simplifiers, on the other hand, have the uncanny ability to grasp a Byzantine tapestry of problems and unrelated facts and come out with the one simple, salient point that links the whole mess together. Simplifiers make lousy scientists but great creative people because they know how to isolate that one most important appeal or feature—and how to communicate it simply. Most good advertising people, on the account and creative sides, solve prob-lems simply.

Aside from their ability to simplify, creative people are just like anyone else, with the same strengths and faults as all of us. With one more exception.

Talent.

All right, you ask, who *doesn't* have talent? Everyone can write. Everyone has some artistic sense. So everyone is convinced that he or she knows all about advertising and can turn out better commercials than the "junk" on television, right? I don't think there's an ad agency in the world that hasn't, over the years, received a deluge of mail from nonprofessionals criticizing its commercials and offering "million-dollar ideas" for future commercials. Quite aside from the fact that it takes time to answer these letters and that the legal implications relating to unsolicited ideas are labyrinthine, I have never, in all my years in this business, received or heard about anyone else receiving an idea from a nonprofessional that could be used. Yet people persist in believing that they can dream up an idea that a battery of creative, trained, talented professionals didn't think of dozens of times and discard. They're not aware of the marketing strategy, the creative objectives, or even the problem. But that doesn't stop them. The letters keep coming. And with each letter comes the conviction that they can create better advertising than the professionals. They're wrong. I hope this book will show them why.

2

Advertising: A Realistic Perspective

Incredible as it sounds, after a business lifetime of learning, creating, supervising, and writing about it, I really don't believe in advertising. Not as most people conceive of it, anyway.

The popular untruths about advertising are these: It is some weird, mystical science by which a chosen few control the masses. It takes advantage of little-known psychological factors plus the mesmerizing effects of the electronic media to sell us things we don't need and can't afford. It is essentially a refined version of brainwashing that is simultaneously castrating and lobotomizing an otherwise discriminating American public. The way we live, the way we eat, the way we work or relax, even the way we vote can be directly attributed to the enormous power advertising wields. And its potential applications in the future are virtually unlimited.

Nonsense.

The perpetrators of this myth (and it is perpetuated by advertising professionals as well as by laypeople) obviously have a very low regard for the basic intelligence of the public at large. After years of trying to sell what I consider to be sound and useful

14

products, I've seen the public's intelligence at work too many times to deny its existence. And when it comes to an attempt to induce people to part with a buck, I find the Chevy crowd at K-Mart to be one hell of a lot more discriminating about spending their hard-earned cash than the limousine crowd at Tiffany's.

Just to prove the truth of this to adpeople at the outset of their careers, I wish I could force them to do their basic training between these two stores, with refresher courses on an annual basis thereafter. The exercise would go a long way toward destroying the myth of consumer stupidity. Then maybe advertisers would cease to show their contempt for and ignorance of the very people they're trying to sell. And the real truth about advertising could be told: Far from being the ultimate persuasive weapon in the hands of a creative superstar, advertising power is shaped by and subject to the modifying influence of people power. And that's just as it should be.

I get furious when advertising professionals inaccurately portray the business to young people eager to get into it. In so doing, they often deliberately give the impression that by being clever and glib and "creative," adpeople can sell anything to a dull, dumb, gullible public. Twice now a leading advertising agency has done just that, teasing eager young hopefuls who think they have the stuff to be copywriters.

The agency ran full-page ads in newspapers and trade magazines headlined "Write if you want work." The ads—purportedly a copy test for aspiring copywriters—contained such requirements as writing a love song about moldy pizza, rancid butter, and flat beer; a "Dialogue in a Dark Alley"; a short welcoming speech, using only visuals and symbols, to describe Central Park to Martians who have just landed; an ad to sell a telephone to a Trappist monk; an ad to make the contents of a can of baked beans sound appetizing; a script for a 30-second TV commercial that would convince millions of viewers to send you a dime each.

What got me so worked up was that the assignment was unrealistic. It perpetuated the myths that advertising is a lot of silly, frivolous nonsense that tries to make lousy products sound good and that copywriters are a bunch of wild kooks with wilder ideas whose job it is to make fools of people. The questions had nothing to do with the real job of a copywriter. The "test" had nothing to do with understanding the real needs and real desires of real people. It had nothing to do with respecting the consumer. It had nothing to do with honesty, sincerity, believability. It had nothing to do with selling a legitimate product in an environment of other legitimate products. In short, it had nothing to do with advertising and what advertising can realistically do.

So what do I believe advertising can do? I believe that *a good practitioner of advertising can convince a logical prospect for a product to try it one time.* No more, no less. Read it again and please pay close attention to the words. I chose them very carefully.

Notice that I use the word "convince." Not "badger." Not "cajole," "intimidate," or "fool." To convince requires a rational appeal to another person's intelligence. And we've already verified the existence of intelligence in the buying public.

I said "logical prospect" because advertisers have to learn to be more realistic about their commercial chances than they are at present. A logical prospect is one who is at that moment in time in the market for such a product, has a need for it (or can be shown that he or she has a need), and can afford to buy it. If you haven't got a logical prospect, your product or service just won't move, no matter how brilliant your advertising is. Cigarettes can't be sold to nonsmokers, for example. Someone who just bought a new car last week is not a logical prospect for your new car campaign. You can't sell a mink coat to a woman who can barely afford a cloth one. It takes desire, need, and capital to make a logical prospect, and there aren't as many of them waiting around to be sold on your product as you might think.

I used the word "try" instead of "buy" advisedly. While it's true that, in most cases, a prospect will have to buy a product in order to try it, I prefer the word "try" because a trier is a tester, while the term "buyer" connotes a steady customer. The best that advertising can hope for is to get a trier, and a one-time trier at that. From then on, the product is on its own. One-time triers are either going to like the product better than the one they've been using (in which case some new customers will be made), or they won't like it better and will revert to their old brands. In that case, they're lost as new customers until such time as a new improved product is developed together with advertising that convinces them to give it another try. Until then, advertising has done all it can do. It's convinced someone to try.

Advertising does not make customers. Only products make customers.

━━━━━━

Let's tread water for a moment.

Over the years I've contributed columns to a variety of publications criticizing (and lauding) the commercials I saw daily on my own TV screen. I chose to write about commercials watched at home instead of viewed by invitation in a studio because I wanted to see them in the same environment that a consumer would—with all the distractions of other commercials and programming around them. Also, I believed, and still do, that the only commercials worth reviewing are the ones that run on the air (as opposed to rejects, tests, or commercials done to update creative portfolios). Most of all, I didn't want my reviews to be influenced by knowing which ad agencies created and submitted which commercials. In most cases, I stuck to this rule so well that I didn't know which agency's commercial I had rapped until I received a threatening letter or call from its president. (I've received dozens. I got flowers only once.)

I've reached a lot of conclusions about advertising during the years I have written about it. You learn a lot about what advertising can do when you review hundreds and hundreds of commercials, consciously analyzing each one. But most of all, I learned what advertising *cannot* do.

It can't sell a product to someone who has no basic need for it.
It can't sell a product to someone not in the market for it.
It can't sell a product to someone who can't afford it.
It can't make a satisfied customer.
And it can't save a bad product.

If anything, good advertising is bound to have the opposite effect upon a poor product. It'll put the manufacturer out of business. Why? Because the better the advertising, the more people who will try the product. The more people who try the product, the more people who will reject it. The more who reject it, the faster the product will fold. It sounds like a semantic Rube Goldberg machine, I know, but it's true.

When the product flops, two things are guaranteed to happen. The agency will blame it on the product. The manufacturer will defend the product and attack the advertising. So how can you identify the culprit? By looking at the sales figures, that's how. If the figures indicate a low initial rate of trial followed by a high repeat-purchase pattern among the few who did try, it's clearly a case of good product/bad advertising. The advertising simply wasn't as good as the product. If it had done its job properly and made enough triers, people would have realized the superiority of the product and purchased it again and again. Fire the agency.

But if the opposite is true—if a high initial rate of trial suddenly slacks off into a low repeat-purchase pattern—chances are good that a brilliant advertising campaign failed to rescue a poor product. The advertising was too good for the product. It created so many triers for the lousy product that it put the client out of business. Fire the product.

Consider the original Gablinger's beer, introduced just before the first edition of *Advertising Pure and Simple* appeared. Gablinger's was the first no-carbohydrate beer. It had tremendous appeal and, for the most part, a very good, very dramatic advertising campaign behind it (see Chapter 5). Yet the sales figures indicated a very high initial trial with virtually no repeat purchasers. Why? You had only to taste the beer to understand. All those first-time triers who rushed to try the new no-carbohydrate beer never came back for a second taste.

Now that light beers have captured more of the beer market than Gablinger's could ever have imagined, it's easy to look back and see where Gablinger's beer went wrong. One problem was that the Gablinger product went too far. By completely eliminating carbohydrates, it completely eliminated taste. We now know that one-third fewer calories is enough to satisfy customers looking for a light benefit along with good taste. Gablinger's didn't need to sacrifice taste completely, and sales along with it.

For those of us who remember Gablinger's, the introduction

in 1988 of Premier—the "smokeless" cigarette from R. J. Reynolds Tobacco Co.—was pure déjà vu. In bold print advertising, Premier heralded a full-bodied but safer smoke—a cigarette you smoke by heating tobacco, not burning it. Premier promised a remarkable smoke and implied (so far as government regulations would permit) that its breakthrough cigarette would not produce the dangerous tar and nicotine found in conventional tobacco-burning cigarettes. Like Gablinger's, it promised vice without price.

Seven years in development and marketing, at an estimated cost of $300 million, Premier made the same exciting promise to smokers that Gablinger's made to beer drinkers. Who wouldn't want to try it? But like Gablinger's, the product failed to live up to the advertising. It was difficult to light, smelled terrible, and failed to deliver the satisfying taste promised by its advertising. After five months in test markets, Premier (pardon the pun) went up in smoke. I wonder if, like Gablinger's, Premier will eventually lead to a new category of product—perhaps a new "safer" cigarette. So far, it seems little more than a pipe dream.

Perhaps the best example ever of brilliant advertising that failed to rescue a poor product (or more accurately, an unwanted product) was the campaign for New Coke that broke in 1985. Panicked by The Pepsi Challenge taste test advertising, Coke blundered into the marketing mistake of the century. The New Coke campaign aimed to convince Coke fans that the bubbly brown refreshment they had been drinking and loving all their lives needed updating. With a flood of publicity and blind taste tests in thirteen cities, Coke introduced a sweeter, bolder version expected to convert its following and stem defections to Pepsi.

New Coke attracted a lot of attention, but mostly in the form of protests. Despite two years of market research, Coke had over-looked the fact that diehard drinkers preferred the ninety-nine year old formula to the newfangled version. Whether the old Coke actually tasted better or just had a loyal public, corporate executives finally acknowledged that they, and research I might add, had miscalculated public reaction. Just months after the fanfare introducing New Coke, the company resurrected the classic formula and gave Coke drinkers back the brand they had grown to love.

Which all goes to show that only products make customers. The best that advertising can do is cause reasonable prospects to try. Once. In a nutshell, that's what advertising can and cannot do. Now that we've defined the ground rules, the rest—how to go about creating an ad—is relatively easy.

———

The first step when creating any ad or commercial, is the most critical: Jot down, as two guideposts, what you're trying to say and the audience you're trying to say it to. If you can't compose one or at most two sentences summing up the key point of your ad, then you're simply not cut out to be an ad writer. Go to bartender school. Learn to tap dance. Become an interior decorator. But please get out of the advertising business! The inability to compose these one or two simple sentences has got to be the cause of much of the confused and garbled advertising I see on TV, in magazines, on billboards. Everywhere I look, it seems, I find advertising copywriters or art directors who didn't really know the one point they wanted to make. An ad or commercial must be single-minded. So an attempt to make three or four points is doomed *a priori* to make none of them.

The creative person must be capable of taking a long, unsentimental look at the audience who is to receive the sales message. Let's assume that you, the copywriter, are taking a bead on a married woman. (Though men increasingly do the family shopping, women are still the biggest customers, particularly in the important area of packaged goods.) Let's further assume that she's now using a product in direct competition with the one you want to convince her to try (a logical assumption, by the way, since almost no monopolies exist on the shelves today). Third, she believes for one reason or another that the product she's currently using is the best one she can buy. (Few consumers buy a product because they think it's the worst.) Finally we'll suppose that when she runs out of her current supply of the product, she'll purchase the same brand again, more or less automatically—a phenomenon known in advertising lexicon as "brand loyalty."

Now then. Assuming that you truly know what you want to

say, do you know your audience well enough to say it as convincingly as possible?

Look at her again—closely, this time. Is that really brand loyalty you see shining in her eyes? Or is it actually brand *laziness?* Based upon what we all know about most busy women, it seems safe to say that brand laziness is what causes her to buy the same brand repeatedly. Because if there's anything in this world she doesn't need, it's another conflict—the very thing your advertisement is trying to create in her mind.

Friend, she's gonna resist your ad. Whether or not she works outside the home, she probably has little time for shopping. Anything that prolongs her trip to the store, like niggling doubts about her regular brand, or a temptation to try another, is going to seem about as attractive as cholera. She *knows* she's happy with the product she's using. Her husband is happy with it. Her kids are happy with it. And here comes your damned ad pushing a competitive product ("Try me! I'm better!"), disrupting her complacency, complicating her shopping, and, incidentally, creating a conflict. A minor one, to be sure, but still another irksome conflict.

If your advertising is going to be successful, it had better be strong enough and convincing enough to overcome this brand laziness. That's a tough order, but it can be done with a good, strong "switching" idea, one that promises the prospect some benefit she will derive from using your product instead of her own, something important enough to make her say, "Hey! I've got to try that" the next time she runs out of her current brand. Can you do it? Sure! Because no matter how passionately they deny it, your prospects are influenced by advertising. Mind you, I don't say they are hypnotized or compelled, but influenced they are, no matter what they say.

But people don't always do what they say they'll do. Think about it. The first reason a woman usually cites for having chosen a particular brand is its price. It happened to be on sale, you know, and since all brands are alike anyhow, why not buy the cheapest one? Having said that, Mrs. Consumer feels satisfied that she is the compleat wife, an excellent mother, a thrifty homemaker.

But that *isn't* why she bought that particular brand. She really bought the brand just because *she always has.*

You don't believe me? Then prove it: Try to tell the woman who says that all brands are alike that the toothpaste she buys for her children is destroying their teeth—and then duck. She'll leap to the defense of that brand, reciting every reason she ever heard the advertiser give for buying that particular toothpaste. Even if the brand she bought was truly on sale that week, you can bet it was a well-advertised brand bearing a name she has faith in, be it a national or store brand. You couldn't *give* her that toothpaste if she's never heard of it before. No matter how cheap it is, she won't buy the unadvertised XYZ brand once you have given her a switching idea compelling enough to overcome the few pennies more your product costs.

Go ahead. Give her a switching idea. It's not as hard as you think, because a powerful switching idea is the result of a process so elementary that it's usually overlooked by most adpeople: listening to your prospects.

I find focus group interviews with representative groups of logical prospects to be the simplest, least expensive, and most valuable research you can do. Get eyeball-to-eyeball with your customers. Talk to them. Question them. And, most important: Listen, listen, listen!

3

The Unique Advantage

The objective of almost all advertising today is winning "conquest sales" (sales taken from your competitors)—unless your product is one of that fast-disappearing breed which controls a 50 percent or better share of its market. To get the edge on your competitors, you're looking for a switching idea that points out your product's distinctive edge, the factor that separates it from the rest of the herd, that characteristic the consumer's going to recognize even blindfolded.

It's called the *Unique Advantage*.

Every successful product has *got* to have a Unique Advantage. Without it, the advertiser is just wasting money (unless the advertiser can overwhelm competition simply by outspending everyone, which in itself becomes the product's Unique Advantage).

Before you can promote the Unique Advantage, you've got to isolate and recognize it in your product. Here are several ways to do so:

1. First and easiest, the Unique Advantage is inherent in the product itself. It's either visible or otherwise readily identifiable. The advertising must then point out to prospects why this unique feature will operate to their benefit. Not all unique features are obvious advantages. You may have to make this bridge for the prospect.

23

These products don't come along every day, so I'm going back a few years for examples.

The Polaroid camera was the perfect example of a product with an inherent and obvious Unique Advantage. Until Polaroid was introduced, you had to wait weeks to see the result of your photography. Now, along comes a camera—the only camera—that allows you to see your pictures in sixty seconds. That's a once-in-a-lifetime Unique Advantage every adperson would kill for. It can make your career, as it did for several adpeople at the Polaroid agency.

The Scripto Tilt-Tip pen of many years back is an example of a unique feature, the advantage of which was not so immediately obvious. Since we have been a ball-point pen writing society for so long, I wonder how many of you remember the joy of writing with a fountain pen? You could lean the pen back in your hand at a 45-degree angle and write almost forever without a hint of writer's cramp. Then came the first ball-point pens, which had to be held vertically in an extremely uncomfortable position. Scripto came out with a new kind of ball-point pen in which the point was tilted in the barrel so that *it* was vertical to the paper while the pen itself was held at a comfortable angle. As all ball-point pens improved and became more comfortable, the Unique Advantage disappeared, and the Tilt-Tip pen along with it.

2. The Unique Advantage may be difficult to find and, once found, may not be an advantage at all, or may not even be unique at all. Cases like these require a back-to-the-drawing-board attitude and an appetite for hard work. But in an overwhelming majority of cases, something will eventually be found in the appearance, ingredients, use, manufacturing process, packaging, or distribution of a product that offers prospects a compelling reason for trying it. It may or may not be truly unique. So long as no one else is talking about it, it becomes unique to your product by reason of preemption.

If you remember my lunch with Rosser Reeves described in Chapter 1, one of the important topics explored in depth that day was how my Unique Advantage (UA) differed from his Unique Selling Proposition (USP). I agreed that they were similar, but with a big difference. I told him that in my experience I had come upon numerous Unique Selling Propositions that were not at the same time Unique Advantages. I proved my point, and to his satisfaction I might add, with several examples. One of the examples I used was the case of Snow Crop frozen orange juice, where I decided not to go with an inherent USP in favor of a preemptive Unique Advantage.

Years ago, the people at Snow Crop could find nothing unique about their orange juice except that it contained more pulp than the others. Research indicated that the presence of pulp certainly was unique, but that was most certainly not an advantage to about 50 percent of orange juice drinkers at that time. Most people born before World War II liked pulp because their standard of excellence was the freshly squeezed juice thick with pulp. But those born after World War II were weaned on frozen juice from which all the pulp had been removed. They hated pulp and strained it out whenever they found it. For Snow Crop, pulp was a Unique Selling Proposition, but it was not a Unique Advantage. Why use a Unique Selling Proposition that strains out half your market? What then? Back to the orange groves.

Careful questioning of company experts revealed that various types of oranges—each with its own characteristics and taste—grow at various times of the year. The logical question is how the quality and taste of Snow Crop were kept consistent throughout the year. The juice from each of the various types of oranges is frozen and stored and then blended together to a specific formula. This "blend" story became Snow Crop's very successful Unique Advantage. Although all other brands blend too, for a long time nobody else was talking about it, and Snow Crop preempted the claim.

Silkience makes a strong preemptive claim for its conditioner by advertising that it goes only where the hair needs it. Its commercials prove it with state-of-the-art scanner photography showing that Silkience conditioner goes to different sections of the hair of different women: to selected places on the head of one woman, all over for another, only on the ends for a third woman. A wonderful, believable, provable Unique Advantage. In reality, any modern conditioner does exactly the same thing. But Silkience owns the claim, since it was the first to make it.

Here's another example. For years Dove had advertised that

its soap was one-quarter cleansing cream. Not all soaps have cleansing creams. And not all soaps with cleansing creams are one-quarter cream. Several similar soaps, including Camay, contain cleansing cream or its equivalent as one of their ingredients. But Dove has used the claim so consistently and for so long that it has become identified with Dove by preemption. Therefore, the other soaps do not use it as the major point in their advertising. And rightly so—they'd only be helping Dove.

3. Sometimes the Unique Advantage is in reality a unique disadvantage that can be quickly turned around to serve the same purpose as a Unique Advantage. I would prefer a unique disadvantage in a product I'm working with rather than have nothing at all in the product that makes it stand alone. Think of Volkswagen. Think of the way it looked. Would you have called its looks an advantage next to the long, sleek, powerful, chrome-adorned American cars the public was used to? Its agency did—and convinced a sizable portion of the auto-buying public to think the same. Sometimes a disadvantage is an opportunity in disguise.

Take the classic example that has found its way into advertising textbooks: the tuna fish story. At one time all commercial tuna fish sold was pink. A new company came on the scene with a white tuna—a tremendous disadvantage, wouldn't you say?—in a market used to pink tuna. The white tuna people didn't think so and advertised their tuna as guaranteed not to turn pink, thereby implying that something was wrong with pink tuna. They made the competition see red. How's that for turning a disadvantage into an advantage? They did it so well that all premium tuna marketed since then is white.

4. Occasionally, no matter how hard you try, you can find nothing unique about a product. It is then the agency's responsibility to recommend to the manufacturer the addition of a particular feature that fulfills an unfulfilled consumer need. Or the agency must create a Unique Advantage for the product by repositioning it. Otherwise, the agency is wasting the client's money. In my experience, there are very few products for which an exclusive claim cannot be made or a new position found. Usually the agency that fails to do so is at fault; it is rarely the fault of the product. As I keep saying, there are far more parity agencies than there are parity products.

The Hamilton Beach Butter-Up popcorn popper is an example of a Unique Advantage that was built into an existing product to fill a need. Home corn poppers had been around for a long time. They all popped corn, and none sold very well until Hamilton Beach and its agency recognized that the overwhelming majority of people prefer their popcorn buttered. No popper then on the market turned out buttered popcorn. Just a simple addition to its existing popper did the trick. Since corn pops by heat, Hamilton Beach just added a little receptacle at the top of the popper to hold butter, which melts and drips onto the popping corn. Although others have since copied this feature, Hamilton Beach owned the market for many years.

An example of a Unique Advantage gained by repositioning an old product is Arm & Hammer. Arm & Hammer was always marketed as a baking soda, a fast-declining market, until a whole new and much larger market was created by selling it as a refrigerator deodorant. Same product. New positioning.

Or take Tums antacid tablets. Until the mid-1980s, Tums' campaign was tagged "Tums for the tummy." But with the increasing awareness of the role of calcium in reducing osteoporosis in postmenopausal women, Tums began to reposition itself as a calcium supplement. During a transition campaign, Tums promoted its dual benefit of antacid and calcium supplement. Later, its advertising focused only on the calcium supplement. The manufacturer even added new packaging, offering a large dispenser of Tums in addition to the traditional candy roll package. Another example of a new market being created for an old product that's larger than the original market the product was intended for. A new need. A new opportunity. A new positioning.

━━━━

And what will you do with the Unique Advantage once it's been isolated? First of all, it should be tested to make sure the advantage has wide appeal. Testing is essential because there are no guarantees that a particular unique feature is going to be viewed as an advantage or switching idea by the majority of cash-paying customers. A lemon-flavored mouthwash is a great idea, for example, provided that it can be proved that consumers will find its unique flavor to be advantageous or desirable first thing in the morning.

When it comes to expressing this Unique Advantage in advertising, there's no sweeping generalization that contains a successful formula. I do, however, believe that every ad or commercial should consist of three fundamental ingredients, and that poor advertising can be traced to one, two, or all three of these ingredients being overlooked:

1. Information about the product and its Unique Advantage
2. A clear statement of the information
3. A unique presentation

If a given ad or commercial contains the first two ingredients (information and a clear statement thereof), you can't possibly have a bad ad. After all, isn't that the definition of advertising—giving information about a product so that people can understand (and hopefully, desire) it? Wholly of and by themselves, these two ingredients are guaranteed to give you a good ad.

They won't, however, necessarily give you a great one. That's where the third ingredient comes in. Advertising messages are worthless unless they're seen. Making your ad stand out from the great mass of advertising is absolutely essential for survival today, and that's what a unique presentation is meant to do. Even so, I hasten to point out that a unique presentation alone, without the first two ingredients, is not advertising. The finest presentation will not cover up the lack of a good, basic selling idea. Similarly, any presentation that gets in the way of or slows down the communication of the idea is not only nonfunctional but counterproductive. Get rid of it.

Occasionally, when I discuss these three ingredients with advertising beginners, my audience puts up a wail about the "restrictive nature" of "1–2–3 formulas." They object (sensibly) to discipline that restricts their creativity. I agree, but that isn't the kind of discipline I'm talking about here. These three ingredients simply aren't creatively stifling. If anything, they liberate the imagination by giving it a focused head start in the right direction. What good is undirected creativity? More often than not, it works up a great lather by producing sensational solutions to problems that just don't happen to exist. To be worthwhile, creativity must be directed toward the solution of a particular problem. Writers or art directors with these three ingredients in mind stand on a creative springboard from which they can solve the problem of selling their product. I call this *creative discipline.*

That's a contradiction in terms, you say. How can creativity be disciplined? I say how can it *not* be and still be advertising?

I check every ad or commercial that goes through my hands for all three ingredients. If the ad is deficient in any one, it doesn't reach the client. But if it does meet these criteria, I find we never have any trouble selling it to a client. More important, it never has any trouble selling the client's product, either.

As for the execution of an ad or commercial, I can't offer any rules or formulas. I have only two words of counsel: *simplicity* (which characterizes all of the very best in advertising) and *believability* (a quality about which you will read more in the following chapters).

The ability to see and present things simply is what makes advertising copywriters a unique breed. I've seen very few fine writers of successful plays or novels who could write good ads. Conversely, I've seen darn few good copywriters who could write novels and plays. They keep trying, but I know they'll never succeed because they're a different breed. (The same holds true for fine painters and art directors.)

Advertising copywriting is an extremely disciplined pursuit requiring a disciplined mind capable of shuffling through stacks of mental index cards until the one precise, correct point to be made is located and extracted. A novelist may have 754 pages to tell his story, and if he feels a little rushed, he can make it 755 or 756 pages. Advertising writers or art directors have a seven- by ten-inch page or thirty seconds of time (if they're lucky) to get a prospect's attention, tell the product story, and try to move the prospect to action. That's tough. For them, the virtue of simplicity is learned during the early stages of their careers out of raw necessity.

As for believability, it is simply the single most important word in advertising. If your prospects don't believe what you have to say about your product—no matter how true it may be—your advertisement is worthless. If they do believe you, you have achieved your primary goal.

It is just this—the ability to achieve believability—that separates the advertising professional from the amateur. It makes the difference between a good creative person and what many people think of as "advertising geniuses," but it really has nothing to do with talent. The ability to make yourself believed is intrinsically tied up with a basic liking for people, a willingness to know them, understand them, listen to them, respect them, and, above all, be honest and sincere with them. You can't fake it, because they're just too smart. So tell it to them straight.

And one more thing. Remember, the product is the hero, not the advertising.

Now you know everything I know about advertising and everything you need to know. What follows is merely substantiation.

4

Concept vs. Execution

Quick! Think of the worst commercial you ever saw.

Got it? Now then, with the camera eye of your mind, pan in on each loathsome detail, then sweep the screen from left to right, lingering where it hurts most. What do you see? Is it the unctuous spokesman mouthing lines you've heard often enough to repeat in your sleep? Is it a plain, dumpy housewife rhapsodizing about a product you've grown to despise? Or a stomach-churningly explicit demonstration of a nasal decongestant? Choose carefully.

Because chances are you're going to be wrong.

The worst commercial you ever saw was not the one that caused you to throw your shoes at the television screen. The worst commercial you ever saw caused you to laugh, dance, or sing along instead of making a decision to try the product advertised. I'll stake my reputation on that.

The unctuous spokesman, the depressing housewife, or the nauseating demo you associate with the "worst" in advertising probably goads you to fury because it contains no real sales message but hard sells as if it did. It insults your intelligence every second of the way.

These commercials belong to the incorrigible *poor concept, poor execution* category. Don't waste your vitriol on them. They're so bad, they don't even bother me anymore. I just shrug them off like so many annoying gnats.

What I find much more annoying than a poor concept, poor execution commercial is a cotton-candy fribble that looks great, sounds great, and yields nothing when you try to bite into it. This is the ***poor concept, good execution*** category. These commercials are annoying because they try to fool me into believing they've got something to say. You get a four-star production created by technicians who know their medium, but the concept fails to live up to the execution.

If you ever saw the Federal Express commercials that once dominated the awards shows, you know what I'm talking about. One commercial featured a fast-talking businessman. This motor-mouth actor creates a highly charged atmosphere. But there isn't a word about the product until, at the very end, a voice-over announcer delivers the "sell": "Federal Express. When it absolutely, positively has to be there overnight." Why don't I like this commercial? Because it's another sad case of execution overpowering concept, entertainment outshining selling point, show business destroying advertising. Saddest of all, this award-winning commercial fooled the supposed advertising professionals who were so dazzled by execution that they didn't even notice there was no selling concept.

This commercial is simply not advertising, at least not by my definition. My definition says that an ad or commercial has a purpose other than to entertain. That purpose is to conquer a sale by persuading a logical prospect for your product or service, who is now using or is about to use a competitor's product or service, to switch to yours. That's basic, or at least it should be. In order to accomplish that purpose, it seems to me, you have to promise that prospect an advantage that he's not now getting from his present product or service, and it must be of sufficient importance in filling a need to make him switch. The only thing Federal Express promises is that it will deliver overnight. But that's generic to the category. Of course it will deliver overnight—that's what I'm paying a premium for in the first place. That's not news, nor is it advertising. I wonder if the same agency would advertise that its food account's products are edible.

Another award-winning commercial in the same campaign was even worse. This 10-second spot pictures a man uprooting an outdoor phone booth as the announcer says, "Federal Express is so easy to use, all you have to do is pick up the phone." What amateurish nonsense. It's an attempt to get attention with a vaudeville sight gag that emphasizes the words "pick up" and not the benefit of the message. But come to think of it, what is the message? How do I get in touch with the other air delivery services, by carrier pigeon?

These two commercials are typical of what Federal Express has been running and winning awards with for years. Funny? You bet they are. Beautifully produced and acted? They're little production gems. In fact, the campaign that included these two commercials won everything from Effies to Clios to One Show Awards to Art Director's Medals. It catapulted everyone connected with it to instant stardom. It was the biggest thing to hit Madison Avenue since Alka-Seltzer . . . and I wouldn't have given it one vote. Why not? Because these ads just aren't advertising. There's not a single competitive selling idea, not a single reason for me to use Federal Express instead of one of its competitors in all those hundreds and hundreds of thousands of production dollars.

For another example of magnificent execution with no selling concept, consider this piece of artificially sweetened confection for Kodak film. Done to the tune of "Daddy's Little Girl," the classic wedding day tear-jerker, the commercial shows a radiant bride dancing with her father. In snapshot fashion, the picture flashes back to childhood scenes. We see the father dancing with his baby daughter, dancing with a girl who looks about seven, and then twirling a slightly older child who is dressed in a tutu. As we hear the lyrics, "You're a little girl, you're spice, you're everything nice," the scene shifts back to the wedding. The bride has finished the dance with her father and is starting to dance with the groom. Father looks on, with a mixture of joy and sorrow.

Get out your handkerchiefs. This commercial certainly captures the mood of the moment. The casting is fine. The song— though hackneyed—is perfectly good schmaltz. But what this commercial doesn't seem to have is an idea. A commercial should be based on an idea, a concept, a specific goal. The Kodak commercial is missing all of these things—beautifully. What kind of idea is "Daddy's Little Girl"? The song tells me nothing about Kodak film.

Visually, this commercial does exactly the right thing: It

builds up to a point where the copy can step in and deliver the sales punch. Only the copy never shows up. In the last moments of this 60-second commercial, the voice-over announcer says, "Don't the pictures of your lifetime deserve Kodak film?" But couldn't these precious moments be just as well captured on any other film? This commercial might just as easily have been sponsored by Fuji. Stop being such an old grouch, you say? How can I knock such sweet, sentimental, heart-wrenching commercials, you ask? Easy. Just take a look at Eastman Kodak's financial statement for 1989. The days of wine and roses and monopoly are over for Kodak. They've got Polaroid snapping at their heels and not just with the camera but with a new film for *all* cameras. And that Fuji blimp flying all over America is not just a lot of hot air, either. They're dropping bombs on Kodak and scoring some direct hits. Kodak can't afford to keep running Mr. Nice Guy commercials anymore. It's time to see the market as it is today. It's not a pretty picture. And all the beautiful executions in the world won't make it look any better. It's time for a big idea. And "Daddy's Little Girl" isn't it.

　　The commercials that really bug me as an advertising man are those in which the sales point gets upstaged or downstaged by the execution.

　　These are the **good concept, poor execution** commercials. There are two distinct types, and once you're on to them, you can pinpoint where they go wrong in a minute—or even fifteen seconds. In the first kind, the first sharp stab of irritation the commercial excites dissolves gradually into lingering pity for a sound idea gone awry. Midway through one Heinz ketchup commercial, for instance, you can feel this phenomenon taking hold as an irrelevant, scene-stealing execution gives birth to a grudging respect for the "slow ketchup" idea. In this commercial, a teenager balances an open bottle of ketchup on a rooftop ledge, placing it above a sidewalk hot dog vendor many stories below. Confident that he has perfectly positioned the bottle, the teenager runs downstairs and orders a hot dog from the vendor. "Mustard on that or what?" the vendor asks. With a quick glance up, the teenager replies confidently, "Uh, no thanks. I've got it covered." Just as the boy is ready to take his first bite, the first drop of Heinz ketchup drips down from the roof right onto his hot dog. This is a wonderful execution, but it completely upstages the concept of thick ketchup. Had Heinz concentrated more on the ketchup and less on the execution, it might have made its unique sales point more effectively. I'm sure everyone who sees this commercial will remember the execution in great detail, but I doubt that many will play back the concept of thick ketchup. This commercial misses the target. Splat!

Or how about the Shearson Lehman Hutton commercial that tries to promote optimism about stock market investments? At a time when people may feel squeamish about putting money in a bear market, the commercial assures them that the market has already hit its low point and that stock prices will rise to higher levels in the coming year. That's a pretty damn good thought for a brokerage house. After all, selling stock is its stock in trade. Sending the message in a form that makes it easily digestible is a praiseworthy goal for Shearson Lehman. So how did they dramatize this concept on TV? They didn't dramatize it at all. They merely displayed the message (plus some additional copy) on the screen like a slide show, while an announcer read it off. Period. That isn't television. That's radio. If the concept wasn't actually *killed* by the execution, it was certainly put to sleep. Watching this commercial for the first time, I felt the way I do when I look at the ruin wreaked by an early frost on a windowbox garden—a minor irritation, a sneaking feeling of sadness, and, finally, resignation. It might have been really nice. Not great. Just really nice.

But I can't work myself up into a similar tristesse over commercials in which the execution actually negates the concept. In this second *good concept, poor execution* category, the quality of mercy is strained beyond endurance. A good or even great concept that is utterly destroyed by execution is a perversion of advertising, a self-indulgence on the part of agencies that is a frightening and growing trend. To see one of these slick little pieces of hoodwinkery is to watch the presentation of a so-called professional's fondest creative dream wrapped in the guise of advertising. Mostly, the execution and the concept proceed independently of one another, almost as if different people were involved at each stage.

A prime example is the Honda Prelude spot that features comedian Jackie Mason. The commercial has a serious purpose:

to promote the Prelude's unique four-wheel *steering*, a feature that makes the car safer on curves on the open road and easier to park in the city. I know this from the first factory spot I saw, which demonstrated how it works and why it's good to have. Subsequent excellent factory (national) commercials explain the advantages of four-wheel steering even more graphically with dramatic, convincing demonstrations of it in action. From these commercials I get the point of the safety and convenience benefits of the Prelude's four-wheel steering. I certainly didn't get it from the Jackie Mason dealer commercials. His delivery is a joke—literally. Jackie Mason stands in a showroom with a Honda Prelude behind him. "Did you hear about the Honda Prelude with the four-wheel steering?" he asks, as if beginning a stand-up comedy skit. Gesturing wildly with his hands, he tries to describe how it works: "The car is goin' like this, the wheel is goin' like that, you're goin' like this because you can't figure out where did the back go. While you were lookin' this way, the car went that way!" As a big Jackie Mason fan, I find the commercial hilarious. But don't ask me to tell you anything about the Honda Prelude's four-wheel steering. I was so busy laughing at Mason's comic routine, I hardly noticed the car, let alone the steering. The execution completely negated the concept and destroyed all credibility. It should be convicted for the murder of a unique feature. What a crime.

Wendy's had a good concept when it decided to show that its hamburgers have more beef than other burgers. But the notorious Wendy's "Where's the beef?" campaign had just the opposite effect. I'm sure you remember the campaign. Everybody does. Clara Peller plays a little old contentious lady with a big bass voice who goes into a fast-food restaurant (not Wendy's) and asks for a burger. Inspecting a tiny meat patty on a huge bun, she exclaims, "Where's the beef?"

In short order, a comedian picked up the line on his network TV show, a candidate used it in a nationwide presidential campaign speech, and off it went into the wild blue yonder of advertising stardom. But think about it. The strength and memorability of the entire commercial is centered on a tiny burger. Clara Peller's now-famous line is based on a tiny burger. The immediate association is therefore Wendy's/small burgers or, at best, Wendy's/where's the beef?

The "Where's the beef?" campaign won all the awards in the year it ran—and drove agency creative people nuts. Jealous advertisers were demanding that their agencies come up with a similar line that would make their commercials a household word. I can remember a week when three of my clients asked for a "Where's the beef?" commercial, and one new business prospect interrupted our pitch to ask my opinion of the "Where's the beef?" spot. Almost every other person I met socially or in business asked the same question: "What do you think of the 'Where's the beef?' commercial?" I told them I didn't like it, but I didn't know why until one evening I got a phone call from my mother. It went something like this:

> **Mom:** Hello, Hank. How come I don't hear from you?
> **Me:** I've been a little busy.
> **Mom:** Too busy to call your mother?
> **Me:** I'm sorry. How are you?

[*Another ten minutes of mother-son guilt conversation, and finally the reason for her call:*]

> **Mom:** I saw such a terrific television commercial.
> **Me:** Which one?
> **Mom:** The one with the little old lady. She's so funny.
> **Me:** What old lady?
> **Mom:** The one with the voice.
> **Me:** What voice?
> **Mom:** The deep voice . . . and she says, "Where's the beef?"
> **Me:** Oh, you mean the Wendy's commercial.
> **Mom:** Yes, Wendy's. Did you do that commercial?
> **Me:** No.
> **Mom:** I'm so disappointed. Why don't you do commercials like that?
> **Me:** I don't know. I'm really sorry.
> **Mom:** I would be so proud if you did that commercial. Your commercials my friends don't even know.
> **Me:** I'm really sorry. What did you like about the Wendy's commercial, Mom?

Mom: Everything. But I love that old lady the most. She's a
         real person. And so funny.
Me: Well, I guess you and Dad are going to eat at
         Wendy's from now on.
Mom: Oh, no.
Me: Why not?
Mom: Who wants such small hamburgers!

Good old Mom. She put her finger right on the problem. The beef I have with the Wendy's commercial is that it doesn't have enough beef. It doesn't carry the story to its logical conclusion. It stops short of proving its point. There's no greater omission a commercial can make.

The "Where's the beef?" commercial cries out for a side-by-side demonstration of a Wendy's burger versus the other guy's burger. That single comparative visual would do more to end the confusion and sell Wendy's than all the one-liners in Henny Youngman's joke book. It would make clear that the small burger belongs to the other guys. The big burger is Wendy's. I assume there is a significant demonstrable visual difference between the size of a Wendy's burger and one from McDonald's or Burger King, or Wendy's wouldn't have devoted its campaign to that point. If the difference in the size of the burgers is important enough to spend that kind of advertising money on, I cannot understand why it isn't important enough to show.

There's no denying the tremendous impact of the Wendy's "Where's the beef?" commercial. The publicity and top-of-mind recognition it got for Wendy's far exceeded anything Wendy's budget could afford. It catapulted Wendy's awareness far above McDonald's and Burger King's despite their far larger expenditures. It just seems a waste that Wendy's didn't get the maximum benefit from all the exposure by making itself clear and convincing instead of just funny. Every comparative commercial (which these Wendy's commercials were intended to be) calls for a comparative demo. By not including one, Wendy's not only lost the worthy concept it started with—that Wendy's has more beef in its burgers—but gave the public exactly the opposite impression. And that's my big beef!

Could it be that good creative advertising people are thinking up the initial concepts and then passing them along to production specialists to finish up? It must be. Because I see too many commercials where the production, or rather the overproduction, strangles the advertising idea. Such production has given birth to an industry that rivals or surpasses the advertising agency business itself, with production houses raking in the dough and their directors becoming the new breed of advertising millionaires. And it's the advertiser who pays for it.

Obviously, perspective has been lost somewhere along the way. Were I the client, my agency would have to do one helluva lot of fast talking to induce me to part with more than $150,000 to produce a single TV commercial. In my heart of hearts, I'd prefer to spend $25,000 less than that. To wheedle more than $200,000 out of me, the agency would have to show me that my money was absolutely essential to make a brilliant concept come off. I sure wouldn't spend it for show biz effects. More about this in an upcoming chapter. Execution, after all, is only the craft we use to express the idea. Far from being an end in itself, it is merely the means to the end. And so, as a rule of thumb, I've learned to be guided by this principle: Any execution that enhances, speeds up, and/or makes more understandable and believable the communication of the basic selling idea is a good one; any execution that slows down, confuses, dominates, or subverts the communication of that concept is dead wrong.

Some years back AAMCO, which guarantees its transmissions for as long as you own the car, destroyed this terrific selling point with a humorous execution. "Ever notice how things break down right after the warranty expires?" the voice-over announcer asks. The commercial shows a pathetic-looking man with a beer belly, who seems to be cursed by problems with appliances. First his TV set explodes, then his dishwasher explodes. He takes a ride in his car and that too falls apart, leaving behind a trail of hubcaps and other automobile parts, including his transmission. This poor soul's one blessing in life seems to be that he has an AAMCO transmission and can get free transmission repairs for as long as he owns the car. I assume that's what he does, but, alas, on his trip home from the AAMCO station, his garage door collapses on the car. The commercial is hilarious, but the laugh is on the advertiser. The poor schnook in the commercial is a born loser. Everything he buys is a lemon, including his AAMCO transmission. But isn't he lucky, his transmission is still guaranteed. Why emphasize the negatives to make the positive point? All the attention is directed at exploding TVs and dishwashers and collapsing garage doors and, particularly, on an AAMCO transmission that falls apart. But who cares about the product so long as the commercial gets a few laughs?

Contrast this execution with a later AAMCO commercial, without a single laugh, done by another agency. With screeching tires throughout, this commercial shows a police car racing to an emergency. The voice-over announcer tells us that police departments can't afford breakdowns, and they rely on AAMCO because it is the expert in transmission repair. Other spots in the campaign convey the same idea using an ambulance and a volunteer fire fighter.

What a clear and believable presentation of the basic selling concept. Unlike the earlier AAMCO spot that focused on a failing AAMCO transmission, this campaign focuses on the positive— emergency vehicles that have to get there. The message is: If AAMCO is good enough for them, it should be good enough for you. And this commercial is good enough for me. In fact, it's great.

That brings us to the fourth category—commercials with **good concept** and **good execution.** Let's talk about what we *should* be seeing on our television screens every night.

Some years back I had the pleasure of reviewing a few of the commercials done for the Chesapeake & Potomac Telephone Company by an agency located outside of New York City. Dramatic, involving, and exciting, without resorting to even a hint of a gimmick, these commercials all put execution into its proper perspective. In one, for example, we are shown a split screen. (The screen is cut in half vertically and two pictures appear simultaneously, one in each half.) Two young men sit in telephone booths calling a girl for a date—the same girl. One of the boys looks up her phone number in the telephone directory while the other calls information. The guy who looks up the number himself finds it, dials it, and starts speaking to the girl right away. At the same time we see the other kid still trying to get the number from the information operator. When he finally gets it and dials it, naturally he gets a busy signal because she's accepting a date from the fellow in the other booth. It ends with the slogan, "Look it up yourself—it's faster." This is what I call the simple, believable communication of a simple idea, and it proves that a good execution needn't be dull. It just needs to be clear.

For a good concept with good execution, you can't beat a commercial for Crest toothpaste that captures the reactions of children in the dentist's chair. "I brush, I really do!" exclaims one little girl eagerly. She looks ashamed when she discovers she has a cavity. "I've got a what?" says another little girl, on the brink of tears as the dentist's drill approaches. In a third dentist's chair, we see a little boy who has brushed with Crest. He grins from ear to ear when he discovers he doesn't have any cavities, then rips off the paper bib and exclaims, "I'm outta here!" Not only does this commercial realistically portray kids, it purely and simply conveys the message that Crest can make a difference.

Here's an oldy but goody: An elegant couple is enjoying a very formal dinner in the ornate dining room of a mansion. Then the doorbell rings. They spring into immediate action, clearing the table and loading all the dishes, glasses, pots, and pans into the dishwasher. Within seconds, they're pressing the machine's starter button. By the time they answer the door, we're on to their secret: This couple is, in reality, the butler and maid employed at the mansion, taken by surprise at the unexpected return of the lord and lady. You can't dispute the fact that it's a great demonstration of how quickly and easily the RCA Whirlpool dishwasher can be loaded, how much it can hold, and, most important, the fact that scraping and prerinsing are unnecessary. These are big points, and they're made with a comic execution that's relevant and functional to the sales point. Who says humor can't sell? When it's used like this, it sells very well.

The long-running commercials featuring Maytag's lonely repairman also show how far humor can go in making a sales point—when it's correctly used to make a sales point and not to make a joke. To convince us that its washers are built to last longer and need fewer repairs, Maytag created the character of the lonely repairman. Over the years, we have seen him in a variety of poses: waiting for the phone to ring, asleep at his desk, dreaming up ways to improve upon Maytag washers. He's always complaining about being lonely, and we always laugh at the irony. But we remember him for a reason: He's not out making service calls. Since Maytag washers are so reliable, there's practically nothing for the lonely repairman to do. Maytag gets the point across with a wonderful comic execution.

What's needed in advertising today—even more than fresh ideas for dramatic development—is a return to what advertising is all about. The basic selling concept, the compelling reason to buy, the unique angle—these are the guts of a commercial and the toughest part to formulate. They're worth their weight in gold and deserve 90 percent of the time spent on the commercial by the agency and the client. The remaining 10 percent should be spent on execution, not the other way around. As a matter of fact, the stronger the concept, the less time and effort and money are required for the execution.

Look at the recent Tinactin campaign if you want to know what a great commercial looks like. Concept is the result of a creative process, true, but most times, with the really good ones, a marketing fact or statistic will prime the creative pump just a little bit. Obviously, that's what happened at Tinactin's agency. They determined that the biggest consumers of athlete's foot remedies are chronic sufferers with recurrent episodes and directed the campaign right smack at these heavy users. A woman sitting on a locker room bench after a workout describes how her athlete's foot comes and goes. Each time she mentions a flare-up, her foot catches on fire. And each time she puts out the fire by spraying Tinactin on it.

This heavy-user concept does several things. First, of course, it concentrates on the right audience. Second, it recognizes that athlete's foot tends to be a chronic problem—that people who have had it once tend to get it again and again. Finally, it promises that the product will extinguish the burning for good if used as directed. A great concept. A great execution. A great commercial. At an inexpensive price.

Another fine concept executed with panache is this Club Med commercial. With soft music in the background, we see idyllic scenes from a Club Med vacation: a woman alone on a beach, a man waterskiing, a couple horseback riding and windsurfing together. With each glimpse of this nirvana, the announcer recalls the stresses of civilization: ringing phones, blaring TVs, wailing sirens, screaming headlines. Somewhere these things still exist, but the Club Med vacationers have found the antidote for civilization.

This spot makes me feel as if I'm on vacation and realize how much I need to get away for one. As an adman, it makes me feel good all over and reminds me how much I need to get away from bad commercials. I can only hope we'll see more commercials like this one, instead of questionable demonstrations, extravagant claims, phony show biz tinsel, and the irrelevant nonsense we've come to accept so meekly. A compelling idea put across in a compelling way to the prospective customer sells the product. Next time you watch a commercial that tries to sell you on the merits or the reliability of a product or service, ask yourself if it succeeds as well as the Club Med, the Tinactin, or any of the other good concept/good execution commercials I've just discussed.

High-caliber commercials like these are what we should be watching on TV. They are incisive, they are simple, and they don't waste the viewer's time or the client's money. And they're not hard to separate from the crowd. Just look for a commercial that actually sells you something, be it oatmeal or a political candidate, by offering you a clear compelling reason for buying, with a believable execution.

When is an execution believable? When it's inseparable from the concept. When it delivers its message unmistakably and dramatizes the benefit of the product. When it leaves you completely unaware of its existence as a separate entity. When it does not obscure or overpower the message and is functional to the idea. Good execution is most often brilliantly simple and shockingly inexpensive to produce. Believe me, good execution is the best friend a concept can have.

To conduct your own acid test of an execution's worth, try asking yourself objectively whether the execution gets the message across faster, more clearly, and more believably than if a stand-up announcer delivered it. If it does, then the execution you're watching is functional to the sales message and an aid to the commercial. If you must honestly conclude that it does not, that a straightforward pitch would be more believable, then some advertiser is pulling your leg.

———

Remember: There are no geniuses in the advertising business. You are as qualified to judge the merits of a commercial as the person behind the camera, probably more so, if you train yourself to regard a commercial as the sum of its parts.

All commercials fall into one of four categories:

Commercials with poor concepts and poor execution.
    They're the worst.
Commercials with poor concepts and good execution.
    They're almost as bad.
Commercials with good concepts and poor execution.
    They're inexcusable.
Commercials with good concepts and good execution.
    They're advertising.

It's easy. Determine the category, and you determine the worth of the commercial.

5

Irrelevance vs. Simplicity

Just to prove that the shortest distance between two points is a straight line, look at the following examples of TV commercials that don't waste time or cloud the issue when it comes to transmitting the sales message from advertiser to audience. Then look at the ones that both waste *and* cloud, asking yourself if their creators were merely clumsy—or desperate to hide the fact that they had no sales story—or so carried away by show biz glitz that nothing else mattered.

Take Gablinger's beer, which we discussed in Chapter 2 as an example of a poor product that could not be saved by a good ad campaign. Although the beer failed in the marketplace, what we could not have imagined at that time was that it would be the forerunner of the most successful beer category since the introduction of beer itself in America. Gablinger's was, in reality, the world's first light beer—a category that now outsells regular beer. Unfortunately, Gablinger's arrived too early with too little. Too early because it preceded the health, fitness, and calorie craze. Too little because it tasted too little like a beer to satisfy beer drinkers. However, as the first beer to be introduced with a really exciting, tangible product difference in a long, long time, Gablinger's was an advertiser's dream. Imagine! The first beer without carbohydrates! The sales message is the product!

In print (magazines and newspapers, that is) the advertiser took direct aim at the audience and fired the sales message in a single, clean, straight line: "Gablinger's: the first beer without carbohydrates." Bingo! Anything else that could have been said about the product at this point would have been superfluous.

The first TV commercial showed us Gablinger's Unique Advantage as simply as possible by stressing the point that every time you drink a glass of beer, you're taking in the carbohydrate equivalent of a whole slice of white bread—without the nutritional value. Two glasses, and you've gobbled down two slices. Three glasses, three slices. Then the commercial introduced Gablinger's as the first and only beer with no carbohydrates at all. Visually the demonstration is great: A slushy, soggy piece of bread floating in a mug of beer reminded us that ordinary beer is filling and heavy. Stare at that glutinous blob long enough, and you begin to imagine how it must look in your stomach. If you're not ready for a diet beer then, you're a hopeless endomorph.

The slogan—"Won't fill you up!"—was emphatic, and it told the heavy beer drinkers at whom the commercial was aimed that they could drink several beers at one sitting without the carbohydrate menace of poor health and beer bellies. The commercial made its single, strong point as simply as possible. Dramatic and believable in its presentation, this commercial sold me on the product's advertising agency, as well as on the product itself.

Now, just to prove to you that advertising is not getting better, only more expensive, take a look at one of my all-time least favorite campaigns—the obscenely overproduced Bud Light extravaganzas that represent the lowest in advertising and the height of irrelevance. In the highly competitive market for low-calorie beer, Bud hoped to overwhelm beer drinkers into thinking that its name was synonymous with light and that all other light beers were imposters. The sales message the ad agency came up with was harmless enough: "Less filling light beer with the first name in taste." This slogan makes two points—one generic and one exclusive. It tells weight-conscious and health-conscious beer drinkers at whom the commercial is aimed that they can drink several beers at one sitting without the carbohydrate menace of poor health and beer bellies. (Sound familiar?) It also lets serious beer drinkers know that they won't be sacrificing taste if they choose

Bud Light beer. Unfortunately, Bud completely distorted the message in a campaign filled with irrelevancies.

In a series of nonsensical spots, Bud showed people in a variety of settings ordering "a light" and getting everything but beer. A cowboy sitting at a bar calls out, "Give me a light." An old-fashioned camera suddenly appears, and a huge flash explodes in his face. In another bar scene, a sportsman orders a light, and the bar is transformed into a crazily lighted disco. When a businessman orders a light, a lamp slides down to his end of the bar, and a woman with a lampshade hairdo tries to pick him up. A man orders a light at a barbecue, and the barbecue pit lights up. These are but a few of the milder executions. What the hell does light, as in electric, have to do with light, as in calories? Nothing! Absolutely nothing! (Which is about what these spots have in common with advertising.) As a matter of fact, these Bud light shows take viewers' minds and thoughts off light beer and thirst and instead make them think about electric lights and shocks. The only good this campaign did was for the agency art directors and producers and their Hollywood directors, who must have had a ball. I'm sure it was and continues to be a bright spot in their careers, but it takes me back to the dark ages of advertising.

I just happen to be one of those dumb, old-fashioned ad guys who continues to believe that a mean, lean sales point the advertiser believes in should come wrapped in a commercial without a trace of fat on it. When *anything* else is introduced that does not in some way contribute to that message—an extra line, a prop that doesn't belong, or a whole sequence of gimmicks that rounds out the commercial itself instead of the product message—I start asking myself why the commercial's producers are distracting my attention from the product.

Imagine how I felt when I saw a commercial for Wendy's restaurants that features a Russian fashion show. Men in military uniforms and women with babushkas on their heads gather around as a hideous, overweight woman with a Russian accent announces the new fashions. As she calls out each line of clothing—daywear, eveningwear, swimwear—the same model (another overweight, dowdy-looking peasant woman) appears on stage wearing the same unattractive shift. All she changes are the props (for evening-wear, she carries a flashlight; for swimwear, she carries an inflatable tube). What does this funny, if tasteless, scene have to do with the taste of Wendy's hamburgers? Here's what the announcer tells us: "Having no choice is no fun. That's why at Wendy's, every hamburger isn't dressed the same." At Wendy's, we can "dress" our burgers with tomatoes, cheese, bacon, and more. I can't think of a more contrived, irrelevant, and unappetizing way to tell what should have been a simple, appetizing story. The bulk of the money spent on this commercial was used to gain attention for the concept of free choice, revolving around "dress" (which provided a far-fetched, irrelevant bridge into "dressing" hamburgers). Instead, the money should have been spent on showing the appetizing results of that free choice on the Wendy's hamburgers. That's the end benefit to the viewer, isn't it? Another case of irrelevant execution doing in the product. Nyet! Nyet! Nyet!

Next in line for the smokescreen award is the "Maalox Moments" campaign. In a series of humorous spots, the campaign depicts a variety of stressful situations. One commercial shows a family sitting around the kitchen table as a father addresses a letter to Maalox. "Dear Maalox," he writes."My daughter's dates give me Maalox Moments." Suddenly the daughter arrives with her latest date, who wears dark sunglasses and an earring. Dad excuses himself to go get the Maalox. The commercial ends with the tag line, "For all your Maalox Moments."

This commercial gives me indigestion. It completely destroys the efficacy of a wonderful pharmaceutical product with a wonderful image of efficacy. It destroys the Unique Advantage of the product, which was previously available only by prescription and is supposedly more effective than nonprescription products. Not only is the execution completely out of character with the product, but it downgrades the product into the category of "candy" antacids. These major criticisms aside, what does the theme "Maalox Moment" mean? All it does is tell you when you're likely to get heartburn. No one has to tell me that. I already know. And how is the "Maalox Moment" different from the Pepto-Bismol moment or the Tums moment? It's all irrelevant! What I'm really waiting for, if I suffer from heartburn, is not what makes the Maalox Moment different, but what makes *Maalox* different? And that question the commercials never bother to answer. So here's an entire campaign based around an irrelevancy. Think about that for a moment!

Speaking of heartburn, how about the commercial for Alka-Seltzer where we're eyewitnesses to a man's stomach catching on fire. Seated at a disco, this poor fellow can't have fun because he has eaten too many spicy chicken wings. After he takes Alka-Seltzer to quell the fire in his stomach, he gets up and dances like John Travolta.

Like Maalox, Alka-Seltzer not only made the mistake of telling us when to take the product (again irrelevant) but, more importantly, damaged its believability with this silly sketch, which was not only irrelevant but totally incompatible with the serious nature of the product and its message. Nobody takes antacid products for fun; they're just not "fun" products. People take antacids to feel better, and I don't believe I will after watching this commercial. And I don't believe I'll be able to dance like John Travolta, either. Fred Astaire maybe, but certainly not Travolta.

Now compare the Alka-Seltzer spot with the Tinactin commercial discussed in Chapter 4. You'll recall that this one also draws upon a fire analogy—to exaggerate the discomfort of athlete's foot. But here the exaggeration clearly works. A woman in a locker room after a workout complains about the burning of athlete's foot as she watches her foot catch fire. She sprays Tinactin on the flame and the fire is extinguished.

Unlike the Alka-Seltzer spot, which is an exaggeration of an unbelievable situation with an unbelievable result, the Tinactin commercial is an exaggeration of a totally believable situation, with a believable result. While the setting of the Alka-Seltzer spot is incompatible with the product, the Tinactin spot takes place in a locker room, where athlete's foot thrives. Once Tinactin puts the flame out, the woman doesn't get up and exercise like Jane Fonda. While the silly result in the Alka-Seltzer commercial undermines the efficacy of the product, the believable result of using Tinactin—relief from a painful condition—enhances the efficacy of the product.

It's useless to try to dope out some ulterior meaning in every commercial that depends upon irrelevancies for its punch because most such nonsense is the result of stupidity, rather than duplicity. Take the Data General campaign that featured a Viking war scene. With dramatic music and elaborate costumes and scenery, this 60-second spot recreated an entire battle—sound effects and all. At the conclusion of the commercial, the voice-over announcer asked, "Are you buying yesterday's technology?" This was followed by a visual of a laptop computer and the line "Data General—a generation ahead." Several other battles of the past were depicted in other commercials in this campaign.

Certainly Data General didn't need the Vikings or a tank battle from World War I to illustrate that slogan. Is someone here trying to associate other computer systems with the era of the Vikings? And, if so, tell me why. I certainly don't need to take a trip back in a time machine to assure you the analogy is grossly exaggerated, inaccurate, and irrelevant. Far better would have been a simple demonstration of some hard facts about the capabilities of Data General computers, contrasted with those of other computers. The fact that Data General didn't do that and instead tried to distract me with the sound and fury of wars of the past leads me to believe the company has nothing to say. Just another expensive smokescreen.

And then there was the ultimate irrelevance in one Honda commercial in which a spokesman, walking around a Honda car, compares it feature by feature with an apple—yes, an apple—perched upon a stool nearby. "This Honda seats four comfortably. This apple holds two, maybe three, worms—tops." At the end of the commercial, the announcer eats the apple, grimaces, and stalks off. He might as well have eaten the car for all the sense it made. I won't even bother to point out why this spot doesn't work; I have too much respect for your judgment. Let me just ask instead: When was the last time you bought a car because it was roomier than an apple?

I was convinced that Honda would hold the prize for the ultimate irrelevant commercial forever until I spotted a commercial for Northern bathroom tissue. A little girl, seated at a baby grand piano, dawdles about practicing. "Cathy! You've only practiced an hour!" her mother nags. Suddenly the little girl stands up from the piano and gets a roll of Northern bathroom tissue. She wraps the quilted tissue around each of her fingers, goes back to the piano, and plays like a virtuoso.

The commercial is supposed to prove that the quilting in Northern bathroom tissue "makes a difference you can feel." Why didn't they prove it with an animated demonstration showing its inherent softness superiority over other tissue? Then I might have believed them. But wrapping toilet paper around fingers and playing the piano with it—come on! What nonsense, and what harm they've done the product. Now I don't believe a thing they tell me. This commercial should be flushed down the toilet.

Irrelevant material, then, that distracts us from the sales message is trying to tell us something. It's trying to say either that there *is* no sales message (or, possibly, that the product's advertising agency has failed to discern it properly) or that the agency has hired a film crew instead of advertising people to do the commercial.

One of the problems with a recent Bertolli olive oil campaign was that it had no sales message. This campaign featured funny faces set against a black background. All the faces were made of vegetables or pieces of pasta: lettuce for hair, cartwheel pasta for eyes, an upturned mushroom slice for a nose, and a string bean for a mouth. All the faces were grumpy until Bertolli came along to perk up the recipe. Creative as this commercial might be (it should give elementary school teachers a great idea for an arts and crafts project for their students), it told me nothing about what makes Bertolli's olive oil different from Progresso's or anyone else's.

When Bertolli changed agencies soon after the pasta faces campaign, I said, "Hooray, maybe now we'll get a selling message." But again Bertolli clouded the picture. This time it chose a spot with beautiful heartwarming scenes of the Italian countryside. The commercial made me want to call my travel agent and plan a trip to Tuscany. Once again, though, Bertolli didn't give me a reason to buy its oil, rather than any other Italian brand. Although the commercial notes that Bertolli has no cholesterol, everyone knows that no olive oil contains cholesterol. The question still remains: How does Bertolli differ from the competition? The answer was staring the agency right in the face. At the end of the commercial, we see a product shot with three varieties of olive oil: One is labeled "Extra Light," another "Extra Virgin," and a third "Olive Oil Classico." Had Bertolli cut through all the irrelevancies, it might have found the Unique Advantage that would distinguish it from its competitors inherently or by preemption: Bertolli offers three varieties of olive oil under one brand name. Neither I, nor any other person I've spoken to, can name any other brand of olive oil with multiple varieties or understands the differences among them. What everybody does know is that olive oil is healthful. What a golden opportunity for Bertolli to educate the market about the different varieties and the unique benefits of each: taste, texture, color, uses, dietary breakdown, fat content, calories, cholesterol-reducing factors, history, price, or any other pertinent or interesting facts. In educating the public, Bertolli could establish itself as the authority in the category and achieve dominance in it. This campaign would also go a long way toward moving the product in all three varieties.

What a sad commentary on our business when two supposedly professional agencies were too dumb or too lazy to search for a Unique Advantage in their client's product that would differentiate it from other brands. Instead, they chose the easy way out by selling generically. Each chose a different generic point—the first, that you use olive oil in Italian cooking, and the second, the equally startling fact that Bertolli is imported from Italy. At this moment, I can't think of which is more obvious, more generic, or more irrelevant. I think it's a tie. I think the creators of both campaigns should be boiled in olive oil.

But as much as I dislike all of the irrelevant commercials we've already talked about in this chapter, none bothers me as much as the campaign for Nynex Yellow Pages. Unlike the others, which are mostly dumb, this one is very clever. While the others appeared briefly to little or no acclaim, this one was all over the tube and was among the most talked-about, most-admired, most-awarded campaigns during the years it ran. And, while the others were merely irrelevant and harmed only their advertisers, this one was not only irrelevant but hurt the entire ad industry because it will be mimicked by impressionable creative people all over the country for years to come.

The campaign begins innocently enough with a simple concept—that "If it's out there, it's in here" (the Yellow Pages)—and then goes on to ask, "Why would anyone need another?" Its objective is twofold: first, to head off competition from other, similar directories that had sprung up and had been making headway in the New York market, and, second, to remind people to use the Yellow Pages in support of Nynex's Yellow Page advertisers. To support this idea, spots were made on many subjects, each superbly produced, each dramatically stark with people against white limbo backgrounds, each hilariously cast and acted, each very funny. And each exists as a monument to the proposition that the gag is more important than the integrity of the message.

Look at the spot for "conductive shoes." An orchestra warms up, and the conductor comes out. After a moment of applause, he stands on his head, clicks his shoes together, and begins to conduct the orchestra with his feet. The orchestra delivers a virtuoso performance of Mozart, as the commercial ends with the "If it's out there . . ." line and a shot of the Yellow Page heading for "conductive shoes."

When I first saw this commercial, I wasn't sure what conductive shoes were, but I was reasonably sure they had nothing to do with Mozart or orchestras. This commercial, which distorts the meaning of the term "conductive shoes," is as bad as the Bud Light commercials, discussed earlier in this chapter, in which beer drinkers order "a light" and get everything except beer. They are a bastardization of the message for the sake of humor.

I have the same criticisms of the Nynex commercial that features "rock drills." Here again, Nynex distorts the message by presenting a military marching band going through a series of dance steps—everything from a duck walk to disco. What's that got to do with pneumatic drills that penetrate rock? Sheer entertainment, this spot is completely irrelevant to the sales message.

Another commercial has us eavesdropping on a very sophisticated, very chic, very "in" New York cocktail party attended by all kinds of egocentric snobs who are all into themselves. The subject here is "vanity cases," but to me it's another case of irrelevance.

And, finally, here's a Nynex commercial I like. The spot for "furniture stripper" features an upholstered chair under a spotlight. With striptease music in the background, the chair slowly sheds its covering until nothing remains but the bare wooden frame.

Of course, this commercial is also a play on words, but it comes close to the topic of the Nynex entry. True, it's inaccurate, since a furniture stripper removes paint or finish, rather than upholstery. But at least I see furniture in the commercial, and the content of the spot has some relevance to the Nynex category heading.

As you've probably gathered, I hate this campaign. It represents all the things I think are wrong with advertising. To my way of thinking, it's dishonest creatively. I'm sure the agency picked the categories that they thought would make the funniest, most irrelevant commercials rather than those categories that people use most and that are most relevant to their needs. To me, that's not advertising for sales. That's advertising for awards.

This is what you should be watching: A basketball player jumps up for a shot as another player tries to block him. Cut (where a scene ends abruptly and another scene begins, in contrast to a dissolve, where one scene fades gradually into the next) to a giant tire gripping the road. Cut to the basketball court and a player dribbling the ball. The scene shifts back to the tire. We see part of the B. F. Goodrich label, and the announcer breaks in: "B. F. Goodrich T/A Radials. Grab. Dig. Perform. . . ." The scene shifts between the car and the basketball court as the analogy continues. When the basketball player takes a giant leap, we get a bird's-eye view of the sole of his sneaker filling the entire screen. The announcer delivers the punch line: "B. F. Goodrich T/A Radials. Athletic shoes for your car."

As a rule, I think analogies are wasteful and unnecessary, since they tend to be farfetched and the commercial's time and production budget are better spent telling the sales story directly. The B. F. Goodrich commercial is a notable exception. What makes the difference here is that the analogy is so relevant, so perfect. If I asked you to fill in the blank: athletic shoes are to basketball players as _ _ _ _ _ are to cars, you would have to answer with the word "tires." The commercial builds up to that analogy with a list of functions common to both: "grab," "dig," "perform." If I thought about it enough, I could probably add a few verbs to the list. But by that point in the commercial, I'm convinced. B. F. Goodrich has made the sales point wi'¹ a dramatic, memorable, and *relevant* execution.

And what could be simpler than this commercial for Head and Shoulders shampoo? Two young, single male yuppies are shopping in a supermarket when one is attracted to a lovely young female shopper. He tells his friend he'd like to meet her. They approach her shopping cart just as she leaves to pick something else off a nearby shelf. They peek into her cart and notice Head and Shoulders. As he flicks some dandruff off his companion's jacket, the friend remarks that Romeo shouldn't make his approach until he, too, buys Head and Shoulders. When Romeo seems embarrassed, the friend confesses that he, too, uses Head and Shoulders. Romeo seems startled and observes, "But you don't have dandruff." Friend smiles knowingly as if to say, "That's because I use Head and Shoulders." Girl returns, all giggle—end of scene. So here is the dreaded Procter & Gamble, you should pardon the expression, slice-of-life format done to perfection—simple, straight, relevant. It contains the product, benefit of the product, and proof that the product works—all in one believable, honest setting that the target audience will relate to. I relate to simple commercials like that.

Commercials like this renew my faith in the power of simple advertising and confirm the weakness of extravagant productions. They reinforce my conviction that the simpler the commercial is, the greater the believability. Stated another way, believability seems to rise or fall in inverse proportion to the cost of the production. That's a little theorem my cohorts have begun to call "Seiden's Law." It holds true, whether you're talking about tires or shampoos or . . .

Doan's for back pain relief. In a simple commercial with nothing irrelevant added, Doan's shows how effective its medication can be in relieving back pain. A man's torso is silhouetted in shadow against a grid. The announcer says, "Doctors measure back pain by how far you can bend." We see the silhouette bend, then stop in pain. The angle of his bend is recorded in red against the grid behind him. The announcer then explains that Doan's relieves back pain better than Bayer, Tylenol, and Advil because Doan's contains an ingredient the others don't have (Unique Advantage). After the man has taken Doan's, we watch him bend again. This time, the man bends all the way, and a much larger angle of bend is emphasized in green against the grid. What could be more simple, more graphic, or more convincing? It's a simple problem/solution format, pure and simple, and it always works. Doan's knew what they wanted to say and said it quickly, honestly, and believably without a lot of double-talk, shaky logic, or irrelevancy to muddy the issue. And one more thing: Doan's ends the commercial by positioning itself as effective specifically against back pain, thereby differentiating itself from the big, all-purpose analgesics which are its biggest competitors. There's not an irrelevant word or visual in the entire commercial. I don't think I will ever get a backache again without thinking of Doan's.

You get the same feeling from the classic commercial that introduced Arm & Hammer laundry detergent. After watching this commercial, you'd feel like a criminal buying an old pollutant for washing your clothes. Not because the commercial makes you feel guilty, mind you, but just because it presents the product's advantages so forcefully and simply. It pictures (and talks about) the natural beauty of our lakes and streams and explains how detergents pollute them. Then, unceremoniously and totally without pretension, it introduces the new, nonpolluting Arm & Hammer detergent. No drums, no bugles, no white tornadoes, no galloping knight. Just a beautifully simple, sincere, and powerful sales message compatible with the product.

It certainly makes the rest of the fanfare and fol-de-rol look foolish, doesn't it? And it tells me that the sponsor is proud enough of the product to want to present it on an unobtrusive velvet cushion that sets off the product's advantages to perfection. That's what a commercial is meant to do in the first place: Highlight the product's advantages. All the hoopla is only a deceptive distraction in an attempt to cover for the lack of an advantage. It never fools anyone.

Now that you know enough to tell the simple from the irrelevant, can you ever again watch a muddled commercial through the same innocent eyes?

6

Show Biz vs. the Advertising Business

I don't know how prime-time programmers feel about this, but for the advertiser, television is a beautiful but unruly beast. If approached correctly, it can enhance the commercial and sell the product as no medium has ever done before. Mishandled, it will devour the advertiser and the message and purr over the remains of the commercial. Just don't try to tell this to the creators of your favorite "funny commercial." They're way too busy writing one-liners to notice that they're being eaten alive by their pet medium.

Commercial funnymen don't want to think that they're stepping on the beast's tail by turning out commercials that are 99 percent show business and 1 percent advertising. They want to think they're advancing the cause of creative advertising a couple of millennia with every sight gag they write. The more medium they apply, the less message we get, but your true technical virtuoso doesn't like to think about unpleasant realities. So long as some sponsor is willing to foot the bill for their creative fantasies, they're going to sugarcoat the sales message with as many layers of entertainment as it will hold. And if they're lucky, maybe they'll win an advertising award for it, too.

To reiterate a point made in Chapter 4, if I had to choose between two extremes to advertise my product, I'd choose a commercial that offered a great selling idea wrapped in a pedestrian execution, rather than the other way around. Because it's the selling idea that's at the heart of advertising, for better or worse, however effective or ineffective it might be. Without a selling idea, you have nothing that even resembles advertising, only a film clip belonging to some entertainment archive somewhere far away from the advertising agency. Clients don't intend to be sponsors of the arts. They're paying the agency for advertising, not entertainment. They want us to sell their products and ideas, to devise new and compelling reasons for people to buy their goods. Their money supports our creativity only as it applies to thinking up new appeals to their logical prospects. That's what advertising people are paid for. And lately, we've been highly overpaid because we're not in the advertising business any more. Too many of us are in show biz.

Look at what some of our extravaganzas cost. Computed on a per-minute basis, they exceed the costliest cast-of-thousands Hollywood epics, making them look like shoestring operations. The $500,000 commercial is not unheard of. And one agency executive bragged to me about the million-dollar commercial his agency had produced. At that rate, a two-hour feature would cost $240 million.

But then, who's crazier, the frustrated Fellinis who create these monsters or the clients who pay for them?

I'm not advocating the kind of commercials that put you to sleep. That would be self-defeating. Nor am I underestimating the role execution plays in delivering the sales message of the commercial. After all, something has to call attention to the commercial in the first place, and that something had better be an attention-riveting execution. I just want to restore that delicate balance which must exist between concept and execution before a commercial can be called true advertising. And if, in the process of restoration, the execution returns to its proper place as the vehicle for putting across the selling idea clearly and believably, I'll consider my time to have been well spent.

———

The Great Show Biz Era—in which execution dominates concept, comedy writers replace copywriters, and film directors supplant art directors—is epitomized by The Great Cola Wars between Coca-Cola and Pepsi-Cola. Both have spent exorbitant sums commissioning celebrities for commercials that really have nothing to do with advertising and everything to do with entertainment. The roster for Coke and Diet Coke has included George Michael, Whitney Houston, Wayne Gretzky, Art Carney, the Pointer Sisters, Kim Carnes, Robert Plant, Sugar Ray Leonard, Jerry Hall, Chris Evert, Phylicia Rashad, Vanna White, Paula Abdul, and Elton John. Pepsi and Diet Pepsi have drafted Madonna, Billy Crystal, Lionel Richie, Tina Turner, Michael J. Fox, Patrick Swayze, Rod Stewart, Ray Charles, Joe Montana, Fred Savage and Kirk Cameron for the teen crowd, and, of course, Michael Jackson.

I've heard some pretty far-out figures for what these commercials cost to produce. Pepsi reportedly paid Michael Jackson $5.5 million for his appearances in its commercials and paid Madonna more than $5 million to perform in another commercial. No doubt such obscene fees to superstars help explain the astronomical annual advertising budgets of Coke and Pepsi. Coca-Cola reportedly budgeted $173 million for advertising in 1988, while Pepsi-Cola budgeted $145 million. Each year since, their budgets have grown even larger. At that rate, Coke and Pepsi are the biggest impresarios of entertainment in the world. You've got to sell a helluva lot of cola just to break even.

But I have a bigger problem with cola war advertising: Though these commercials win all the awards, they say nothing about the product and even less about differentiating the products. I don't find one sales point, one functional reason to buy Coke rather than Pepsi (or Pepsi rather than Coke) or anything else in these commercials that remotely resembles advertising. Not only that, I can't remember whether George Michael works for Pepsi or for Coke. In fact, the stars of these commercials are so interchangeable that Don Johnson first appeared for Pepsi and subsequently switched to Coke.

If you can find one reason to buy Pepsi (rather than Coke)

after seeing the two-minute "Like A Prayer" commercial featuring Madonna, I'll buy a whole concert hall full of Pepsi. The commercial begins with a darkened room and a home movie of Madonna's eighth birthday party projected on a screen. The adult Madonna, seated in an armchair watching the movie, begins to sing, "Life is a mystery, everyone must stand alone. I hear you call my name, and it feels like home. When you call my name, it's like a little prayer. I'm down on my knees, I wanna take you there." As the song continues, the adult Madonna, clad in a slinky black dress, trades places with the little girl. The little girl sits in the chair watching the movie as the adult Madonna appears on the screen, revisiting scenes from her childhood: a classroom, a piano recital hall, the corridor of a parochial school, and a church aisle. Over and over again she sings, "Just like a prayer, I'll take you there, it's like a dream to me." By the end of the commercial, child and adult have again switched places. The camera pulls back to Madonna seated in a lounge chair, holding a can of Pepsi and still watching a home movie of her own birthday party. "Go ahead, make a wish," she says, as the little girl on the screen prepares to blow out the candles. Once she has extinguished them, the screen darkens to form a border around the Pepsi logo. The slogan below it reads "A generation ahead."

I'm not sure what this commercial is about, but I know it's not about advertising. There's no mention of Pepsi (not even a visual of the product) until the very end of this two-minute spot. And the commercial never gives me a reason to drink Pepsi, rather than the competitor's cola.

It simply isn't enough justification to say that its objective was to build brand awareness in a market dominated by another brand. That's a cop-out excuse that could be used by any product in any category that isn't number one in its class. For Pepsi it's ludicrous. Pepsi-Cola and Coca-Cola are probably the two best-known brand names in the world. Moreover, building brand awareness isn't what you'd call a specific objective, or even a worthwhile one when you think about it. People don't buy products simply because they know of their existence. Building brand awareness is not enough; I expect a lot more from a commercial than that. It has to give me a reason to try the brand over the brand I'm now using.

And this commercial offers no such reason.

So it simply isn't advertising, and the person who could create a commercial like this one obviously knows a whole lot more about show biz than about advertising. And more about the private lives of show people than about the American public. So many viewers objected to the religious imagery and explicit sexuality of this commercial that Pepsi yanked it off the air after only a few exposures.

Who says there is no God? Not only does God exist, but he/she knows something about advertising, too.

Here's another one that makes me see stars. To the sound of eerie music, a little boy makes his way down a dark alley. "Mr. Jackson?" he asks, timidly knocking at Michael Jackson's stage door. The boy enters the dressing room, and the music turns magical. The boy tries on the singer's sunglasses, hat, and jacket, and has a vision of himself as Michael Jackson performing. As the fantasy develops, the crowd noise begins a gradual crescendo. Finally the music fades away, and a bottle of Pepsi appears on the screen. We hear Michael Jackson's voice inquiring, "Looking for me?"

Actually, I was looking for the commercial to tell me something about the product. But what I got instead was pure show business. The personality is a show biz personality. The production, gimmicks, and glitz are all props from the world of show business. Even the endorsements are Hollywood props. In fact, Pepsi, in a public statement, actually said it was unconcerned about reports that neither Madonna nor Michael Jackson drinks Pepsi. The company was interested in "Michael Jackson's ability to provide some entertainment, not whether or not he drinks the product," one Pepsi spokesman told *The New York Times.*

Perhaps that helps explain the fact that most, if not all, Pepsi commercials could just as easily have been commercials for Coke, and vice versa. Consider the one that features Glenn Frey and Don Johnson driving through the center of town on a rainy night. Frey is whistling the tune "You Belong to the City," which is playing on the car radio. With some difficulty, the two men navigate various obstacles—speeding through a dark tunnel, being tailgated by a truck, being blinded by headlights—as they try to find their way. Even when they're stalled by engine failure, the car radio keeps playing "You Belong to the City." Johnson turns off the music, but Frey protests, "That's my song." The two men leave the car and enter a noisy nightclub to look for help. Inside, a disc jockey drops a can of Pepsi on the record to get the crowd's attention. When the music stops, Johnson calls for a mechanic as Frey begins to sing, "We've got freedom, we've got soul. We've got Pepsi and rock 'n roll. There ain't no choice, it's Pepsi in the U.S.A." They find a woman mechanic who repairs the car's engine, and the two men drive off, cheered on by a waving crowd. A super (words superimposed over the picture) reads, "Pepsi, the choice of a new generation."

In two full minutes of airtime, there's not a word about what makes Pepsi different from the competition. In fact, the same plot and same lyrics, with Coke substituted for Pepsi, would have worked just as well in a commercial for Coke.

Some industry observers seem unconcerned about the millions of dollars being spent on commercials that say nothing about the product. "In the cola wars, there is very little product differentiation, so the point is to make very creative commercials that people notice," one self-appointed expert told *The New York Times*. "Most of the role of advertising is to reinforce current use of your product, to make sure people know you're still there. It's to maintain the status quo, not increase market share."

What a revelation that is, and what a surprise to every advertiser and every advertising agency in the country. Can you imagine justifying spending all that money to remind people that Coke and Pepsi are still around and that you should continue drinking the same brand you're drinking now? Only someone completely ignorant of even the basics of advertising could make an idiotic statement like that. Increasing market share is what clients pay ad agencies to do. Good commercials, concepts, and executions are *not* interchangeable. Good commercials are tailor-made for a specific product according to that brand's marketing strategy. Every product is entitled to a Unique Advantage—even colas. And if the ad agencies are too lazy to find it, they're pouring their clients' money down the drain.

That's why I bristle when I see both sides in the cola wars relying on the same ammunition. Take a commercial for Coke in which Robert Plant sings "Tall Cool One" in a rock-concert setting. At first it sounds like he's singing to a woman: "I'm a strange cat running in the heat of the night. I got a fire in my eyes, got a taste for delight. Lighten up baby, I'm in love with you." Only when Plant displays a bottle of Coca-Cola Classic do we suspect that the soft drink may be the real object of his desire ("You're so tall, you're so cute"). The scene shifts back to Plant, and with strong sexual innuendo, he sings, "You stroke, you jump, you're hot and you tease, 'cause I'm the tall cool one and I'm built to please."

Not a word about taste, nothing to distinguish Coke from Pepsi. Except for a couple of quick shots of the cola bottle and a display of the Coca-Cola logo, this commercial almost lets us forget about Coke altogether and get swept away in the seductive lyrics. Thanks so much, Coke Classic, for that entertaining production number to break up the tedium of our nightly television fare.

While the Robert Plant routine only hints at the product, another commercial for Coca-Cola Classic incorporates the product into the song. This one features Kim Carnes singing, "It's a splash in the heat of the day, a shiver that's coming your way. Just a sip and you're gonna say, can't fight it. No, you can't hide it—the feeling you get from a Coca-Cola Classic." At least these lyrics relate to a soft drink and they make a noble effort to describe the feeling you get when you drink a cold Coke on a hot day. The problem again is that the commercial could just as easily be describing Pepsi or any other soft drink or beer.

The same, happily, does not hold true for a commercial in which Whitney Houston sings the praises of Diet Coke. Here, at least, the song is Diet Coke's exclusive theme, and the lyrics reflect the long-term strategy of the brand—"Just for the taste of it." "Diet Coke . . . just for the satisfaction . . . just for the light of it . . . just for the taste of it . . . just for the fun of it. One calorie." Better than the others, but still all entertainment.

Both Coke and Pepsi are so concerned with show biz and entertainment that they seem to have forgotten the good competitive advertising that marked the early years of their rivalry. When Pepsi first came into the cola business in a serious way in the 1930s, Coke was the industry leader. Pepsi, a latecomer to the market, launched a new product before the age of television with a heavy campaign in newspapers and magazines and a wonderful radio jingle: "Pepsi-Cola hits the spot/Twelve full ounces, that's a lot/Twice as much for a nickel, too/Pepsi-Cola is the drink for you."

Notice the competitive spirit of this jingle, which emphasized Pepsi's Unique Advantage over heavily entrenched Coke. Although the products looked and tasted similar and had the name "cola," Pepsi gave Coke's customers the irresistible switching idea that they could get twice as much Pepsi for the same money. By creating a Unique Advantage and emphasizing that advantage in its advertising, Pepsi was able to gain a foothold and make a two-horse race of the cola industry.

Coca-Cola eventually gave up its long-running generic theme ("The pause that refreshes") and responded with a much more competitive strategy, "Coca-Cola. The real thing," implying that Pepsi was a fake. This campaign stabilized the situation, leaving Coke unchallenged as the king of the colas—until Pepsi's second major advance, accompanied again by highly competitive advertising without even the slightest trace of show business.

I'm referring to The Pepsi Challenge campaign that began in the mid-1970s and continued into the early 1980s. The commercials in this campaign had no celebrities, no gimmicks, no entertainment value, and probably cost less than $50,000 each to produce. Yet they caused Coke to commit one of the biggest marketing blunders in advertising history.

Pure advertising, The Pepsi Challenge was based on that old standby, the taste test. In their simplest form, the commercials in this campaign showed real people sitting side by side at a table, participating in a blind taste test. Without identifying the brands, Pepsi asked the participants to taste two colas and to state their preferences. In test after test, avid Coke drinkers chose the taste of Pepsi over Coke. Pepsi went national with the taste test and showed that around the country, it repeatedly beat Coke among Coke's own customers. Based on these results, Pepsi now had, or implied it had, the ultimate Unique Advantage: taste!

The taste tests were very convincing. Those people most convinced were the Coca-Cola people in the company's world headquarters in Atlanta. They secretly replicated the Pepsi taste test, got the same result, panicked, went back to the drawing board, and came up with the formula for New Coke. As we've already seen in Chapter 2, New Coke was a marketing blunder. But it was largely inspired by the success of good competitive advertising known as The Pepsi Challenge.

These are the lessons Coke and Pepsi have forgotten in fighting a battle of stars instead of a battle of products. Don't they realize that all the big advances in the war of the colas have resulted from competitive claims and competitive advertising? The entertainment commercials they are both running lack any competitive claims, or any strategy at all. I can just see Coke or Pepsi marketing executives ready to do battle with me after reading that last sentence. In defense of the campaign, they might argue that there *is* a strategy and that it *is* competitive. The strategy, these executives would argue, is to appeal to the youth of the world, who are the big drinkers of colas, and to convince them that their cola is the "in" cola. My answer is: That's no strategy, and even if it was, it has been neutralized by the competitive brand doing the same thing in the same way. The trouble with Coke and Pepsi is that they underestimate young people—their own customers. These customers are a lot smarter, a lot shrewder, a lot more demanding than Coke and Pepsi give them credit for. Young people, like all people, respond to reason. They respond to a meaningful benefit. They respond to a Unique Advantage. Want proof? They responded to The Pepsi Challenge, didn't they? The Coke and Pepsi entertainment commercials are the lazy—but very expensive—way out. That's a lot of money to spend to avoid thinking.

If I were sponsoring a cola commercial, I'd damn well demand less cute entertainment and more cutting sales talk for my advertising dollar. Nor would I spend one cent on a memorable commercial that may be mistaken for my competitor's commercial. I hope that some day Coke and Pepsi will realize once again that they need to distinguish their commercials from those of their competitors by identifying the Unique Advantage of their product. When that happens, they will have come full circle to what started their rivalry and their great success in the first place.

In fact, Coke did resurrect an earlier campaign—its highly successful "the real thing" theme, and I thought that at long last,

Coke was beginning to see the light and was going back to a competitive line with a distinguishing switching idea. But before the smile of satisfaction could even form on my face, I learned that Coke had also signed country music star Randy Travis, produced a new spot featuring Michael Jordan, and was about to produce another new commercial teaming Art Carney and Brian Bonsall. Oh well, you can't win them all!

In case you haven't already guessed, I'm heartily opposed to advertising that treats entertainment as its first priority. So is there any place for big name stars in advertising—not to give testimonials, but merely to entertain?

My answer is a loud and unmistakable *no!* Advertising and show business are two different things. When stars do their routines with no reference or relationship to the product, they have no business in advertising, just as there's no place for advertising within a star's act. They're both out of place and detract from the main attraction. The star on stage is the entertainer. The star of a commercial should be the product.

Before we leave the cola battleground, we should look at another cola that would dearly love to fight in that war but, alas, is too small. This cola doesn't have the vast war chest to take on the two supercolas. But the company does have enough to get into show biz. If it can't afford Michael Jackson, at least it can afford an elaborate Hollywood production—one of the most blatant examples I've ever seen of show business overpowering advertising. This huge production, sponsored by RC Cola, features knights jousting on horseback. One is knocked off his horse, and a swordfight ensues. In a conciliatory gesture, the knight who is losing the battle offers his opponent an RC Cola. When the victorious knight hesitates, the loser urges him to take it with this "immortal" selling line: "With all due respect, your majesty, we're not talking about a Magna Carta. Just try it!"

With all due respect, we're not talking about advertising here. We're talking nonsense. Why should I try the product? Just because RC Cola did a nonsensical commercial that cost a bundle?

With Coke and Pepsi busy out-entertaining each other, what a golden opportunity for RC Cola to slip in with solid, product-based, competitive commercials and take a big gulp out of both of them. But no, RC Cola would rather get into the entertainment competition—a battle it can't win—by belittling its own product. Which just goes to prove, you don't have to be big to make a big mistake.

———

Show business commercials have reached extreme proportions in the cola wars. But they are not new. Consider, for example, an earlier Alka-Seltzer commercial that committed some of the same mistakes. I'm referring to the great granddaddy of show biz commercials—the "Try it you'll like it" series. Think of it—the two creative originators of this campaign were lionized as heroes of Madison Avenue. The famous lines they created for this series, "Try it you'll like it" and "I can't believe I ate the whole thing," slipped effortlessly into common parlance. Decades after these campaigns appeared, the tag lines are still being repeated, although I bet not many people could tell you where they came from.

Throughout the "Try it you'll like it/I can't believe I ate the whole thing" era, I stoutly maintained, "I can't believe I *hate* the whole thing," because this campaign wasn't advertising.

The slogans built public recognition for Alka-Seltzer (in short order, they appeared on sweatshirts, in supermarket windows, and as punch lines for stand-up TV comics). But again, recognition is not the criterion for advertising success when it comes to a product as well known and heavily advertised as Alka-Seltzer. Believability, conviction, persuasion, and, of course, conversion of nonusers and users of competitive brands—these factors determine whether a well-known product's campaign is successful or not, and they add up to *sales.*

Secondly, although it's very nice for the copywriters that their lines were being repeated so enthusiastically, I'm not sure what advantage that gave to the client since the product's name was not included in the lines. Because this series was far better entertainment than advertising, the waggish punch lines were far better remembered than the reasons for buying the product. The "entertaining" commercial can be a well-financed ego trip for its creators.

The much-awarded Alka-Seltzer campaign also gave birth to a new generation of humorous advertising. The creators of the campaign unfortunately confirmed that their formula for creating these commercials was first to come up with a funny, memorable punch line and then to write a commercial around it. In short, suit the sales idea to the execution, instead of the other way around. This may be the right way to sell funny lines to the buying public, but I can't believe it's the right way to sell a product.

While the Alka-Seltzer campaign was garnering all the awards, the president of the agency that created the commercials had this to say about the American consumer: ". . . The overindulgent American is an average consumer. We understand him . . . because we're average consumers ourselves. We're *now* people. We use Alka-Seltzer, we talk like people in the commercials, we can identify with smiley situations. I'm fascinated with the American consumer today. He's just so smart."

And those may be the funniest lines of all. (The agency president was married to a major airline president and owned three residences, including a villa on the French Riviera, at the time she called herself an average consumer.)

Agency people just aren't average consumers. They are, as she noted, "now people," marketing-oriented and far too hip to have much in common with average anybodies. She was right about one thing, though. American consumers *are* smart. So smart that they quoted the punch lines and didn't buy the campaign. Or the product. Shortly thereafter, the smiley situations were replaced by real commercials that sold Alka-Seltzer instead of *bons mots*. And suddenly, I loved the whole thing.

The creators of the new ads got rid of the show biz. The entertainment. The jokes, the punch lines, the actors, and the elaborate productions. In their place, they introduced some of the simplest commercials they've ever done, and some of the best. Each one consisted of a close-up of an on-camera spokesman— not a famous personality, but a plain, believable, next-door-neighborly human being—who delivers the entire message face-to-face, person-to-person, with no frills and no bull. His message was straightforward and honest, stressing how effective Alka-Seltzer can be in combating upset stomachs and headaches. He offered us solid reasons why we should use Alka-Seltzer instead of a competing brand: first, for its specially buffered aspirin and antacids, and, second, because it's the best remedy you can buy without a prescription. If it doesn't work, you'd better see your doctor. (A strong statement like that instills consumer confidence in the product.) Third, you should buy Alka-Seltzer because it's a potent medicine, not a candy store patent remedy. (A repositioning statement that treats the product with the seriousness it deserves as a cure for a serious problem. After all, what's funny about an upset stomach?) Finally, the commercial established the efficacy of the product by warning us not to take it every time some little thing bothers us but, like any medicine, to save it for when we really need it. The advertising even took advantage of Alka-Seltzer's long history on the American scene by promoting its history in commercials aimed at the older market. It's been around for a long while, these commercials said, and we have faith in it.

The concept and positioning of that campaign was absolutely right. The execution was brilliantly simple, completely believable, highly persuasive, and totally honest. It made the old show biz Alka-Seltzer spots look a little distasteful, a little silly, a little contrived, a little inappropriate, a little incompatible with the nature of the product—and then, suddenly, the whole dumb series seemed about as appetizing and as convincing as a big spicy meat-a-ball. If I'm wrong, I said at the time, and this straight-from-the-shoulder campaign didn't do a better job of selling Alka-Seltzer than the ethnic situation comedies, then I threatened to get the hell out of the business.

And as a reward, if I was right, I'd settle for the difference in production costs between the "Try it you'll like it" campaign and the later one.

(Well, it's now many years later and I'm still in the business, but nobody has come forth to give me the difference in the production costs. No matter, I was a winner anyway, because everything I believed about advertising was confirmed.)

I have a lot of respect for Alka-Seltzer for diagnosing and correcting its own mistake. The unfunny sales results produced by its funny campaign prove that cause-and-effect is truly a factor in advertising and that the buying public has a say in the kind of advertising we see on our TV screens. It also proves that jokes, entertainment, and big-budget commercials don't sell the product if the sales idea isn't there to begin with.

———

Do I believe in humorous approaches to advertising? Of course I do! But I also believe that an ad maker owes it to the client to consider these three questions before communicating a sales message with a funny or "clever"execution:

1. Is it compatible with the nature of the product being sold? If your client is the local funeral home, you'd better think it through again.
2. Is it likely to detract from the seriousness, believability, or sincerity of the message? Again, an upset stomach is no laughing matter. When humor minimizes the importance of the malady, it also minimizes the importance of the cure.
3. Does it overpower or slow down the communication of the message? If it does, you're selling humor at the expense of your product or service.

Some people who should know better think humor is just fine for all occasions. An ad in the advertising trade press quoting one of advertising's top gurus told about starting on beginners' row in a large ad agency and being told to keep writing humorous radio spots until he started to laugh at his own jokes. In retrospect, this veteran adman thought it was a good exercise. After all, he reasoned, good advertising should leave them smiling.

Who cares if they're smiling? I only care if they're buying. Funny executions leave them smiling. Not so funny sales points leave them buying.

———

While I'm on the topic of slowing down the communication of the message, I'd like to sing out about jingles, one of the most used and abused devices of both radio and television.

Generally, I don't believe in jingles as effective selling devices. By themselves, they're not advertising. The best and most effective advertising is what comes closest to duplicating the one-on-one encounter of a salesperson and a prospect. If you were a salesperson, would you sing your message? Not unless you were selling songs.

People may wind up singing the words of your jingle without ever understanding or thinking about their meaning (as they do with "The Star Spangled Banner," for example). They remember the jingle, but not the message.

I think jingles can be used effectively to do two things, provided they are used with reasonable frequency. As an audio tag, they can help register a product name. Recall the famous "J-E-L-L-O" tag that made Jack Benny famous, the Jolly Green Giant jingle, and "N-E-S-T-L-E-S, Nestles makes the very best chocolate." For years, Kellogg's signed off with "K-E-double-L-O-double-good Kellogg's best to you" at the end of every commercial. And Nabisco still ends every spot with one word set to a tune: "Na-bis-co"—a terrific registration of a product in two seconds. Campbell's soups, which for several years dropped its wonderful jingle, "That's what Campbell's soups are M'm! M'm! Good!" recently had the good sense to bring it back. M'm! M'm! Smart!

Jingles can also act as a reminder of an already well-established fact or concept. Repetition of the "Twice as much for a nickel, too" jingle used to launch Pepsi kept driving home for years the reason people should buy it. Burger King kept telling its customers to "Have it your way" and Budweiser said it all with "When you say Bud, you've said it all." McDonald's hit the mark with several memorable jingles. Who could forget "You deserve a break today" or "Good times, great taste"? But my favorite McDonald's jingle by far was the tongue-twister that catalogued the ingredients of a Big Mac: "Two all-beef patties, special sauce, lettuce, cheese, pickles, onions on a sesame seed bun." The purpose of this jingle was to sell a Big Mac with everything on it. The jingle worked because it was catchy and fun enough to make you want to learn it. And even if you didn't know it perfectly, you wound up with a pretty juicy idea of what's in a Big Mac.

Jingles should never be relied upon to carry, deliver, or establish a basic selling message.

But I do admit they're great for the shower.

The only reason for the existence of any commercial is to communicate an idea from the advertiser to the viewer. It is not a vehicle for entertainment. If it leaves you howling with glee or whistling a tune, the chances are good that it didn't simultaneously leave you making plans for the purchase of its product. You simply haven't got time to concentrate on both. As an advertiser, I'd much rather let you arrange for your own entertainment through movies, plays, books, sex. Show biz isn't the advertising business, and the two make strange bedfellows on the TV screen. This is not to say that commercials cannot or should not be entertaining. So long as the entertainment is functional in communicating the idea, I'm all in favor of it. But I get mad as hell when I see Hollywood people, sets, and budgets taking over my business.

The kind of people who belong in the advertising business are adpeople with bright new ideas about how to *reach* and *convince* other people in thirty seconds or less. That's damned hard to do. Which is why these people, the real innovators and professionals, should stay in complete control of a commercial from start to finish. The alternative is for them to surrender their brainchild, the single most precious product of our business, to the swash and swagger of a loud, wasteful, and unnecessary swarm of technical parasites. And that would be untenable. It would be suicidal. It would be cowardly.

And it wouldn't be advertising.

7

The Seven Deadly Sins of Advertising

Some advertising practitioners will look you right in the eye and tell you that the single worst fate a commercial can suffer is death by neglect. Proponents of this position insist that they would rather have their commercial noticed and hated than ignored. To them, it's better to have the product name registered negatively than not registered at all. This is the old "spit-on-the-table" George Washington Hill school of advertising.

(To all of you who have not seen *The Hucksters,* a movie based on a novel about advertising by Frederic Wakeman and starring Clark Gable as the good guy—ad agency man, of course—here is the background for that label. There is a scene in the film where the mean old client spits on a conference room table, to the utter amazement and disgust of the assembled executives. He then makes his point—they didn't like what he did, but none of them would ever forget it. That, he remarks, is what he expects of his advertising. The scene and the character were rumored to be based on the legendary George Washington Hill, chairman, president, marketing director, advertising director, and everything else at The American Tobacco Company at the time, who had the reputation of being the world's toughest client. This kind of advertising became known as the George Washington Hill school.)

I couldn't disagree with it more. While its proponents may be right in saying that being ignored is the worst indignity *advertising* can suffer, being ignored is infinitely preferable to the worst indignity an *advertiser* can suffer: that of watching the public turn against his product. For the public to ignore his advertising is one thing; to be revolted by it is plainly another.

In short, bad advertising is curable, but advertising that turns the public against the product is fatal. Most often, advertising that alienates a client's market has committed one of these seven deadly sins:

1. *Bad taste.* Happily, we don't see too many commercials in genuine bad taste anymore, a fact that makes the occasional clinker all the harder to swallow. But if you see as many such clinkers as I do, you begin to get the trembles about the future of the advertising business, and a whole rash of them confirms this feeling of apprehension. The bad-taste syndrome must eventually hurt the client as well as outrage the public, and it can do irreparable damage to the entire advertising business. That's what makes it so dangerous.

This is what I mean by bad taste.

Dr. Scholl promoted his foot odor antiperspirant spray with the same old theme that every soap, deodorant, toothpaste, and mouthwash has used at least once: "You may be the last to know. . . ." The commercial is divided into the familiar three-scene format. (The three-scene format has become quite common in 30-second commercials. To build suspense and interest in the commercial, three vignettes are used to dramatize and drive home the same point. One scene would stretch out too long for the time span and be dull. Two scenes aren't convincing or memorable enough. Three scenes seem to be just right to make the point, add interest, and fit perfectly into the allotted time.) In the first, a man removes his shoe and hands it to a shoemaker for repairs. The shoemaker passes out. The second scene takes place in a bowling alley: One of the bowlers on a team takes off his shoes to change into his bowling shoes and his three teammates faint dead away. Predictably, when a man removes his shoe in the third scene, his dog topples over.

Come on now, Dr. Scholl. When dealing with so personal a problem and product, shouldn't you have bent over backwards *not* to be insulting? This commercial goes out of its way to do just the opposite. It's insulting to the very people who are the product's prime prospects—those who are aware of the problem and are embarrassed by it!

Wouldn't Scholl have been better off handling the problem seriously by offering the delicate reassurance to "sufferers" that their problem is quite common and can now be easily eliminated? And wouldn't it have been more compatible with the ad's theme ("You may have it without knowing it") to have directed the message to the far larger market that may not even be aware of the problem? Instead, Scholl chose to dramatize people with such obviously severe cases that, unless their nasal passages have been blocked with portland cement, they've *got* to know.

Something else about this commercial irks me: Why is the problem limited to men only? Don't women, particularly those who wear boots all day, have the same problem? (Now there's a marketing segmentation idea: a foot deodorant specifically made for a woman's special foot odor problem.) And just look at the people they chose to be the offended parties: Who cares about offending a shoemaker, a bowling team, or a dog? The shoemaker, let's face it, must regard foot odor as an occupational hazard, the bowlers couldn't care less, and the dog likes to lick feet anyway, the smellier the better.

The people we are most concerned about offending are those with whom we have some significant social contact. A wife, for example, or a girlfriend. Neighbors, associates, clients. One's peers. My point is that this commercial, besides being needlessly insulting, is downright dumb.

A happy footnote to this commercial is that Dr. Scholl no longer resorts to insensitive, insulting advertising like this. Its subsequent campaigns have been much more sympathetic to and understanding of their customers' feelings.

Or for pure nausea, how about the Scope commercial that shows three different couples revolted by their own morning breath, or the breath of their spouses? One husband rolls over in bed to give his wife a kiss in the morning. "Ooh honey, don't come near me, please," she responds, pushing him away. Another man runs to the bathroom before he'll let his wife get near him. A woman backs off in shame with her hand over her mouth. "Oh sweetie, you don't want to get too close," she warns her mate. All three offenders rinse with Scope and are ready to smooch.

Another Scope commercial shows an attractive woman reporter who has revolted a male colleague with her halitosis. As she approaches him in the newsroom to talk about a story, the co-worker finds he cannot get away from her bad breath. "I moved to the right, the left, there was no escape!" he says. Suddenly the woman catches on. She grabs a bottle of Scope from her desk drawer, excuses herself to rinse, and returns confidently to the office. So what's the point?

Just this: Advertisers should never commit the bad-taste error of trying to insult people into buying their products. Convince them? Yes. Reason with them? Of course. Debate them? Always. But insult them, never.

And speaking of insulting, how about this one for Surf detergent? It's the hottest day of the year in Houston, and a teenager anchors an amateur news bulletin, using members of his family and neighbors as on-the-scene reporters. The whole spot is done like an amateur home movie. "What's it like out there?" he asks his father, as the scene shifts to a tree-lined block in a Houston suburb. The boy's father is standing with his arms raised and a pail on either side of him. "It's so hot today, I'm sweating buckets!" he answers, as the sweat pours off his body into the pails. Next we hear from a group of neighborhood teenagers. "Some smell has created the sock monster, and it's raining stinky socks everywhere!" complains one boy. "A most disgusting specimen!" gripes another, holding up sweaty clothes. Suddenly Surf comes to the rescue. The family washes its clothes in Surf, and the whole neighborhood breathes easier. The commercial ends with a child holding a hand-lettered sign that reads "THE END." A child's voice announces, "Hope you liked our commercial!"

Frankly, I think it stinks. It's trite, unbelievable, insulting, sophomoric, and "ichhy." In fact, it reminds me of the sort of cruel lunchroom humor that teenagers sometimes use to make fun of each other. Sweat and body odor are not funny, and neither is this exaggerated rendition of these common problems.

Another Surf commercial is almost as bad. This one shows father and son going one-on-one playing driveway basketball.

"Did I ever tell you they retired my college jersey?" the father asks, putting his arm around his son as they wind up the game. Catching a whiff of Dad's sweat-soaked T-shirt, the son exclaims, "The way your shirt smells, they probably burned it!" Whereupon Dad lifts his arm, sniffs his armpit, and groans. When he washes his shirt in Surf, all the dirt and odors come out. Happily, he returns to the game with his son.

How grotesque. No doubt Surf hoped to win customers with these commercials. They probably lost more than they won. I hope so.

Equally insulting is a print ad for Marriott's Residence Inn. To compare the average stay at most hotels with the average stay at a Residence Inn, the ad shows two pairs of men's jockey-type underpants accompanied by the label "most hotels." For Residence Inn, it shows ten pairs. Maybe Residence Inn had a good concept. But the execution is completely offensive. Why choose underpants as a symbol of the length of a stay? As one woman observed in a letter to the editor of *Advertising Age,* why not choose laundry bags, toothbrushes, pillows, or even "DO-NOT-DISTURB" signs? I'm so offended by the ad, I wouldn't visit a Residence Inn for ten minutes, let alone ten days. It doesn't represent the quality I'm looking for. And, at a time when increasing numbers of women are traveling on business, the ad seems to alienate a large group of potential clients.

2. *Bad Judgment.* Second only to bad-taste commercials are those that use bad judgment. A case in point was the Dodge Colt commercial that featured two priests (actors, of course) to deliver the sales message. They are an obvious takeoff on the old Barry Fitzgerald/Bing Crosby team that sold so many tickets to *The Bells of St. Mary's.* The young priest shows the older priest the new car he has bought for the church to offer as first prize in the church raffle. He then makes all the sales points about the car's luxury features, and when he tells the old priest the price, the older man (in his thickest Barry Fitzgerald brogue and over-the-top-of-his glasses twinkle) declares that there's really no need for the parish to know how inexpensive the car really is.

In other words, let's pull a fast one on the parish.

Depicting men of the cloth in a commercial is always risky,

and forcing the priest to make the actual sales pitch is even more questionable. But implying that the priests would even entertain the thought of deceiving the parish is highly improper, and I've got to believe that a large segment of the people who saw it (and not just the churchgoers, either) were offended and were left with a negative impression of Dodge. Was it worth it?

Another example of bad judgment is a Roy Rogers commercial that tries to pitch a summer special to an audience of school-aged children. The commercial features a number of middle-aged women who look like prison matrons dishing up cafeteria grub. Each woman is identified by name and by school. As the picture flashes from one unappetizing plate to the next, we hear a chorus of "See You in September." The voice-over announcer says, "You know what September means! So head for Roy Rogers now." At the mention of Roy Rogers, the picture changes to juicy-looking cheeseburgers and roast beef sandwiches. Yum! The commercial ends with a reprise of one of the lunchroom ladies offering up a plate of unidentifiable mush. The voice-over reminds children to hurry before the summer and the promotion are over and they go back to school food.

Is Roy Rogers suggesting that these poor kids will be force-fed gruel come September? In any event, Roy Rogers showed terrible judgment with this distasteful view of school cafeteria workers. If Roy Rogers really cared about kids, the commercial would dwell less upon the cafeteria workers and crummy school food and more upon healthier meals to serve children. Luckily, the commercial didn't last too long. School cafeteria workers from around the country threatened to beat Roy Rogers, Dale Evans, and Trigger to death with their giant serving spoons.

Commercials that perpetuate ethnic stereotypes are the worst kind of bad-judgment advertising. And sometimes the groans they elicit are real. Consider these side-by-side 15-second spots for Continental Airlines. The first shows a Samurai warrior, complete with sword, standing in front of a mound labeled "High Fares." In halting English, the warrior asks, "You wish to travel to Denver, but have little money and hate restrictions?" With dramatic Oriental music in the background, he slashes off the top of the mound. The second spot shows the warrior standing behind two airline seats. "You long to travel, but hate to fly alone?" he asks. Again, he whips out his sword, this time slashing one seat in half to show that you can take along a friend at half the normal fare. Why an Oriental warrior? I could begin to understand it if they were talking about flights to the Orient. But these are domestic destinations. The choice of a Samurai warrior is completely irrelevant, incompatible, misleading, and confusing, to say nothing about insulting to Asian-Americans.

This campaign brought an outburst from Asian-American groups. The Chinese for Affirmative Action called it racist, and Continental canceled the spots in Seattle and Spokane, Washington, after a threatened boycott. Another campaign grounded by poor judgment.

3. *Insensitivity.* Sometimes advertisers offend potential buyers by showing extreme insensitivity to the user of the product.

Remember the Safeguard soap commercial in which the daughter comes home from a date in tears because her boyfriend has given her a bar of Safeguard as a subtle hint? Her father becomes incensed, storms outside to rake the boyfriend over hot coals for implying that his little girl has body odor, and returns a minute later saying, "The boy makes a lot of sense." Daddy bursts into tears. Mother bursts into tears. Daughter is already weeping buckets, so the whole family joins together for a cozy sobbing session.

This is advertising? I can't imagine a more tasteless, insulting, repulsive way to sell a deodorant soap. There's a complete lack of sensitivity and tact and human feeling. I think it's a crying shame.

Here's another one that makes me want to cry: a commercial for Oxy-10 acne medication that features a war game and uses military terminology to describe the battle against acne. The battle is labeled "operation mop up," and the commercial begins with a strategy session. The targets—giant oily spots on a boy's face—are projected on a screen. Of course, the weapon is new improved Oxy-10. To simulate the way the medication works, a general blasts a laser at the screen, and the giant oily spots disappear from the boy's face. The commercial makes a game of acne.

Anyone who has ever suffered the frustrations of acne knows that it's not a game and it's not funny. It's the most serious, most embarrassing thing in a teenager's life. A company making a remedy for acne certainly should know that, too. This commercial is insensitive to the feelings of its target audience and could very well turn teenagers off. I hope it does, because not only is the commercial insensitive, it also gives users false hopes for an immediate cure and sets them up for disappointment. And that's cruel!

Among the worst and most insensitive advertising I've seen, though, is a print ad for The Prudential Property Company that ran in *Manhattan, inc.*, a business magazine centered on New York. The ad shows an assortment of disgruntled passengers packed into a crowded subway car. Amidst all the men in business clothes stands a rumpled bag lady. The headline reads, "Some of America's most successful companies have chosen our wildlife over yours." At first glance, I couldn't even tell what this ad was about. As I read on, I realized the purpose: to convince New York City-based companies to move to the New Jersey suburbs. The assumption is that if the subway passengers had offices in New Jersey, they wouldn't have to share a crowded subway car with a bag lady. That may be, but the language of the ad is completely insensitive and offensive, not just to the homeless but to the entire audience of the magazine who just happen to be New Yorkers. It compares the wildlife of the suburbs to this "wild" woman of the city and treats homelessness as a problem people should run away from, rather than solve.

No wonder the ad sparked angry protests from New Yorkers, as well as from advocates for the homeless. Prudential quickly pulled it and issued a public apology.

4. *Double entendres.* Double-entendre commercials created for their shock appeal can also hurt an advertiser's image. In a memo to his staff many years ago, John E. O'Toole, then president of Foote, Cone & Belding (now president of the American Association of Advertising Agencies), honed in on two specific examples. Air France's "Have you ever done it the French way?" campaign was one. These provocative lines are uttered in a provocative tone by a provocative bikini-clad woman in a provocative pose. The other campaign was Mennen's "Get off your can. Get on the stick" campaign for their underarm stick deodorant. Mr. O'Toole concluded his memo with this statement:

The conventions of vaudeville dictated that when laughs weren't forthcoming, a sure way to bring the house down was for the comedian to drop his pants. Advertising, despite the misconceptions of a few, is not vaudeville. And a sale is more difficult to achieve than a laugh.

Still good advice, John, and a client's good name is still more precious than any commercial.

Speaking of dropping pants, let me drop this campaign for Sansabelt slacks on you. It's a blatant example of double-entendre advertising under the theme line of "What women look for in men's pants." In one spot, a sultry, sexy lady turns provocatively toward camera and purrs, "My mother always told me to look at a man's eyes first. [*Pause.*] What did she know?" In another equally provocative spot, an equally provocative woman says, "I've always considered a man's lower half his better half." And still another siren, in a room sans furniture except for a bed, tells us that "All men are alike until they put their pants on."

That's pretty rough stuff, even for adults. But a double-entendre commercial that bothered me much more was one for L. A. Gear footwear aimed at teenagers: Two teenagers flirt. The boy asks, "Why do you think they call all cars 'she'?" Slowly sashaying and lowering her eyes, the girl responds in a series of double entendres: "They're responsive, temperamental, and very expensive. And they have great curves [*on this one, she bends over the car while the camera pans the obvious*] . . . and if you try to start them too fast [*the boy is moving toward her, his hormones all ajangle as she backs away*] . . . they stall!" The boy's response? "You are such a brat!" Maybe this commercial aims to be cool and talk to kids in their own language. But it speaks the language of double entendre to teenagers and that does not speak well for L. A. Gear. In the long run, it can't help the image of the company.

5. *Harmful spokesperson.* As we will see in Chapter 13, the right spokesperson can help sell a product. But there are also times when the wrong spokesperson can actually do the product harm. The most stunning example is Jacko, the loudmouth brute with the ugly face, the blond crew cut, the bulging biceps, the bully personality, and the Australian accent, who shouted at us for sev-

eral years in commercials for Energizer batteries. There were several executions of the same theme, all loud, all obnoxious, and all featuring Jacko dressed in a wrestling outfit, screaming at the top of his lungs. In one typical commercial, he boards a commuter train filled with businesspeople and shocks the mild-mannered crowd, first by shoving a battery under one man's nose and then by lifting an oversized Energizer as if it were a barbell. In another spot, Jacko comes barreling down an office corridor and forces his way through a set of closing elevator doors, trapping a less-than-delighted captive audience. I'm sure they all had burst eardrums by the time they got to their floors.

The first time I saw these commercials, it was hate at first sight. It was hard not to hate Jacko. Will Rogers would have hated him. Dale Carnegie would have hated him. Even George Washington Hill would have hated Jacko. I was never charged up by Jacko's energy or by his power as a spokesman, either. In the windup, neither was the consumer. The louder he yelled, the softer sales got. Energizer eventually pulled the plug on Jacko, but not before he did great harm to the company's image.

6. *Inappropriate.* Advertising that is inappropriate to the product can hurt the image of the company. The Prudential's agency learned that lesson the hard way when its "Happy Endings" campaign reached a sad demise. The campaign featured 60-second black-and-white simulations of schmaltzy old movies. You know the plot: Boy meets girl, boy marries girl, everybody lives happily ever after. One spot shows a romantic parting shot in a European-style train station à la the famous Bergman/Bogart airport parting shot in *Casablanca*. Another is a 1930s nightclub scene in which two lovers featured in the floor show are reunited after years apart. In both, the message is the same: In the movies it's easy to make dreams come true, but in the real world it takes financial planning. So come to the companies of the Prudential and build your future on the Rock.

Pure show business, the Prudential campaign piqued the interest of vintage movie buffs but ruffled some feathers in the corporate board room. It seems that serious-minded financial planners thought the "Happy Endings" spots were too frivolous to support the tough-as-a-rock image Prudential wanted to convey. So did I. They were incompatible with the image of the company and the product the company was trying to sell—confidence. I wouldn't have a great deal of confidence in a company that did make-believe advertising like this. I certainly wouldn't trust them with my retirement money. The real-life ending was that Prudential moved its $70 to $80 million account elsewhere. Not such a happy ending for the agency.

7. *Misleading.* Advertising that misleads the public about the benefits of the product is a sure way to lose buyers. It's even worse when it's a clinical product—like Tylenol.

Consider a Tylenol spot that features a real-life teacher who is also the school football coach, telling how the stress of his job has led to headaches and an ulcer. He tells us his doctor told him to stop taking aspirin, so he switched to Tylenol and his ulcer has been fine ever since.

By the end of the commercial, we are so focused on the guy's ulcer that we have totally lost sight of the fact that initially he took aspirin for his headaches. To be clear, the commercial should have let us know that now when he gets headaches, the coach takes Tylenol instead of aspirin, and it doesn't irritate his ulcer. Without making this point clear, the commercial suggests that the man took Tylenol for his ulcer and completely misleads the public about the benefits of the product. Tylenol didn't deliberately mislead us with this commercial. The company had no intention of suggesting that Tylenol cures ulcers. It happened because the commercial was unclear. That can be a fatal mistake.

———

I've saved the worst for last. The Reebok bungee divers commercial commits most of the deadly sins, with poor taste and bad judgment heading the list. (Bungee divers, I found out, are thrill-seekers who dive headlong off high places with elasticized cords tied to their ankles to stop their plunge in the nick of time.) In this spot, two such divers jump off a bridge; one is wearing Reebok's new Pump basketball sneakers, the other, Nike hightops. We witness the fall in dramatic silence except for the eerie "whooshing" sound of the straining cords. The fall finally comes to an end with the Reebok diver dangling upside down from his cord while the Nike diver is nowhere in sight—only his sneakers remain, swaying from the end of his cord. A narrator coldly, matter-of-factly announces that the Reebok Pump "fits a little better than your ordinary athletic shoe." Advertising like this to any audience is questionable. The fact that its target is impressionable teenagers is unforgivable. It does great harm to the image of all honest, responsible people in advertising. Fortunately, the commercial ran only briefly before a public outcry forced it off the air. (Interesting, isn't it, that two of the three networks approved it for airing in the first place.)

Eventually, the commercial was re-edited, a 7-second disclaimer was added assuring us that no one was injured during the filming of the spot, and it was put back on the air. Although the spot was slightly changed, I haven't changed my opinion in the least—I still think it's a horror.

—————

Any of these seven deadly sins of advertising may alienate a client's market from his product or cause the public to think less of the company. So what can be done to guard against these sins?

All who are charged with preparing or approving advertising at the ad agency must always think first, before irreparable damage is done, of the company that is footing the bill. The single most important responsibility we who create advertising have, even more important than selling the client's product, is protecting the client's good name. The client's reputation is more important than all the creative advertising awards in the world. It's the client's name that is on the line, not our own, and though we may choose to take certain risks with our own reputations, we have no right to take any risks with our clients' reputations.

8

The Demo – TV's Ultimate Weapon

Television was made for demonstrations.

And that's very fortunate, because nothing achieves believability like a good, simple, relevant demonstration. Why? Because a mere claim of product performance or superiority told in words and pictures, no matter how earthshaking in concept or perfectly realized in execution, is just one more claim among thousands competing for the consumers' credence. As such, a claim will be accepted or rejected by the viewer almost at whim, and most whims are inclined to be negative.

A good solid demo, on the other hand, is proof positive of the claim made. It lifts that claim out of the controversial world of opinion and positions it firmly within the realm of absolute fact.

Of course, there are demonstrations and demonstrations, and the use of this technique is not an automatic guarantee of believability. Some demos I've seen, for example, have demonstrated an irrelevant or inconsequential feature. No one will care (or buy) unless the feature demonstrated offers a substantial advantage. Other demos simply do not prove their sales point

85

convincingly, and some get so complicated that they lose their believability.

I insist upon seven basic ingredients for making good, convincing demonstrations:

1. *Make it interesting, exciting, suspenseful, or dramatic.* I'm talking about execution here, and everything I said about execution in Chapter 4 still goes. Execution is the soulmate of your concept. It's what keeps audiences in their seats when their favorite shows break for a commercial. It's the setting that displays your jewel of an idea to perfection, so prepare it with care.

I point to the classic Sears power mower commercial that combined a simple, believable demonstration with an element of uncontrived suspense to make a near-flawless sales point with maximum impact. A live commercial, it demonstrated the easy starting capability of the Sears mower as the mower started up almost every time the test was run. A tally of successes and failures was kept throughout the campaign right on screen, and if the score was less than perfect, it was close enough and honest enough to be convincing.

But nothing could top that split second of suspense falling between the activation of the starter and the answering roar of the motor. Would it make it? Would the mower prove itself on live television, where precious little can be faked, or would it flop, die, and see its failure recorded in big, black letters on the public tally?

Now that's exciting—a critical feature of the product demonstrated on live TV in a manner guaranteed to stop viewers in their tracks when on the way to the refrigerator or to the hardware store to buy a mower.

A more recent demonstration for the Sears power mower makes the same dramatic point. One hundred men and women who look like they could be your next-door neighbors line up on the sideline of a football field. Each stands poised, ready to start a Sears Craftsman power mower. Again, there's the uncertainty: How many will start on the first pull? At the sound of the referee's whistle, ninety-nine people move on to the field behind their purring mowers. Just one lonely man is left standing behind. True, this commercial doesn't have the suspense of the live version. But it's still a great demonstration. It shows us dramatically that the Sears power mower is so reliable, it almost always starts on the first pull. And the one-in-a-hundred failure makes it all the more believable.

2. *Make sure it's relevant to the point you want to make.* To do this, you've got to think hard about what you're trying to say, then make your demo say it.

Consider Saran Wrap. The Unique Advantage advertised is the ability of Saran Wrap to keep odors in. So a commercial was created that features a ferocious tiger and two steaks. One steak is wrapped in Saran Wrap, while the other is double-wrapped in both Reynolds and Glad Wraps. The commercial tells us that a tiger never goes after anything it can't smell. The tiger rips apart the steak wrapped in Reynolds and Glad Wraps, and ignores the one wrapped in Saran. The point: Saran prevents smells from getting out. Although the execution of this commercial is exaggerated, it never strays from the point, and it gets the message across in a dramatic, memorable way. And it's so believable that I would not hesitate to stare down a hungry tiger if I were wrapped in Saran.

For a dramatic demonstration accomplished almost without audio, I'd give an A+ to Cheer All-Temperature laundry detergent. The entire commercial is a magic act, accompanied by music, to demonstrate the effectiveness of Cheer in cold water. A poker-faced magician, clad in a tuxedo, uses a handkerchief to wipe the bottom of his shoe. He holds up the filthy cloth to show his audience, then drops the cloth into a cocktail shaker. With considerable flourish, he adds ice cubes, water, and Cheer, and gives the brew a shake. Presto! The handkerchief is white again. What an innovative demonstration of the power of a detergent. Not only is the ad relevant to the point—that Cheer works well in cold water—but it makes that point with such flair and élan that it not only captures our attention but stands out from the usual detergent format. It's all reinforced by a visual warning at the end: "We do not recommend trying this demonstration with just any detergent." I doubt anyone will.

Another great, relevant demonstration shows us clinically how Mobil 1 motor oil withstands the heat of a car's engine. The commercial starts with a man in an asbestos suit standing in the middle of a roaring fire. He tells us the fire is 570 degrees—as hot as it gets inside a car's engine. Next, he pours Mobil 1 into one frying pan and conventional motor oil into another. Both pans are heated to the temperature of a car's engine. The conventional motor oil is scorched black and sticky and has to be scraped off the pan. Mobil 1 remains liquid and clear.

Have you ever seen a more believable demonstration of a product's Unique Advantage? Or one that sells the product any better? A relevant demonstration eliminates the need for much explanation. Good demonstrations are self-explanatory.

3. *Prove your point conclusively.* Some people, when telling an anecdote to illustrate an important point, drop the ball on the two-yard line by failing to make the moral of the story sufficiently clear. To them, and to everyone who has ever labored over the creation of a demo, I offer the following object lesson in proving a point:

Two short pieces of board are glued together right before our eyes with Elmer's, then put in place at a pool for use as a diving board. Then, in a demonstration that had me cringing in my seat almost afraid to look, a diver jumps up and down on this glued board to show how firmly the pieces adhere. The commercial ends by reminding us that Elmer's is stronger glue than you'll ever need for most household jobs.

In a similar show of strength, Krazy Glue suspended a burly construction worker in midair by gluing his hard hat with him in it to a steel girder. After viewing a demo like that, it's not hard to believe that Krazy Glue will work for more pedestrian uses.

And how about this classic commercial for Master Lock? A marksman using a high-powered rifle fires at a Master Lock. Bull's-eye! Slow-motion photography dramatizes the tremendous damage done to the lock at the instant of impact. Yet the lock will not open even when forced.

Conclusive? Absolutely. To the point? Utterly. Proof? Positive.

4. *Keep the staging uncontrived.* This is a toughie. Because the temptation is to think that the bigger and more elaborate the demonstration, the more resounding the proof.

Not so.

Take a look at this lovely bit of simplicity sponsored by Clean & Clear hair conditioner. In one transparent container filled with water, an ordinary conditioner leaves a heavy, greasy trail. When a comb is dipped in the water, the conditioner sticks to the comb. What woman wants that gook in her hair? In a second container, Clean & Clear is poured into the water, completely and invisibly dissolves, and a comb dipped in the container comes out clean. What a superb demonstration to prove that Clean & Clear is not just another greasy conditioner.

More important, though, the demonstration is so simple and uncontrived you can prove it to yourself. All you need is water, Clean & Clear, and any other conditioner. What could be simpler? Or clearer.

And what could be less contrived and more convincing than this little giant of a demo from Volvo? Volvo has been promoting the safety of its cars for years, so when the company did an ostensibly public service spot promoting the use of seat belts, it was in sync with its marketing strategy. And right on the nose. The commercial didn't use cars or even people. Instead, it used a block of wood with wheels attached (car), and two eggs sitting in indents on the block (people). One egg was secured with a tiny belt. Then the block was released down an incline until it hit a barrier at the bottom. The belted egg survived without so much as a crack. But the other egg flew forward and splattered like Humpty Dumpty, spilling its yolk all over the place. Yuck! How's that for uncontrived? You don't have to be an egghead to understand you've got to be cracked not to wear a seat belt.

5. Be sure it's simple to follow and understand. Even if the concept is more complicated than you would like, you'd be surprised at how simply it can be demonstrated. Like this one: A torrent of water resembling a waterfall pours down on a car, almost obscuring it. When the water stops, the only remnants of the deluge are beads of water on the car. Raindance car wax is still protecting the car's finish.

To be sure, the execution is an exaggeration. But the procession of ideas is orderly and easy to follow. It doesn't take much brainpower to grasp the simple, solid point it makes (Raindance won't wash off), and no one is going to drown in boredom in the process.

An equally simple commercial shows two pots cooking side-by-side on a stove. One pot is Corning Visionware, made of see-through glass. The other pot is made of aluminum. The aluminum pot boils over, spilling sauce on the stove, while the see-through pot by Corning remains under control. Again, the message is easy to understand: Visionware lets you keep an eye on your cooking so food won't boil over.

In all, these commercials illustrate how demonstrations must flow—and not stumble—if they are to be believed.

6. *Make it preemptive.* By this I simply mean that a demonstration, if it is to be any good at all, must be so memorable and so closely identified with your product that no one would *dare* use that demonstration after you've done it.

No other paper towel is going to get away with a crumpled towel-in-glass absorbency test since Nancy Walker preempted that demonstration for Bounty. In the original no-frills commercial, Ms. Walker demonstrated Bounty's extra absorbency by crumpling two different paper towels and putting each in a glass of liquid. Only Bounty absorbed all the liquid. Later commercials still fortify the image of absorbency for Bounty, but the plot has thickened. One commercial features an Old Flame who looks and talks like Humphrey Bogart, visiting his former sweetheart (played by Nancy Walker). Old Flame spills his coffee, and Nancy Walker wipes it up with Bounty. Again there's a side-by-side demonstration comparing Bounty's absorbency with that of an ordinary paper towel. Bounty swallows it all, while the ordinary paper towel leaves a puddle behind. Old Flame observes nostalgically that his former sweetheart is still using Bounty.

This commercial is certainly more complicated than its low-budget predecessor. But when you strip away the show business, it's the same convincing demonstration.

Another variation on the theme shows Nancy Walker about to go over Niagara Falls in a rowboat. As the danger intensifies, she reaches for a sheet of Bounty, and it absorbs all of Niagara Falls. Though not at all believable, and not really a demonstration, this commercial still reinforces the image of absorbency for

Bounty. Absorbency is so much a part of Bounty's image that the brand can get away with making fun of its own demonstration and still reinforce its Unique Advantage. No one else could do that, but frankly, I much prefer the old simple demos.

Demonstrations become preemptive if they've been fashioned with enough originality. Wesson oil cooked up the idea of frying a crustless loaf of bread. This demonstration grew out of a simple desire to show that the product won't make fried foods soggy inside, a point every oil manufacturer is eager to make. The commercial shows a loaf of white bread being fried in Wesson. It gets golden well-done on the outside, but a knife cuts into the bread to reveal that the inside is still white and soft and fluffy.

Another Wesson demonstration makes the same point, using fried chicken. The commercial shows one measuring cup of Wesson poured into a frying pan. Next we see a batch of chicken frying in the pan. When the chicken is done, the oil is returned to the measuring cup. All but one spoonful remains. The entire batch of chicken contains just one spoonful of oil. Wesson has sewn up the idea of making greaseless fried chicken.

Other products that have become closely identified with demonstrations include Charmin bathroom tissue and Heinz ketchup. Not a soul would advertise "squeezability" in connection with a bathroom tissue after the Mr. Whipple Charmin series. Nobody but nobody is going to promote "slowness" as a virtue of ketchup after Heinz has used it in demonstration after demonstration to illustrate the richness and thickness of its product.

7. *A demonstration must be believable beyond the shadow of a doubt.* And that means you've got to see the point proved before your very eyes and have absolute faith in the method of proof.

Let me give you an example. For total believability, Volkswagen put its own engineers in a series of life-threatening demonstrations. One of my favorites shows a Volkswagen accelerating on a race track. Two engineers sit unperturbed at the end of the track with their backs to the oncoming speeding car. The brakes screech, and the car stops—just inches from the unconcerned, completely confident engineers. Who could ever forget or doubt the claims made for Volkswagen brakes after witnessing this demonstration? And what could be more convincing in a demo than people who made the product and are then willing to risk their lives on the results?

To demonstrate the reliability of Volkswagen steering, the company relied on a similar theme. This time, it constructed a human slalom with a team of its own engineers and sent a Volkswagen speeding through the slalom. Again, these men were willing to bet their lives on their product. That has to be the ultimate demonstration, and the ultimate in believability.

Demonstrations like these are unquestionably credible, and that too makes them memorable. For the same reason, I like the old Memorex commercial in which an operatic tenor shatters a glass by hitting a high note. As he sings, his voice is recorded on a Memorex cassette. When the tape is played back, a second glass is shattered by the recording, proving that Memorex records and plays back original sounds with magnificent fidelity.

Effective as TV demos may be, sometimes a demo works even better in print. Consider an ad for Brother's full-color copier, which compares the quality of a photograph with a reproduction of the same photograph made on the Brother copier. To do that, the ad shows a split image of a tulip. The left half is from the original photograph. The right half, which completes the colorful picture, is a copy of the photograph made on the Brother copier. The copy, produced on the Brother machine, is as vivid as the original.

One of the things that makes this demonstration in print even more effective is that the item it promotes is a print product. It's much more effective to compare printing techniques in print than on TV.

———

Ads and commercials like these are good for our conscience. To the escapades of all those Hollywood hotshots, they say, "Hey! Stop the nonsense! This is what advertising's all about!" There is damned little showmanship for entertainment's sake involved in these commercials. No casts of thousands. No tricky camera angles, special effects, jingles, dancing girls. There is not one complicated story line.

No saccharine "slice-of-life" situation comedies. Not even a single funny line. Just good show-and-tell demonstration.

Yet I found them more engrossing, more interesting, and more suspenseful than any of the engineered hilarity that passes for advertising on television today.

Long live the demo. Long live effective and believable advertising.

9

Comparison, Fear, Naming Names, and Simulation

If there were an easier road to believability than the standard show-and-tell commercial, you can bet I'd take it.

In fact, I'd even be willing to stand up before the nation on TV and tell everyone just how wonderful my clients' products are. (At least one agency president has already done that.) One look at my winsome smile and sincere, catch-in-the-throat delivery, and you'd trip over your own feet getting out the door to buy the product, right?

Wrong. And that's why commercials are so hard to write. It's not enough that they be sincere; they have to make you *believe*— somehow, anyhow, or they're no good at all. So how does a commercial achieve believability when the audience and the teller of the story are divided by thousands of miles, millions of dollars worth of technical equipment, and scores of executives and creative people who have reshaped, refined, edited, and re-edited the message every inch along the way?

It's easy. You simply pick the technique that will do the most convincing job for your product, letting it display the product to full advantage, like a picture frame. There are so many techniques to choose from that I can't really list them all here. But I've done the next best thing by narrowing the possibilities down to four that are tried and true routes to believability. And to reinforce my point, I won't just tell you how well they work. I'll show you how they've lent credence to commercials you've watched on your own living room set.

Comparison Commercials

Right in the middle of an episode of "Murder, She Wrote," with Jessica Fletcher about to trap the elusive killer, your screen goes dark, then lightens into a shot of two couples—the Cinchells and Wimpoles—carrying their garbage out to the curb for collection. Mr. and Mrs. Wimpole, clad in dreary black clothes that look like Salvation Army discards, struggle with a big, heavy, dirty, old garbage bag overflowing with refuse. Their neighbors, the Cinchells, in dapper white outfits, nonchalantly present a clean, neatly tied Hefty Cinch Sak. The Cinchells explain to the Wimpoles that the Hefty Cinch Sak is a cinch to close, a cinch to lift, and a cinch to carry. The Wimpoles take the hint, pack up their trash in a Hefty bag, and are suddenly transformed from a wimpy, sorry-looking couple into a dazzling twosome.

It's a cinch to figure out what part the Hefty Cinch Sak played in this sudden transformation. The commercial builds believability for its product by dramatizing the end result of using the product and comparing it to the end result of not using it or of using another product. And although the execution is silly and contrived right down to the names, the dramatic comparison is strong enough to overcome it. The commercial gets an A+ for comparison because it contrasts what the product can do against a less attractive alternative. Unfortunately, I would give the commercial an F for execution, since it's so unbelievable it detracts from the comparison. But the side-by-side comparison is so strong it overcomes the silliness.

Let's look at another example of a comparison commercial:

the Folgers taste test. But unlike a side-by-side comparison, this commercial compares its coffee to another in absentia. To prove that discriminating coffee drinkers can't tell the difference between Folgers instant and freshly brewed coffee, Folgers installed a hidden camera in an upscale New York City cafe. Sophisticated customers are served Folgers, which has been secretly substituted for the cafe's usual brew. As patrons rhapsodize about the richness, the smooth aroma, and the taste, the camera records their reactions. Of course, they are stunned to discover that they are drinking instant.

Convincing? You bet. Taste tests almost always are. Combine that with the equally convincing hidden camera technique, and it's all the more believable because it involves real people in a real environment expressing their real thoughts. Despite the fact that the technique has been used before by Sanka, it's so convincing that it works every time.

In a more contrived setting, ScotTowels stages a race between its paper towels and the other leading brand. While both brands unroll at a furious pace down a hilly track, the voice-over announcer makes the single sales point that ScotTowels consistently outlast the competition. Finally, the leading brand comes up empty as ScotTowels keep rolling merrily along. The announcer tells us that when the other brand runs out, ScotTowels keep on running with 40 percent more sheets.

This commercial doesn't say a thing about quality. It doesn't have to. One assumes that with a trusted name like Scott, the quality is at least parity. Scott uses the campaign to focus on the one reason you should buy its towels instead of the leading competitor's: You get more of them for your money. Economy has always been and will always be a compelling Unique Advantage.

Kraft, on the other hand, talks of nothing but quality in its comparison commercial for salad dressing. The spot, which compares Kraft ranch dressing with the leading brand, gradually takes us through a logical thought process worthy of Socrates. With strong visuals, it contrasts a big, leafy head of fresh lettuce with flaky shreds of dehydrated lettuce, and a big, juicy, ripe tomato with pathetic slices of dehydrated tomato. Since you wouldn't put dehydrated lettuce or dehydrated tomatoes in your salad, the announcer reasons, why use the leading salad dressing, which is made with dehydrated buttermilk? That makes good sense. With this effective comparison, Kraft not only makes the point that its ranch dressing is made with fresh buttermilk, but that the leading brand is not. Pretty compelling reason to buy Kraft, wouldn't you say?

Comparison commercials stick in the consumer's mind, or in the following case, to their arms. One Light Powder Arrid deodorant commercial opens with a voice-over announcing: "I'm going to try something nutty" (an apologetic line the commercial could have done without). A man sprays ordinary deodorant on one arm, presses a cotton ball to it, then turns his arm over so the cotton is dangling from his arm. "Aaaahhhhh," muses the announcer gratuitously. "It's sticky."

Now the man tries the same thing on his other arm, this time using Light Powder Arrid. Of course, the cotton ball falls off because (as the announcer carefully explains) light powder isn't sticky.

In spite of a few sticky lines, the commercial makes an excellent point: Nonsticky Arrid powder won't cause your clothes to stick to you. You've seen it with your own eyes and judged between the two with your own brain. Now do you believe in Arrid?

I think so.

Just for good measure, take a look at this classic commercial, which shows what the comparison technique can do for an inexpensive, frequently purchased, and highly competitive product like potato chips. Two plain brown paper bags appear before a time-lapse camera, one filled with ordinary potato chips and the other with Chipos brand. They are allowed to sit for a couple of hours until it becomes obvious that the bag containing regular chips is spotting badly with grease stains. The Chipos bag, on the other hand, is almost as clean as it was when it was placed there. Now do you believe Chipos are almost greasefree? And which chip would you rather put in your mouth? This is a simple, effective commercial that puts the evidence before your eyes and invites you to compare. People believe in comparisons, and when they believe, they buy. Unfortunately, people didn't buy enough Chipos, and the brand has been discontinued. However, I'm sure it was for reasons other than this commercial, which is a superb example of comparative advertising.

Fear in Commercials

Caught in a torrential rainstorm when her car breaks down, a teenager calls her mother from a pay phone. Mom is on the phone talking to a friend, but since she has Call Waiting service, she hears a tone letting her know someone is trying to reach her. She excuses herself from the first conversation to take her daughter's frantic call. "Don't worry, honey, I'll call the service station and be right there," she reassures her. The announcer reminds us that New York Telephone's Call Waiting service not only puts an end to annoying busy signals, but lets the important calls get through.

I find this commercial devastatingly believable. I'm afraid *not* to believe it or to tempt fate by not getting Call Waiting and missing an important call, especially from young children or old parents. With skillfully pointed commercials like this one, New York Telephone rings my bell and a lot of other bells, too.

Fear sells other services as well. Take the terrific American Express commercials that demonstrate all the ways in which you can be relieved of your money. One shows a couple beginning their summer vacation in a museum. As they ride the up escalator, a pickpocket observes them on his way down. Just when they pass, he reaches out and snatches the woman's handbag off her shoulder. It's scary. It's also believable and promotes belief in the necessity of the product.

American Express has also relied on fear in a series of commercials that sell American Express Card Purchase Protection. In one, Dad unpacks his new TV/stereo/VCR combination while toddler Peter looks on. Dad explains how it works in terms the child will understand. "Now, it eats these things. I open the mouth," Dad explains, inserting a cassette into the VCR. Mom calls to Peter, "No TV until you've had your breakfast," as she sets down his bowl of oatmeal. With dramatic classical music in the background, we next see Peter secretly feeding oatmeal to the VCR. Dad later tries to insert a video as the oatmeal is ejected. Yuck! But not if you paid for it with your American Express card.

A quick call to American Express, and Dad is assured that the VCR is covered by Purchase Protection. The announcer reminds us that lost, stolen, or damaged purchases are automatically insured if they were paid for with the American Express card.

Another commercial in the same campaign shows a woman buying an expensive vase for her parents, only to watch it fall and shatter soon after she gets home. No need for her to break down. Since she paid for the vase with her American Express card, it's automatically covered by Purchase Protection.

"*Don't* believe," these commercials seem to be saying, "and see what happens."

I'd rather believe.

Part publicity, part public service, these next two commercials, which talk about breast cancer detection, use fear in a positive sense. One, from General Electric, shows a woman going for a mammogram, as we hear the voices of other women who are putting off the test. "I was too busy, too busy," says one. "I have to cancel," says another. "I'll go when I have the time," says a third. The announcer breaks in with some reassuring information about G.E.'s breast cancer detection system, which uses mammography equipment built by G.E.: It can detect tumors too tiny to be felt and can help increase the breast cancer survival rate to 91 percent. All the while, we watch the woman in the doctor's office calmly getting this painless test. As she leaves the office, reassured, the doors slam behind her, and the announcer breaks in, "There's one thing it can't do. It can't make you go." For all the women who are so busy making excuses, this commercial provides a reason to take action.

Du Pont, which makes X-ray film for mammography, got the same point across with a commercial that shows a woman examining her breasts. "Mary Brody won't feel the tiny lump in her breast for another two years. But she'll discover it tomorrow, after her first mammogram," says the female announcer. For Mary, early detection means a two-year head start on the rest of her life.

G.E. and Du Pont both use fear not to sell the product but to sell the service for which their products are used. Both companies will eventually benefit. And so will the women who pay attention to their messages.

Naming Names

I'm in favor of telling the world that your product is superior to your competitor's if that superiority can be proved. It's only a step from that premise to naming your competitor and showing his product losing out to yours. Now that's believability!

Coke and Pepsi always name each other in their comparative commercials. In one award-winning spot, Pepsi shows an archeological dig in the twenty-fifth century. Accompanied by their inquisitive professor, a group of students unearths various objects found in a split-level house. As one student stands by drinking a can of Pepsi, another turns up an antique Coke bottle. "Professor! What's this?" she asks. "Hmm . . . I have no idea," he muses, totally baffled. While Pepsi has survived for generations, Coke was buried in history.

Of course, Coke fought back with an equally competitive spirit. A commercial for Diet Coke lets us know that in one year, almost two million families stopped buying regular Pepsi, and almost half a million of them moved to Diet Coke.

And listen to the "name calling" commercial MCI devised to show that its lowest long distance rates start at 7 P.M., while AT&T's don't begin until 11 P.M. Two women sit in lounge chairs beneath a large clock. At seven o'clock, the woman using MCI picks up her phone and makes a long distance call. The other woman, who relies on AT&T for long distance service, must wait until 11 P.M. for the rates to go down. As the MCI caller spends the evening gabbing, the AT&T caller passes time reading, watching the clock, and looking bored. By the time the rates go down four hours later, she is fast asleep in her lounge chair. The MCI caller is still happily gabbing on the phone. After seeing this commercial, could anyone miss the point that MCI's Primetime rates apply all evening long, while AT&T is more expensive until 11 P.M.? More important, could viewers question the authenticity of the claim?

Only if they were busy gabbing on the phone at the time.

Another example of how strongly name-competitive advertising sells is the Doan's commercial discussed in Chapter 5. In this commercial, as you may remember, we see a man trying to bend and then being forced to stop because of back pain. After the man has taken Doan's, he is able to bend all the way. The commercial explains that Doan's relieves back pain better than Bayer, Tylenol, and Advil—the all-purpose analgesics that are its biggest competitors—because Doan's contains an ingredient that the others don't have. The implication is that Doan's has a Unique Advantage. Once you've seen this commercial, you really believe that Doan's has it all over the other analgesics for back pain. I'm sure this commercial caused considerable pain to Doan's competitors as they watched their products on the screen while Doan's pointed out their deficiencies. You can't get more competitive than that. Or more believable.

What makes this and other name-competitive commercials so totally believable? The fact that people believe commercials that mention competitors' names, that's what. They assume (and not without justification) that what gets said about the competitor's product must be true, or it wouldn't be aired on TV. What's more, they know you'd be sued for your last nickel by your competitor if you bent the truth by so much as a hair.

A commercial that names names achieves a level of believability that one making unilateral claims for its product can't reach. A noncompetitive commercial is always subject to a great deal of skepticism. A name-competitive commercial, on the other hand, is rarely questioned when presented in an honest, factual way.

Take Sorrell Ridge preserves, which used name-competitive advertising to launch a direct attack on Smucker's and Polaner's. The concept: Sorrell Ridge is 100 percent fruit and fruit juice, while the other brands have sugar and corn syrup added. Sorrell Ridge got the point across by lining up three jars of Smucker's preserves and three jars of Polaner's. To get the same amount of fruit that's in one jar of Sorrell Ridge, you'd have to eat three jars of either of these other brands.

Total cereal had the same idea in a commercial that compares the vitamin content of Total with that of Special K, Grape Nuts, and Shredded Wheat. This spot shows a hungry pack of hard-

working cops ordering breakfast in a luncheonette. The first officer orders Total. Another chooses Special K, only to be told by
the announcer that it will take three bowls of that cereal to deliver
the vitamins of one bowl of Total. Still another orders Grape Nuts
and gets a stack of four bowls of cereal (the amount it takes to
equal one bowl of Total). When a fourth cop asks for Shredded
Wheat, a stack of twelve bowls of cereal arrives (he would have to
eat all twelve bowls to get as many vitamins as he would get from
one bowl of Total). Seeing this, another cop jokingly asks for separate checks. But by this time, Total has checkmated the competition. Total delivers more nutrition in just one bowl. Even the
dumbest flatfoot couldn't miss that clue.

Simulation

If I told someone just starting to flirt with drugs that taking
drugs could do great harm, would the person believe me? Possibly, but I'd be a lot more convincing if I illustrated that statement
with a convincing visual.

The Partnership for a Drug-Free America did just that with
a hard-to-ignore simulation of the effect of drugs on the brain. A
man standing in a kitchen prepares to fry an egg. He reaches into
the egg carton and holds up one egg, which he tells us represents
the brain. Next, he points to the skillet heating on the stove. "This
is drugs," he says, as the pan begins to smoke. With a flick of the
wrist, the man breaks the fragile shell and dumps the egg into the
sizzling pan. As it crackles and expands, he boldly concludes,
"This is your brain on drugs. Any questions?" Simply and unmistakably, the commercial lets us know that taking drugs is like
frying your brain. That just might be strong enough to stop someone from starting on drugs. Let's hope so.

The Volvo demonstration discussed in Chapter 8 is another
excellent example of simulation and coincidentally uses eggs—
this time to simulate automobile passengers, with a tiny wooden
block simulating a car. The "car" rolls down a steep decline and
hits a roadblock. One egg, secured with a tiny strap, survives the
crash. The other splatters. Now do you see why you should use
your seatbelt? Now do you see the power of simulation?

Simulations can be just as effective in selling a product as they are in conveying a public service message. Remember the Tinactin commercial, discussed in Chapter 4, in which the woman uses Tinactin to put out the flame of athlete's foot? Or how about this commercial for Butter Buds Sprinkles which simulates the unhealthy effects of butter? A man asks if we've ever wondered why they call it a stick of butter. The answer: because it sticks to your hips, your stomach, and your heart. Saying that, he attaches Velcro sticks of butter to his suit jacket in the appropriate places. Behind the simulation is a sound concept: Butter Buds have the natural flavor of real butter without unhealthy fat, sodium, cholesterol, and excess calories. I might not believe that when a spokesman tells me so, but watching the sticks of butter attached to the man's jacket helps to convince me. It's not as dramatic or as realistic as the Tinactin simulation, but it sure does remind you what butter can do to your body. And that's good enough.

Often simulation can make a point that a realistic film sequence can't accomplish as effectively, if at all. To illustrate its skin-close shaving system, Norelco simulated a magnified hair entering the razor's chamber, being individually lifted and then cut by a blade a split second later. The simulation helped me understand how Norelco shaves so close without the blade even touching the skin—a concept no other technique could have illustrated. When it was over, I really believed that Norelco shavers are different from the others.

———

That's really what it's all about, you know, getting those prospects to believe you enough to try the product. You might say we're really in the believability business. No matter what else the consumer remembers about your commercial—whether it's a foot catching fire, a taste test, a cotton ball adhering to a sticky arm, a brazen pickpocket, or a side-by-side comparison of products—first, last, and always the consumer must believe your message. Comparison, fear, naming names, and simulation are all persuasive techniques for sending prospects to checkout counters believing beyond a shadow of a doubt in the promise of the product.

10

Print: The Mother Medium

Just because most of the chapters in this book concentrate on television, don't get the idea that this is a book about television advertising.

It's not.

Because everything I've got to say about good advertising pertains to all media. I've merely used TV commercials rather than print ads as examples throughout this book because television is the single most dramatic, effective, and dominant medium for mass communication in the world today. More national advertising dollars are being poured into it than into all other media combined—$26 billion in 1988. And it's going to become even more dominant in the future. You can bet on it.

But print isn't dead yet. It's just changed from what it was a generation ago.

It's important to understand that change and what caused it, because it changed the lives of almost everyone in America and eventually the world. It also changed advertising and the lives of everyone working in it.

Close your eyes for a moment and imagine yourself back in the 1950s. Magazines were the glamour girls of the media parade. Everyone subscribed to quite a few. Magazines were beautiful, they were entertaining. They were an unhurried pleasure on a winter's night, a faithful companion of the lonely, the curious, the shut-in. Everybody loved magazines. But no one more than the advertising people who prepared ads for them.

There was nothing more exciting for an art director or copywriter than creating a full-page, full-color ad for a big, prestigious mass magazine. Some of us remember them—*Life, Look, Saturday Evening Post,* and *Collier's,* known as the Big Four to folks on the inside. To see your work in any of these publications was to feel that, at long last, you had arrived. Who would have dreamed that within the space of a few short years, these institutions would be gone (it would be the equivalent of CBS, NBC, and ABC suddenly disappearing). They live only in nostalgic tales of the Good Old Days, told by old men to their uninterested, unimpressed grandchildren whose eyes are glued to the TV, their ears covered by Walkman radios. Must we really ask, "What happened?"

Television happened! And magazines would never be the same again.

A revolutionary change in America's life-style had taken place. This change brought excitement and entertainment into the homes of Americans who never had much of either. How many people are going to pay to read a book when they can see the movie free? It soon became clear that television would overtake magazines as the dominant medium, as more and more sets found their way into more and more living rooms across the country. Magazines could never again compete with television for the mass general audience. And the Big Four became three . . . then two . . . then one . . . and then there were none.

Nothing could halt the TV juggernaut. Television was, and is, the most intrusive and far-reaching means of mass communication ever developed.

But television is obviously not the *only* medium, and in many cases not even the best medium, for delivering an advertising message. From a communications perspective, television's greatest strengths are its intrusiveness and its mass reach. However, for many advertisers, the virtues of print media often vastly outweigh these formidable strengths of television.

Without a doubt, the virtue that distinguishes television from any other form of advertising is its unique ability to command your attention regardless of whatever you might be doing. Even if you are reading a magazine or a newspaper, television will get to you. Picture yourself reading a magazine, while another member of your family is watching television in the same room. Even if you were totally engrossed in an article or immersed in an ad for a product you've always wanted, I dare you to keep your eyes glued to the printed page. You'll lose. The lure of television will reach out and grab your attention to anything on that magic screen, be it a newscast, sitcom, game show, movie, or even a commercial.

TV's inherent ability to command one's attention is so formidable that the great majority of us, if asked, would say we were exposed to the advertiser's message while reading a magazine when in reality we had reacted subconsciously to what we had seen on the screen.

This strength would seem simply to overpower print media. But herein lies the first chink in television's armor and the best way for print media to do battle with television. It has to do with the *quality* of the exposure.

A print exposure differs greatly from a television exposure. A prospect must make a conscious decision to read a print ad. The exposure involves active participation by the reader. While this may tend to somewhat limit opportunities for exposure, it greatly increases the value of each exposure. Prospects must be interested in the advertiser's message or they wouldn't make the effort and take the time to read it. All of it. Every selling word. Every little detail. And over and over again if they choose.

While this may not have seemed so compelling during the exciting early days of television, it is a tremendous advantage for print in an era when television commercial unit lengths are continually shrinking. Where once a 60-second commercial was standard, we now find more than half of all network television announcements are only fifteen seconds long. All of television's many virtues—its sight, sound, color, and motion, its mass reach, its ability to demonstrate the product in use, even its intrusive strength—can be offset or even negated if the complexity of the advertising message requires a greater length. Television is becoming more and more a reminder medium.

Print has always been able to provide whatever detail is necessary to deliver the message effectively. From the smallest fractional ads to multi-page spectaculars, print ads can include as much information as the advertiser thinks necessary to an active and involved reader who craves all the information you can provide.

Print can take all the time in the world, for example, to convince an affluent reader to pay more for a motor car than most people pay for their houses. Arguably, the most famous of all automobile ads did just that with this headline: "At 60 miles an hour, the loudest noise in this new Rolls-Royce comes from the electric clock." The headline was followed by 607 words of factual copy covering thirteen topics ranging from the making of the engine to the optional extras (including hot and cold running water and a bed) to the price, which is mentioned almost casually as an afterthought. This elegant, to say nothing of successful, campaign proved beyond a Silver Cloud of a doubt that print is the Rolls-Royce of media.

Print is also the Mercedes-Benz of media. The ads that were responsible for the enormous success of the Mercedes in America contained even more words—a page or spreadful, in fact. I remember the campaign vividly. I read every word of every ad. One of the headlines I remember particularly well read "You give up things when you buy the Mercedes-Benz. Things like rattles, rust, and shabby workmanship." I gave up a lot more. Money. I bought a Mercedes-Benz from those ads. No television commercial or campaign of commercials could have sold me like that fact-packed print campaign did. And I needed every last fact to convince myself to lay out those kind of bucks for a car. And what short, superficial snip of a commercial could have sold tourists on visiting Britain as did the magnificent print ad featuring Westminster Abbey, carrying the equally magnificent headline "Tread softly past the long, long sleep of kings"? The long, long copy tells of the kings entombed within and describes the historic wonders of the Abbey and of Great Britain. I'm sure it woke up all the history buffs who ever dreamed of visiting the United Kingdom and sent them scurrying to catch the next flight.

This is not to imply that print is only for those advertisers who require a deep or involved message. Some of the best print advertising ever created had only limited copy. One such ad, for Volkswagen, had only four words. The graphic showed a simple cartoon character holding a gas pump nozzle to his head as if it were a gun. The copy simply said, "Or buy a Volkswagen."

One of the most famous Volkswagen ads had a one-word headline, "Lemon." The illustration was of a brand-new VW, and the copy told us quality control had rejected this car because of a blemished chrome strip on the glove compartment. Another great ad in this great campaign had only two words in the head-line—but what big words they were: "Think small."

Another short and sweet ad, this one for Dannon Yogurt, showed only a photo of a deserted beach. The copy warned: "Bathing suit competition starts May 15th."

None of these print ads could have come off as effectively, as boldly, as dramatically on TV as they did in print. They point out another hidden power of print—its greater ability to provoke or encourage thought. Print can be less obvious than television be-cause readers get more involved. Good print stimulates us to think about the message and its relevance to us. You're lucky to even *see* a message that whizzes by in fifteen seconds, let alone think about it.

And think about this: Anything TV commercials can do, print ads can do—often better.

Print can sell with empathy: An ad for Johnson's baby sham-poo will reduce even the Wicked Witch of the West to tears with just a peek at the sweet little tot in the ad with tears in his eyes from someone else's shampoo. The headline says: "In his eyes all baby shampoos are not alike. . . ." A second picture of the baby, this time all smiles, with Johnson's baby shampoo in his hair, will make your tears dry up, too. The second part of the headline delivers the sell: "Only Johnson's baby shampoo has the unique 'no more tears' formula." When it comes to selling with empathy, this ad is a real tearjerker.

And when it comes to frightening us into buying, print can be a monster of a medium. For example, as AIDS became more widespread, advertising began to appear promoting condom use as a precaution against the disease. One ad for Lifestyles condoms pictured a close-up of a young woman's face in dramatic, docu-mentarylike black and white. She is speaking to us, and her words appear as the headline: "I'll do a lot for love, but I'm not ready to die for it." After being exposed to a killer of an ad like this one, how many women would take the chance of being exposed to a killer of a disease like AIDS? I'm sure it has led a lot of young women to insist that their lovers use prophylactics—and even supply them.

Another product category that often uses fear as a selling device is sunburn products. Skin Cancer Garde, by Eclipse, ran a print ad picturing a woman sitting outdoors. The copy was a testimonial from her, informing us that she has had skin cancer and that she now uses Eclipse Skin Cancer Garde to protect herself from the sun. If that ad doesn't get you to think twice about protection from the sun, how about this one? It's a print ad introducing Block Out for Children, from Sea and Ski. We see a close-up of a badly sunburned child's face. The headline warns, "Today it's sunburn. Tomorrow it could be skin cancer." The subhead quotes a medical study that confirms that even one sunburn in childhood dramatically increases the likelihood of developing skin cancer later in life. Does that get you? Of course it does, because few parents will take a chance with their child's life.

Another powerful print ad we came across was for Du Pont mammogram film, which was discussed in Chapter 9 as the subject of a TV commercial. The print ad uses a discreet photo of a woman examining her breasts. The headline tells us that a mammogram will discover a lump in her breast two years before she can feel it. The copy informs women that now they can start having mammograms earlier than ever before, thanks to a new Du Pont film. It urges each woman to do just that and perhaps, like the woman in the ad, to get a "two-year head start on the rest of her life." A very compelling print ad that I think makes an even greater impact than the TV version. There's something about print that makes it more urgent, more immediate, more believable than television.

These ads don't pull any punches. AIDS, skin cancer, breast cancer, children's health. That's scary stuff. And, somehow, because you can linger over the thought and the picture, they're even scarier in print.

Competitive advertising is not a TV exclusive, either. Here's a print ad involving a type of advertising we're seeing more and more of lately—trying to get a patient to ask the doctor about a specific prescription product. This ad's for NEE birth control pills and begins, "Announcing good news for users of Ortho-Novum and Norinyl." (The illustration shows these two pills, in addition to NEE.) The FDA has determined that three birth control pills are equally safe and effective. "Yet, one costs up to 50% less." You don't have to be a gynecologist to guess which one—NEE, of course. Or how about this three-page ad for Merit cigarettes? The format is a right-hand page, followed by a spread. The right-hand page sets up the challenge: "Which cigarette tastes as good as these but has up to 50% less tar?" The cigarette packs pictured are Winston, Salem, and Camel. Turn the page and the spread reveals the answer: Merit!

And nobody has to introduce print to introductory advertising. Again the format is a right-hand page, followed by a spread. The right-hand page features a small photo of an elegant spa that appears almost to be floating on a full-page of light blue effervescing water. The copy reads: "Nothing relaxes, rests, rejuvenates like the naturally carbonated baths at the great spas . . . except one thing." Turn the page and we see a spread of a beautiful young lady relaxing in the light blue carbonated water as though at a spa. "Introducing Actibath, the first carbonated bath tablet." That's an introduction that holds water!

Nothing sells quality like a beautifully photographed, richly printed, full-color page or spread: the gleam of a gold watch, the sparkle of a diamond, the luster of fine leather, the softness of fur, the texture of a fabric, the richness of a fine wine. Even the actual fragrance of a perfume. And, of course, for appetite appeal, print is a gourmet's delight. No TV system yet invented, including High Definition TV, will ever match print in capturing the juiciness of roast beef, the refreshment of a soft drink, the crispness of a salad, the steaming goodness of a casserole. You can almost eat them off the page. Eat your heart out, TV.

Okay, okay, all you TV defenders. I know what you're thinking—that only TV can do justice to a dramatic demo. Your verdict is wrong, and here's my evidence: Picture three sweat socks on a page against a limbo background. Sock number one is filthy with dirt and mud. Sock number two is partially clean but just a little discolored where the mud and imbedded dirt had been. Sock number three is sparkling white. Headline: "Introducing Tide With Bleach." Each sock has a caption under its toe. Caption one asks, "What do you do with a sock this dirty?" Caption two says, "Wash it in a regular detergent, like the one you're using now, and it will get only *this* white." Caption three delivers the clincher: "But it'll get much whiter with Tide With Bleach, because you'll have the cleaning power of the best Tide ever *plus* the whitening power of a liquid bleach." The whole ad is summarized by the sign-off line: "It'll knock your socks off. And it'll get 'em whiter." That demo is as good, as simple, as believable, as dramatic as any you'll see on TV. It knocked my socks off. I rest my case.

———

As a result of competing with television, print advertising is better than ever. But it wasn't easy. If it was difficult for the magazine industry, used to being the unchallenged king of the hill, to compete with as formidable an opponent as television—it was darn near impossible for adpeople who knew only the print medium to compete with so ostentatious an opponent as the television maven.

The impact of the television revolution on the people who create advertising for all media was disastrous.

With the growth of television, a whole new breed of creative people emerged. They looked different. They talked differently. They dressed differently, in jeans and long hair and beads and beards; they spoke a language of their own, a cross between hip and Hollywood.

And that's where they came from, in the figurative sense. Hollywood. Eager to cash in on the new entertainment craze sweeping the world, and the advertising world in particular, this new breed thought entertainment was the objective of all advertising. The more entertaining the commercial, the better advertising it must be.

Who was to argue with them? After all, they were paid incredible salaries, salaries out of all proportion to their worth, by an industry hungry for people to show how this scary new medium should be used. And the new creatives thought it beneath them to learn anything about advertising. Does one ask Steven Spielberg to cut his teeth on trade ads, promotion pieces, brochures, packages, instructional booklets, catalogs, or point-of-purchase displays? Should a budding genius be required to finish up ads created by experienced senior people? What are you, crazy or something? And, surely, such show biz whizzes couldn't be bothered with as dull a medium as print. It was an insult to their talent. Print was for "noncreative" ad people. When they did attempt to create a print ad, they treated it as a stepchild of television. The new creatives tried to apply TV techniques to a medium that wasn't made for them. They tried to use humor in a medium they didn't understand, and it was laughable. They tried to use noise in a medium that's silent, and it was deafening. They tried to use flash in a medium of ideas, and it was blinding. Without their actors and music and production techniques, they were lost. And advertising was following them down a yellow brick road to oblivion.

It didn't bother these egotistical interlopers that they didn't understand marketing objectives. That they couldn't write a creative strategy or reposition a product. (It takes an adperson, not a showperson, to change the end benefit of a product in order to appeal to a completely new, and hopefully larger, market.) These "entertainers" looked down their creative noses at advertising people who could do all those things. They were establishment squares. Understanding the public ("those *hicks!*") was a bore, so they used themselves and their friends as representative American buyers. As a result, they turned out lousy advertising, if it was advertising at all.

It consisted of "insider" comedy, little jokes, and musical extravaganzas that bore no more resemblance to advertising than the Grade B comedies and musicals that had nurtured them. These were dark days for advertising. For a while it looked as if the business would become an East Coast franchise of West Coast TV and movie studios. The crowning absurdity was the introduction of those obscene Academy Award-type orgies to the advertising industry. Hollywood reigned supreme.

Then suddenly there was light. It took a good ten years, but gradually, professional advertising people, having solved the "mysteries" of television, wrested the business back again. And it happened not a moment too soon. There are still some show biz personalities around, but for the most part, the smarter ones who took the time to learn something along the way have prevailed. The "entertainers" are gone. The awards shows remain as their legacy, but fortunately, there are fewer of those left, too. However, just when I thought it was safe for advertising again, I am seeing a whole new generation of "entertainers" cropping up. I see more and more of their entertainment winning awards. The threat, for the first time, is coming not just from within, but from outside our shores as well. Having lived through the last advertising holocaust, it frightens me to see it happening all over again!

———

Television dealt a heavy blow to magazines and newspapers by depriving them of large numbers of readers and huge amounts of advertising income. Some print media were destroyed altogether. Those that survived did so only by making adjustments and learning to live with television. Advertising, too, had to adjust to the new medium and learn to use it best. The learning period was long and painful, but the message is now clear: The medium is *not* the message.

Television not only came close to destroying magazines and newspapers, it damn near killed advertising as well!

To me, print is the purest form of advertising. It pits the creative mind one-on-one against a blank sheet of paper. With no outside influences. No tricks. No gimmicks. No hiding behind actors or music or jokes or props. When it comes to print, it's just you, that blank sheet of paper—and the moment of truth for the creative person.

Those who can meet the challenge of print are the truly gifted. Those who can't, no matter how creative they look or dress or talk, are not—and never will be—adpeople. Why? Because print (including newspapers, magazines, outdoor posters, even matchbooks) is the one medium that separates the Simplifiers from the Complicators.

Print is the mother medium. The basic medium. So basic that it can even be used as a guide to creating better television commercials. Turn the page and find out how.

11

How to Create Better TV Commercials

Believe it or not, it's really a lot easier to create a good television commercial than it is to create a good print ad. TV is an easy medium for creative people. For one thing, they've got the added dimension of time that they can count on—anywhere from ten to sixty seconds or more. For another, the creatives have motion to work with, and nothing commands more attention. There is sound, everything from a single voice to the London Philharmonic. There are professional actors. Producers. Directors. Editors. If they can't communicate an idea with all that going for them, well maybe they don't really have an idea at all.

A print ad, on the other hand, requires real discipline because it has none of that magic going for it. No time sequence. No motion. No voice, music, or effects. All you've got is a piece of paper and some printing ink. And from that, you've got to create something that will attract someone's attention, entice someone to read your words (an act requiring effort, unlike the passive business of watching and listening), communicate the selling idea, and then convince the prospect to try the product.

That's tough. Much tougher than creating a TV commercial.

I tend to judge the conceptual thinking ability of the writers and art directors I've interviewed, beginners and old pros alike, by their print ads. I'm convinced that anybody who can create good print ads can create good TV advertising, even if he or she has never done it before. Conversely, it doesn't always follow that someone with a proven track record in TV advertising can create good print; it's been my experience that those with a background of heavy TV lack the sharp, disciplined thinking of writers who started out by writing print ad after print ad after print ad, first trade and then consumer. The same is true of art directors.

You don't believe me? Let me describe the kind of people who come looking for a job with a portfolio consisting of a cassette full of TV commercials and a few grudging print ads. Their thinking is fuzzy. They can't isolate a single salient point—or make one quickly. They think in terms of scenarios instead of sentences that have beginnings, middles, and ends. They make vast plans for lighting, casting, camera angles, ECUs (that's Extreme Close-Up in TV jargon, part of a huge lexicon of initials meant to intimidate the poor average adperson, and a language I've never bothered to learn), and a whole panoply of other techniques long before they ever have a real idea. Give them a print ad to do, and they're lost. Utterly lost. I feel like Simon Legree even asking people like this to describe in a single, succinct sentence the basic selling idea behind a commercial they've worked on. Precision isn't their bag.

They're in show biz.

Now picture the people who come to me with a satchel full of great print ads and no TV. It usually turns out that once they start working in TV, they find it so much easier than what they've been doing that they create the best TV commercials in the place. They're crisper, cleaner, fresher, simpler, and more convincing than those being turned out by the so-called TV pros. These people may not be familiar with the techniques or the nomenclature, but they know how to think and how to communicate the results of their thinking quickly and clearly. It's easy to teach a new technique to someone who thinks. What's hard is trying to teach a master of technique a new way to think.

Right at this point I'd like to defend myself against all the TV specialists who are crying "foul" because I seem to be boosting print at the expense of their beloved medium. Not true. I no more believe in the intrinsic fuzziness of all TV creative thinking than I believe that all print people are necessarily masters of decisiveness. A smart person is a smart person in any situation, just as a good adperson is a good adperson in any medium. He or she will create good advertising in print, TV, radio, outdoor, direct mail, skywriting, matchbooks—you name it. If the person's smart, the ads will be smart. What concerns me here is the dangerous likelihood that we will get more medium than message from creative people who have concentrated on TV to the exclusion of every other medium. Too many of our creative people are more in love with TV technique than with advertising, and as a result, too much of today's TV advertising is entertaining, witty, funny—and pointless.

What is it about the magical medium that calls forth the Steven Spielberg in us, anyway? I'm not just talking about TV adpeople whose hearts are really in show business. I've watched good, print creative people whom I've seen think simply and clearly under normal circumstances metamorphose into temperamental, paranoid, raving maniacs on a TV shoot. Gone are the quiet, decisive habits of mind that made them good adpeople in the first place. Quite simply, they've been seduced by the newfound wonders of TV technique, by the intensity a big-budget project demands, by the glamour of makeup men scurrying around a celebrity. Hordes of other professionals watching them as they create. Grips and gaffers, electricians and carpenters, cameramen and sound technicians ready to spring into action at their every word. The immediacy of enforced teamwork, so different from the lonely evenings spent perspiring over a typewriter or a set of multicolored magic markers to produce a great print ad. In a way, the pinwheel eyes and megalomania on the set are all very understandable, but it's the commercial result that suffers. And that's dangerous.

I've spent some years working out a modest proposal for saving our good and righteous adpeople from the forbidden lures of Madame TV. I can't guarantee success for it 100 percent of the time, but it works for me and a lot of other people who now use it to turn out some outstanding TV work. I hope it turns out to be a trend that spreads.

If Marshall McLuhan was right in believing that intelligence begins with the ability to condense, then intelligent advertising should begin with the ability to condense a complicated sales message down to its basic form: a headline and a picture. The further away we get from these two elements, the poorer our communication becomes. So, far from being ends in themselves, TV techniques should operate only to make the headline and picture more interesting, more exciting, and more convincing as clearly, quickly, and simply as possible.

With that in mind, I ask you to consider my plan: Every creative team, before starting a TV campaign or commercial, should first rough out a print ad communicating the same message to be communicated in the TV commercial. Needless to say, the team members should execute this print ad, consisting of headline, rough visual, and copy points, just for themselves. No one else should see it. To be on the safe side, the team should also consider several approaches before deciding on the best way to go. In the end, it's not only conceivable but entirely probable that the team will spend more time on the ad than on the actual television storyboard, because the storyboard will come easily after this basic conceptual groundwork has been laid.

If nothing else, this technique is bound to sharpen creative thinking by forcing a team to determine, first, the single most important point to be made, and, second, how best to make it.

As for the rest, it's easy. The print ad should be used as a blueprint for the TV storyboard and the final execution. All along the way, the storyboard should be judged against this ad to see that the idea hasn't been lost, obscured, or slowed down in translation from print to TV. And it would be a good idea if, in the final production of the commercial, the print ad was prominently displayed so that every time a production technique begins to crush the basic idea, it could be stopped then and there.

As a guide for the final editing, nothing could beat the print ad. It should also be compared to the finished commercial, just to see how closely the techniques of one medium have approximated the other.

The print ad, you might say, is ideally suited to serve as the conscience of our industry. If we paid more attention to our consciences, as theologians and thinkers have advised for solid centuries, we would see better and more effective TV commercials in the future.

I can guarantee it.

12

The Making of a Television Commercial

I really debated whether or not to include this chapter in this book.

It's not necessary, you know, to understand the ins and outs of television production in order to tell good advertising from bad advertising. If it were, every ex-Hollywood film technician would be an authority on advertising. As we already know, this just isn't so.

But since so many of the points I make in these pages about advertising are illustrated by commercials, and because most of the production money spent on advertising today is spent on commercials, and because I refer so often to television execution—it might be helpful to know what goes into each brief spot that rolls across your screen each day and night. You may be surprised to know how detailed a process commercial-making is.

The first thing you need to make a TV commercial is a good idea. (You'll find this statement repeated over and over again throughout this book.) A light bulb has to go on over someone's head before the lights go on on a television stage set and the cameras can start rolling. Usually it's the creative department of the

118

agency that accounts for the wattage. When the copywriter and art director assigned to the account sit down together to thrash out their ideas, they first develop a storyboard—a comic-strip-like device that has a pictorial representation of the commercial drawn in frames, with the words typed below each frame. Usually this creative team will develop quite a few storyboards. From these, the agency chooses, often with the help of research, the one storyboard that seems to best solve the problem. This one is recommended to the client.

Once the client approves the storyboard, it is turned over to the agency producer. As the title implies, the producer is in charge of producing the commercial and is responsible for overseeing every aspect of the production from start to finish. The producer must worry about costs as well as creative considerations, carefully balancing the two so that neither suffers. Much of the eventual success or failure of the commercial rests in the hands of the producer.

The first thing a producer or someone from the production department must do is to submit a copy of the storyboard to the Continuity Clearance Departments of the three major television networks, so that they can make certain it meets their standards of truth, fairness, and taste. All the networks require that advertising claims be substantiated with written proof and documentation, but each network sets its own standards of fairness and taste. What one network will accept, another may not. So you can imagine how difficult it is to get a storyboard that all three networks will agree upon. And what was agreed upon one day may well be rejected the next. Without going into detail here (because I'm saving my big guns for Chapter 22, "The Regulation of TV Advertising"), let me just point out that the decisions taken by the networks at this stage can be quite arbitrary, and getting final copy approval can be a *very* frustrating experience. Quite often, it ends in defeat; one network reported that over one third of the storyboards initially submitted to it are rejected for one reason or another!

While the struggle goes on to get the storyboard approved by the networks, copies are sent to a select group of outside TV production companies for competitive bids. Interestingly enough, production companies tend to specialize in various subjects. Some specialize in food, some in people and dialogue, some in fashion. There are production companies that perform better in a studio, just as there are some that are better out on location. Some are very expensive, some less. All of these factors are taken into account in determining which production houses are asked to bid on the commercial. On the basis of their bids (and the aforementioned creative considerations), a production company is chosen to do the commercial.

All right. The preliminaries are out of the way, and at this point we're ready to attend the pre-production meeting, at which agency, client, and production company go over every aspect of the commercial and finalize all of the details. This meeting of the minds is crucial, as you can well imagine, to eliminate costly mistakes that might be made on the day of the shooting. The details discussed will include everything from what exactly the people in the commercial will wear to what props will be shown in each scene, precisely how long each scene will run, what camera angles will be employed, how the product will be shown or demonstrated, and the myriad other questions that must be answered *before* the camera begins to roll. If the commercial involves actors and actresses, it is at this meeting that final casting selections are made from a list of people who have auditioned for the part. Final wardrobe is chosen, final set designs or locations are agreed upon, and the shooting date is set.

And then, the shooting. First off, it isn't cheap. The standard time frames for TV commercials today are fifteen seconds and thirty seconds. They can cost anywhere from $60,000 to $1 million, depending on the talent chosen and the complexity of what is to be shot. The average national TV commercial shot in 1989 cost $196,000 to produce—a 12 percent increase over the year before.

The people who participate in the shooting of a commercial are highly trained and highly paid. They are not employed by the agency but are part of the package supplied by the outside production house. The average TV commercial requires the services of these professionals:

- *The director.* The director is responsible for the overall look and quality of the commercial and is involved in every aspect of production, from camera angles to lighting to directing the actors and actresses. A production company is judged by the talent and capabilities of its directors. They are the people agencies rely upon to take the glorious idea on the storyboard and translate it successfully into film.

- *The assistant director (A.D.).* As the title suggests, this person is the director's right hand. He or she generally coordinates the whole commercial and makes sure that everything required for the commercial is there when it's needed. The assistant director is responsible for keeping the production moving smoothly and efficiently. You'd recognize an A.D. by his or her familiar chant, "Quiet on the set!"

- *The cameraman.* He (this job is still done mostly by men) has responsibility for anything and everything that has to do with the camera. The cameraman makes sure that the exposure is correct, the camera is in focus, the correct lens is being used, the camera is functioning properly, and so on.

- *The assistant cameraman.* This person assists the cameraman in all of the above. The assistant cameraman is also responsible for seeing to it that there is enough film in the camera. If the camera runs out of film in the middle of a take, you will see the assistant cameraman with smoke curling off his or her heels running from an irate director.

- *The sound man.* The sound man (or woman) lives in the world of microphones and tape recorders. Where there is dialogue or other on-camera sound in the commercial, it is the responsibility of the sound man to make sure that it is all properly and clearly recorded. When the job is done right, you won't notice the sound man. But if you can't hear something clearly, or if you see a microphone in the picture that shouldn't be there, you know the sound man has failed. Mostly, though, sound imperfections are corrected long before the finished commercial reaches your television screen.

- *The electrician, or gaffer.* This professional makes certain that everything in the commercial is lit the way the director wants it lit. The electrician works with the director and the cameraman to make sure there is enough light for a proper exposure, to eliminate unnecessary shadows, and to enable the viewer to read the name of the product on the box. He or she also moves cables, prevents blown fuses, and even turns off the lights when the shooting is over.

- *The script person.* This is the person who makes sure that everything that is supposed to be shot *is* shot and that nothing is forgotten. The job includes timing each sequence on the storyboard as well as each "take" to ensure that it is the right length within the overall context of the commercial. In addition, the script person keeps track of which "takes" should be developed and which should not because of their unsatisfactory quality. He or she assigns numbers to each "take" to assist the editor later on. When you hear the shout "Take eight" and see the slam of the sticks, you know it is the script person who has supplied the correct number.

- *The grip.* This is the person who moves the camera around at the behest of the director, principally so that all shots can be covered with the desired moves and from the desired angles. In general, he or she helps move anything heavy that has to be moved, like furniture or scenery. The grip is the muscle behind the production.

- *The prop person.* You guessed it! This is the person in charge of all props. He or she makes sure that the props are all in good shape and positioned properly for the camera and that all special props are functioning properly.

- *The set designer.* This person designs the set and supervises the building of the set until he or she is satisfied that it will give the desired effect. If Rome has to be built in a day, it's the set designer's worry.

- *The makeup person, hair stylist, and wardrobe stylist.* It's up to these people to make certain that all the people in the commercial are dressed, coiffed, and made up properly.

- *The home economist.* If food is to be shown in the commercial, it is the home economist who prepares it on the scene and makes sure it looks as luscious as possible. More important still, the home economist works to ensure that the food will photograph as luscious as it looks.

• *The video playback specialist.* This crew member helps with a process known as "perfecting" the film. Before the filming begins, the video playback specialist sets up the monitors and video recorders. While the camera records the commercial, it simultaneously displays a video on TV monitors near the camera. Though the image is generally black and white and of notoriously bad quality, it provides enough information to make technical and aesthetic decisions about the commercial. The video playback specialist records each take and, together with the script person, notes whether it was good or bad. The playback specialist must be very alert to commands to play back instantly what has just been filmed. Some of the most exuberant and heated moments on the shoot occur in front of the video monitor.

So there they are. By working together, these people apply their diverse talents to capturing on film what was originally conceived on a storyboard. When they finish, the next stage of the commercial process can begin: editing.

Editing is done by the *editor*—the person whose responsibility it is to take all the film that has been shot and piece it together into the finished commercial to fit the allotted time. Most often, the editor is hired by the agency and works with the director, the agency producer, and the agency creative team.

Editing starts with the viewing of the *dailies,* or *rushes.* The rushes consist of all the film that has been selected to be developed by the script person—that is, all the "good" takes from the shooting.

At this point the agency creative team, producer, and the editor, working together, separate the wheat from the chaff by selecting the best takes (there are sometimes dozens of different takes for each individual sequence of a commercial) from the raw footage.

Now the magic of editing begins. Following the storyboard, the editor puts the selected takes together to form the first *rough cut* of the commercial. The resulting bit of film is called the *work print.*

Believe me, the work print gets worked and reworked. The editor may, for example, substitute one take of one scene for another to see which works better. Or one scene may be lengthened while another is shortened. A close-up may even be substituted for a long shot to see if it improves the commercial. It's done over and over and over again until a satisfactory version is achieved.

Since the work print represents only the pictorial part of the commercial, the next step is to concentrate on the audio part. Now all the off-camera voices (announcers, for instance), sound effects, and music are recorded. Each of these elements is laid down on a separate track. Then it is all mixed together into one sound track at a special recording session called, appropriately, the *mix*. At the mix, all kinds of subtle adjustments can be made in the sound track. The music can be lowered, for instance, and the voices can be made louder. Sound effects can be raised or lowered. Bass and treble can be balanced. The latest techniques in this area are synthesized sounds, which can be created electronically, and "sampling" of sounds, which is a technique where live sounds are recorded and manipulated electronically to create new sounds which were impossible to achieve just a few years ago. The sound is "mixed" at the same time as the work print is being viewed, to ensure that the music, words, and effects are happening in exactly the right places—"in sync" (synchronization).

Once the picture and sound have passed through all the levels of approval required, the commercial is ready to be finished for broadcast. The broadcast standard format (tape size) today is one-inch videotape. That's what gets sent to the stations, and what viewers see on their sets. So now the original film is prepared by the editor for *film-to-tape transfer*. The technician who works the highly sophisticated (and expensive) film-to-tape transfer equipment is called a *colorist*. Creative team and producer work with the colorist to transfer the film image to reels of one-inch videotape. The highly sensitive equipment can shade and color the original film with incredible accuracy and subtlety. Every scene is carefully considered for its own color tones and lighting, as well as its relation to the overall look of the spot.

These transferred scenes now go into another highly sophisticated (and expensive) edit room, where the last stages of production begin. This is the room where all of the optical effects are added. *Opticals* include things like dissolves (where one scene fades into another), wipes (where one scene is "wiped" off and replaced by another), and special effects (such as things popping on and off the screen and titles). Special 3-D electronic animation makes it possible to create complex title and action sequences. The agency creative people and the film editor work closely with the videotape editor in this process, which is highly creative because computerization allows them to view many options quickly. When the optical effects are in, you've got a final picture. It's now time to combine the final picture with the final sound mix. Together they become the "master" tape, from which copies are made and distributed to every station that has been selected to run the commercial all over the country.

So now you know what goes into the making of a commercial. What makes a commercial into *advertising* is the subject of the other chapters of this book.

13

How Not to Use a Testimonial

I don't know about you, but it takes a bit more than some famous star's say-so to convince me of a product's intrinsic merit. I'm not as easily impressed as I once was, and the days when I might have rented O. J. Simpson's or Arnold Palmer's favorite car just because they told me to are long gone. These days, I demand a good solid switching idea before I'll try *anything*, even from a spokesperson whose face is as familiar to me as that of an old and trusted friend.

After all, I expect more of my friends than charisma. I expect the honest truth.

I tend to devote something less than full, rapt attention to commercials using famous people as crutches. So you can imagine how much attention I paid to the Hertz commercial with not one, not two, but—count 'em—three rich and famous celebrity spokespeople in the same spot.

For years, Hertz car rental commercials teamed golf star Arnold Palmer and football pro O. J. Simpson. They've since become the longest-running comedy team since Abbott and Costello. But in case we weren't starstruck enough, Hertz recently added Jamie Lee Curtis, almost to set off their comic routine.

126

Talking into the camera, Curtis announces that Hertz's low prices enable us to see the United States for a song. The scene shifts to Simpson and Palmer riding in a car together. In California, Simpson blows the harmonica as Palmer sings, "California, here I come. . . ." In Hawaii, Palmer plays the ukelele as the two men sing a few bars of "Aloha Oe." In Florida, they join in a chorus of "Moon Over Miami." As the commercial ends, Curtis makes fun of their singing and speculates about the cost of voice lessons.

Why add a third celebrity to this already star-studded commercial? Like so many who saw it, I was too blinded by stars to catch any of the critical sales points. Curtis, the Hollywood star, seems to be in the wrong constellation. I know why Hertz chose Arnie and O. J. years ago as spokesmen. It was because of their recognition and appeal among the largest single segment of car renters: businessmen. Everybody knows all businessmen play golf and are in awe of Arnold Palmer, a businessman himself and a pretty fair golfer. And when businessmen aren't digging divots on the links, they're planted in their easy chairs digging football on the tube. And when you talk football greats, who pops into mind initially? O. J.! So where does Jamie Lee Curtis come from? (And don't tell me Tony Curtis and Janet Leigh.) And why? Maybe because Palmer and Simpson aren't doing so well. Latest sales figures show Hertz's share of market dropping dramatically over the last few years to competitors who are appealing to more women and more leisure travelers. Enter Jamie Lee Curtis, star of the smash hit movie *A Fish Called Wanda*. She should star in her own commercial aimed at women and leisure travelers. Instead, Hertz cast her as third banana to a couple of jocks.

Not only does Curtis fail to add anything to the commercial, she actually detracts from it, since we spend most of the time trying to figure out what important mission she is supposed to accomplish. When professional announcers can be had for the asking, why push a famous actress into the part? If you're going to get a star, let her play a starring role.

None of this is meant to be critical of Jamie Lee Curtis, who happens to be one of my favorites. It's not her fault that she wasn't used to her best advantage. By failing to make her a functional part of the commercial, Hertz made a very expensive mistake. What a waste! This is simply no way to treat a celebrity!

If I may invoke Seiden's Law again for a moment (the believability of a commercial is in inverse proportion to its cost), I'd like to do some rapid finger counting to pinpoint what this commercial cost in relation to what it yields. I don't have any idea of Curtis's fee, but I happen to know that stars of top magnitude have been commanding anywhere from $1 million to $10 million for their commercial appearances. I'm not saying Curtis got several million, but whatever she got, it was more than the part Hertz gave her was worth.

Contrast the Hertz commercial in which all those celebrities do nothing for the product with a commercial for the Bowery Savings Bank in New York, in which one well-chosen celebrity works wonders. I'm referring to the Joe DiMaggio campaign. A widely admired superstar from the glory days of New York Yankee teams, DiMaggio is as much a landmark to New York baseball as the Bowery Savings Bank is to New York banking. DiMaggio is more than a ballplayer. He's an institution. Everybody trusts Joe DiMaggio. He is solid, thoughtful, conservative, admired—someone we assume is sensible about money. Just in case you wonder what an old ballplayer knows about the Bowery, DiMaggio answers the question by saying, "Those folks take their pinstripes as seriously as we did ours." For all these reasons, the Yankee Clipper hits a home run in the Bowery commercials.

Hertz might have done as well—or better than—the Bowery if instead of choosing Palmer, Simpson, and Curtis, it had chosen celebrities who could enhance its product. I'm not quite sure this likable trio does. In fact, I strongly disagree with the view, expressed by one veteran adman recently, that "people like to buy from somebody they like." All things being equal, I will buy from someone selling a better product—or someone offering a better price—even if I don't like the person. To have any value at all, a spokesperson must be believable (Joe D. is a lot more believable than jokesters Palmer, Simpson, and Curtis combined) or at least uniquely suited to a particular situation, product, or strategy. For example, Al Unser, Jr., the racing car driver, is the perfect spokesman for Valvoline motor oil. Lynn Redgrave, who recently lost weight after years of being plump, is a perfect choice for Weight Watchers dinners. I might choose elegant Dina Merrill for a luxury product, fastidious Tony Randall for a grooming product, and beautiful Raquel Welch for cosmetics.

The spokesperson should also be compatible with the product. That's why Texaco, which used Bob Hope as a spokesman for fifteen years, made the right decision when it decided not to use Hope in launching System 3 gasoline. The product, a potent fuel billed as a technological breakthrough, was clearly designed for a younger audience. I'm sure Hope would still be a convincing spokesman for other products. Life insurance, maybe. A retirement village, an airline, a resort, golf clubs, or fishing gear. But he's an inappropriate spokesman for a state-of-the-art breakthrough product.

Claude Akins is the right spokesman for AAMCO Transmissions because he played a veteran trucker in the TV adventure series "Movin' On" and because he looks the part. He is very reassuring, has a friendly approach, and sounds as if he knows cars. We believe him and are reassured when he tells us that even if a small transmission problem sounds like a big one, chances are it's not. Akins helps eliminate the fear of a simple car repair turning into a huge, expensive job. In contrast, Jack Klugman seems out of character as a spokeman for Canon copiers. Klugman's role in these commercials is as adviser to a little old lady about how Canon copiers could make her cottage industry more efficient. But Klugman, who played a disorganized slob in the popular, long-running TV sitcom "The Odd Couple," is hardly a model of efficiency and is totally miscast in the role of efficiency expert.

Linda Ellerbee, a former newscaster, and Willard Scott, an NBC weatherman, were interesting and promising choices in a recent campaign for Maxwell House coffee. In this spot, my problem is not with the spokespeople but with how they were used. The whole purpose in using newscasters is to achieve the highest degree of believability. So when they are cast in executions that destroy their believability, you destroy all need for them. That's what Maxwell House did in this commercial. The commercial, done in the form of a newscast, reported the results of a taste test in which Maxwell House beats out its rival, Folgers. Ellerbee, who is in the newsroom, announces the results of the test, treating it like news. So far, so good. Then Scott does silly, nonsensical, whimsical man-on-the-street interviews, getting people to react to Maxwell House. All believability in Scott, the interviewees, Ellerbee, and Maxwell House is destroyed. But, don't blame the newscasters, blame the creatives who forgot, once again, what the purpose of advertising is.

An interesting side note to this commercial was the uproar it caused in the trade and consumer press. Newscasters and other broadcast people condemned Ellerbee for "selling out" and compromising her integrity. What a bunch of holier-than-thou nonsense. I'm sure any of these critics would do the same thing if only someone would ask. Writers do it. Artists do it. Industrial giants do it. Tiny jockeys do it. Astronauts do it. Actors do it. Even politicians do it. Which brings us to . . .

Tip O'Neill, former speaker of the House of Representatives, has done it at least twice—for American Express and for Quality Inns. In the motel commercial, first we see a suitcase filled with gavels and American flags lying on a motel room bed. Suddenly O'Neill's torso pops up from the suitcase like a jack-in-the-box. How's that for dignity? How's that for believability? How's that for stupidity? Rather than making good use of O'Neill's obvious expertise as someone who has presumably traveled a lot all over the country and knows something about motels, this commercial degrades the spokesman. And devastates his credibility. I feel ashamed for Tip O'Neill and surprised that he allowed himself to be used in such a tacky way. I also seriously doubt that a man of his stature would actually stay in a chain of motels that would do a second-rate commercial like this. When you have a quality spokesman, let him be the star of the commercial, not a silly visual gimmick that takes attention away from him. It's a waste of the money spent for the spokesman.

Celebrity spokespeople are sometimes overused. Bill Cosby, cashing in on his popular TV comedy show, has been a spokesman for so many products, it's hard to keep track (Jell-O, Texas Instruments, Ford, Coca-Cola, Kodak, and E. F. Hutton, to name a few). If he was ever credible, he lost his credibility after so many testimonials for so many products. I no longer get excited when I see Cosby endorsing a product. I get excited when he's not!

When it comes to credibility, commercials that use animals in testimonials are one of my pet peeves. Animals are believable endorsers only when they have a particular link to the product. The prime example is Morris the cat, for years the spokescat for 9-

Lives cat food. Morris is the perfect animal "spokesman" because he's a satisfied user of the product. But I could never understand the Spuds MacKenzie campaign for Anheuser-Busch's Budweiser beer. What does a dog know about beer, and why should I choose a brand on the dog's say-so? I hate the damn ugly dog. He insults my intelligence. The campaign has given birth to a whole litter of other commercials in which dogs tout beer, including spots for Ranier Special Dry beer and Stroh's. They're all dogs. I can almost understand what prompted Pabst to launch a commercial making fun of all the beer commercials that use testimonials from dogs. Almost, but not quite. That spot was a dog, too. And what about Smokin' Joe, the chauvinistic cartoon camel for Camel cigarettes, who uses macho caveman tactics on women? Talk about ugly—he makes the dogs look good. After a public outcry, the camel was dropped, but it'll take a long time for the product to get over the hump this mangy mammal left behind.

Cartoon characters don't do much better. Imagine, Howdy Doody is selling Cherry Pepsi, Peanuts characters are selling life insurance for Met Life, and Beetle Bailey is a spokesman for Federal Express. Lovable as some of these characters may be, none of them seems to have any connection to the products they are endorsing. Even less believable is the campaign for the Chevrolet Lumina line that uses Disney characters to sell cars. I don't know about you, but I won't take the word of Mickey Mouse or Donald Duck or even Dumbo when I spend $15,000 for an automobile. Would you listen to Mickey before you listened to an automotive engineer? As pure advertising, it's pure nonsense. Obviously the public thought it was nonsense, too, because Chevrolet decided to drop Walt Disney characters from its advertising for Lumina cars. You don't drop a campaign that's working.

———

All these cases of misused endorsers lead me to believe that there are a few simple rules that advertisers *must* observe when using spokespeople for commercial testimonials, lest the commercial and the product suffer a loss of credibility.

1. Advertisers must realize that an endorsement is only as good as the believability of the endorser.
2. The endorser must be appropriate to the product endorsed.
3. The endorser should never be allowed to overpower the endorsement, nor the execution overshadow the endorser.

Finally, there's one more vital question: Is the personality really needed at all? Will he or she add credibility to the commercial? Does the commercial work just as well, or maybe better, without the personality? A celebrity may make a good commercial great, but he or she can never make a bad commercial good—just more expensive. This is why sometimes it's infinitely preferable to skip the famous-name celebrity altogether and turn the testimonial over to another kind of spokesperson, the unknown (but knowing) expert.

Why? Because the point of all this testifying is to make the audience believe in something. If you, the advertiser, use a celebrity spokesperson from the unbelievable, unreal, make-believe world of show business, you risk having your audience pooh-pooh your commercial on the grounds that your show biz celebrity is just mouthing another part written for him or her. Testimonials, remember, are believable only to the extent of the specific expertise of the people who deliver them, so stars (unless they are attesting to some matter about which they are acknowledged experts) are usually less credible than non-celebrity experts.

This is what I mean: In one Volkswagen commercial, a contingent of Volkswagen engineers, dressed in white coats, arranges themselves in a giant circle. Within the circle, a Volkswagen races at breakneck speed. Its tires squeal as it travels around the circle's circumference, at times dangerously close to the engineers. But instead of backing off, the engineers move in closer, making the circle even smaller. They believe so strongly in the car's control at high speeds that they are willing to risk their lives to prove it.

This is a great commercial because it's completely believable. The automotive experts are authentic, obviously not actors and obviously not acting. As a result, the commercial is more believable than all those show business productions starring singing ath-

letes, Disney characters, and funny weathermen. With one simple
(and, I daresay, inexpensive) commercial, Volkswagen makes its
point a lot more convincingly without the celebrities.

What about these other real-life examples? A pediatrician
who washes her hands more than thirty times a day tells us that
she prefers Jergens Eversoft hand lotion to keep her hands soft.
An emergency room doctor who has seen the damage automobile
accidents can do chooses a Volvo as his car. An aeronautical engi-
neer who services planes for an international airline uses Sears
Craftsman tools. These are all good, solid, honest, believable experts who have good reason to tout the products they are endorsing. They're bound to have an impact on anyone in the market
for those products. How can you ignore them? They're just too
believable to be disregarded.

Can an "expert" testimonial ever make use of humor? Sure,
as long as the humor doesn't detract from the sales message. Remember the Progresso spaghetti sauce commercial that sought to
establish Progresso as an authentically Italian sauce? So who is
more qualified to testify as an expert than a real Italian mama?
This commercial showed us a series of three honest-to-goodness
Italian homemakers from Brooklyn, photographed in their own
kitchens and dining rooms, each of whom urged a steaming platter of spaghetti upon us with great determination, large smiles,
and wheedling cries of "Mangia!" meaning "Eat!" The voice-over
tells us that for years Italian mothers have been serving Progresso.
Now it's time for everyone to try it: "Mangia, Goldberg, O'Brien.
Mangia Lopez, Armstrong."

This is an awfully good commercial, one that properly combines warmth with humor. But most of all, it establishes Progresso's authenticity beyond a doubt, just as an expert testimonial
should. (Who knows more about authentic Italian spaghetti sauce
than authentic Italian mothers?) All hail to the power of believability!

Another commercial includes a testimonial by three elderly
women who supposedly wrote the company praising Murphy's Oil
Soap. The voice-over announcer extolls the virtues of the product
as we watch close-ups of the women happily scrubbing various
wooden surfaces. At the end of the commercial, the camera pulls
back to reveal the three workers, equipped with pails and mops,

framed by the wooden church pews they have just cleaned. The punch line is, "If Murphy's Oil Soap is good enough to clean this house, it's surely good enough to clean yours." Amen!

Sometimes company founders, owners, and presidents are very believable spokespeople—but only sometimes. I generally subscribe to the following piece of advertising folklore:

> *If the client sobs and sighs*
> *Make his logo twice the size.*
> *If the fellow still proves refractory*
> *Stick in a picture of his factory.*
> *But only in the direst case*
> *Should you ever show the client's face.*

To be sure, using a founder, owner, or president is an easy way to sell the campaign to the client (clients love it). But the campaign won't sell to consumers unless the company spokesperson is believable. One terrific example is Frank Perdue, the chicken man, who made history as the first brander of chicken and who for years has been winning customers with his uniquely sincere manner, look, and sound in radio and TV commercials. Another big hit is Orville Redenbacher, who not only assumed the role of the popcorn king with a folksy, benefit-oriented campaign, but introduced his (equally believable) grandson and provided us with a successor. Frank Perdue and Orville Redenbacher are probably the two most believable spokespeople in America—if you don't believe me, look at their sales results.

Rich Davis is believable as a spokesman for KC Masterpiece barbecue sauce, since he is able to tell us how he came up with the formula and which ingredients make a difference. Lee Iacocca is a wonderful spokesman for Chrysler since he's Horatio Alger himself, and who doesn't believe in and root for Horatio Alger? What are you, a communist or something? He stands for the proposition that all things are possible and has a reputation for being blunt and telling it like it is. The founder of Wendy's hamburger chain, R. David Thomas, hits close to home with the message, "Our hamburgers are the best in the business, or I wouldn't name the place after my daughter." He also offers customers their money back if they disagree. I think I believe him.

Sometimes company spokespeople are not quite as believable. Take Bill Farley for Fruit of the Loom's Activewear line. Farley, the president and chief executive officer of Farley Industries, which owns Fruit of the Loom, tries to convince me to buy Fruit of the Loom products by telling me they are made in America. Somehow Farley, a nice-looking fellow and a nice guy, doesn't give me a warm feeling or do anything for the products. In fact, I can't think of any reason to use him in the commercial except possibly if he showed up in his skivvies. The same goes for Victor Kiam, who tells us he liked Remington shavers so much, he decided to buy the company. I don't believe him. I think he bought the company because he got a good deal.

For sheer believability, no famous person can ever match an expert, whether an authority in the field or an anonymous expert. Does that mean that big-name celebrities should never be used as spokespeople if we can get an expert? Of course not! Sometimes a famous person can also be an expert, and if he delivers the message with the conviction and panache of Wilford Brimley, he's worth his weight in oats. Wilford Brimley is the perfect spokesman for Quaker Oats Company's Old Fashioned and Quick Oats. Honest, straightforward, and believable, Brimley played the grandfather in the family-oriented TV series "Our House," and he dispenses good sound grandfatherly advice. He appeals to the older audience to whom Quaker targets its product.

One of the best examples of celebrities well-used is the American Express print campaign, which drafted an impressive roster of celebrities to show that "Membership has its privileges." Beautifully conceived, the campaign features celebrity portraits by photographer Annie Liebovitz of everyone from Olympic diver Greg Louganis to comedian Alan King. The ads have very little text: They identify the people pictured, along with the year they became "cardmembers," and remind us not to leave home without the American Express card. In this case, the pictures speak louder than the words. They tell you that if you get an American Express card, you join a very prestigious club with quality members such as Jessica Tandy and Hume Cronyn (photographed on the boardwalk at Coney Island), Ella Fitzgerald (shown in a leopard coat next to her 1956 convertible), Mikhail Baryshnikov (dancing in a rowboat), Neil Simon (cuddling a puppy), Candice Bergen (poised on a horse), or any of the others in the extensive American Express gallery. They even persuaded Paul Newman to appear for them in what may be his first American commercial endorsement. In contrast to the Quality Inns commercial, which downgraded Tip O'Neill's image, American Express treats the former speaker with the respect he deserves, thereby upgrading its own image and the image of every other American Express member.

Disarmingly honest and simple, these ads do exactly what a celebrity testimonial should do: They make us believe in the sincerity of the spokesperson and in the value of the product endorsed. Who wouldn't want to join a club that has these people as members? This campaign is extremely compatible with American Express' Unique Advantage over its competitors—it's the most prestigious, most exclusive, most desired, and hardest to get of all the credit cards. The campaign makes my list as one of the most admired of the decade.

In the final analysis, a commercial is a selling vehicle that must be able to stand on its own feet without a spokesperson before I would consider using a spokesperson at all. A famous (or nonfamous) spokesperson cannot be the entire creative strategy but should merely add excitement, memorability, and believability to an already sound package of sales points. *A spokesperson is an executional technique, not a concept.* Used properly, he or she can tip the scales in favor of believability every time.

And that's the name of the testimonial game!

14

How Not to Talk to a Woman

The women's movement has made great strides since I wrote the first edition of this book. We've put a woman on the presidential ticket, sent three women into outer space, and seen a woman appointed to the United States Supreme Court. Women comprise 50 percent of most professional schools, occupy key positions in Fortune 500 corporations, and play a major role at many advertising agencies. That's why it always surprises me when I see advertisers caught in a time warp as they try to sell to women. Let me refer you to several commercials that represent the epitome of how *not* to talk to a woman!

A commercial for Noxzema skin cream pictures a beautiful young woman bending over her sink. The offscreen voice asks what she's doing.

"Washing my face," she replies.

"With soap?" inquires Mr. Voice.

The woman looks up at the question in surprise. "At my age?" she asks. Surprise gives way to emphasis: "I use Noxzema."

At this point, her boyfriend enters the picture to deliver the clincher.

137

"So," he muses, "that's how you stay so young-looking!"

I didn't know whether to laugh or cry. For one mad moment, I actually toyed with the idea that it was a big put-on concocted by the Noxzema people as a gleeful bit of self-satire.

It wasn't. They were dead serious.

Here is this beautiful young thing, who looks all of 18 and certainly no older than 25, supposedly concerned about her aging skin and revealing her secret for staying so "young-looking." I know her real secret, of course: She's practically a baby.

Can you imagine how this commercial must make women viewers in their thirties, forties, and fifties feel? How they must writhe to hear from this little woman-child's own baby lips her worry about her aging epidermis? I'm not sure about the age of the women who represent Noxzema's prime target audience, but my common sense tells me that the vast majority have got to be over 25. But if any commercial was ever designed to turn off women who are over 25, this is the one.

The Noxzema commercial is a classic from the past. But advertisers are still making the same mistake. I can't understand how people in the business of talking to women and selling products to them could be so insensitive to their feelings. In the long run, this commercial had to alienate the vast majority of the product's prospects. It could have been a wonderful commercial if a beautiful woman in her thirties, forties, or fifties with a beautiful complexion had been used as its subject. Then it would have been believable. As it stands now, this Noxzema commercial is laughable—or cryable, depending upon the age of the woman viewing it.

It's no way to talk to a woman. Especially an older woman.

Oil of Olay sure knows how to talk to a mature woman. Its commercial pictures a beautiful older woman who defiantly declares that she doesn't intend to grow old gracefully but to fight it all the way—with Oil of Olay. Now, *that's* the way to talk to a woman!

Here are two commercials for Puritan oil that women will fight all the way, too. We're following a handsome, vital, energetic, high-powered corporate executive as he scurries around the office. He rushes from meeting to meeting, dashes up a flight of stairs, grabs a quick bite of an apple while on the run—all under great stress and time pressure. As we watch him hustle, his wife worshipfully informs us via voice-over: "This is my husband, Michael. He's under a lot of pressure and now he's doing things differently . . . like taking the stairs, eating more fruit, and cutting down on cholesterol and saturated fat. That's why I cook the foods he loves with Puritan oil." The commercial goes on to extoll the health virtues of Puritan. At the end, we watch little wifey pick up her lord and master after work to drive him to the health club, assuring us that "Michael is feeling wonderful." It ends with the theme line: "His oil for life."

I'm very relieved that Michael feels so well. I don't know what the world would do if King Michael's heart suddenly attacked him. But I do know what his dumb, doting, dutiful wife would do—throw herself on the funeral pyre. This commercial might be a big hit in countries where women live only to serve their husbands, but in today's America, depicting a woman in such a subservient state of mind is absurd. Our self-sacrificing little housewife's only concern is keeping her husband healthy and feeding him food he likes. I wonder what *she* eats? Probably franks and beans. That's good enough for her.

The second Puritan oil commercial in this campaign features high-and-mighty husband as a school principal and a wife who hasn't learned a thing about self-respect. He spends his day under pressure at the school, while she seems to spend her day in the kitchen worrying about his health. At the end of this commercial, the wife walks hubby home from school to see that he gets his exercise. Again, the line "His oil for life."

Can you imagine talking to a woman (and these commercials are pitched to women) this way in this day and age? I know at least a thousand women, including my wife, who would be glad to throw a party in honor of the creator of this insipid, insulting, insensitive campaign. And they'd have plenty of Puritan oil on hand—to boil him in.

Here's another candidate for the male chauvinism award. A commercial for Cascade dishwashing detergent shows the horrors and impending doom a woman experiences when she discovers that her husband is bringing his boss home for dinner and there are spots on the wine goblets. This commercial makes her look ridiculous. Could she really think her lousy housekeeping would put her husband's job at risk? If his relationship with his boss (and her relationship with her husband) depends upon the condition of her glasses, they're both pretty fragile relationships. I'd break them both off!

Cascade probably thought it was on more solid ground with women when it ran a similar commercial featuring three women partners in a catering business. The commercial never praises them for their business acumen or ambition or their food. Again, lousy housekeeping is the only issue. One woman fears the business will be forced to close because it catered a party using spotted dishes. Is she for real? Even as this commercial tries to depict independent women in their own business, it chastises them for being bad housekeepers.

As did Minute Rice in many commercials. For years, the product's campaigns centered around women who were failures in the kitchen because their rice came out sticky. One spot features a cooking class with women showing off the chicken and rice dish they have just prepared. While her classmates win kudos for their culinary skills, the class flunky gets scolded for a recipe ruined by sticky rice. The implication is that she is a bad wife and mother because she can't make perfect rice. The answer is to use Minute Rice for perfect rice every time, in five minutes.

Rather than pointing the finger at a woman who has fouled up in the kitchen, later Minute Rice commercials accentuate the positive. These commercials show a variety of recipes, all of which have been prepared with Minute Rice, and people sitting down to enjoy these delectable meals. And there's a new tag line too: "Fits the way you want to cook today." No longer is Minute Rice telling women they have to be perfect. They're now telling them that Minute Rice is perfect for their new life-style—it's versatile for today's new recipe favorites, it's fast, and it's foolproof. That's the way to talk to today's woman. Minute Rice has learned you can't scare her into buying your product.

Smith & Wesson learned that lesson the hard way when a print campaign for handguns backfired. Pitched as public-service information about self-protection, one ad pictures a woman approaching her car in a dark parking lot. The headline reads, "You thought no one could fit in your backseat." The copy suggests you check the back of your car before you open the door. "Cramped as it looks, there's actually room in the back of your car for a hefty six-footer—to hide," it warns.

Though the ad never mentions guns, it sends the implicit message that in addition to checking the backseat of their cars, women should pack a Smith & Wesson. (In fact, one month before the campaign ran, Smith & Wesson introduced the LadySmith, a .38-caliber revolver especially designed for a woman's smaller grip.)

The ad sparked an outcry from gun-control groups, who argued that it preyed on women's fears. A number of women's magazines refused to run the ad. And women were scared off. Smith & Wesson shot themselves in the foot by offending the very audience it was trying to woo.

Equally offensive are commercials that treat women as sex objects. (Yes, they're on the decline, but they're still around.) A spot for Silkience conditioner, for example, plays on the double meaning of the word "chick." "All kinds of chicks want beautifully clean hair," chirps a woman with a luxurious blonde mane. She cuddles a baby chicken in the palm of her hand, continuing the double entendre: After hours of play, the chick conditioned with Silkience "would stay cleaner, fluffier, more beautiful" than one who wasn't. New Silkience ("just hatched") repels up to 75 percent of the dirt hair can attract.

And this commercial repelled 100 percent of the women who saw it. I doubt that they even heard the sales points. They turned off the minute they heard themselves referred to as "chicks."

Another commercial that turned women off with an insulting reference was one for Hawaiian Tropic suntan oils. The commercial begins by panning up a woman's almost nude body, starting at her feet, as she sunbathes on the beach. The copy begins, "In Hawaii the sun shines on all kinds of beautiful babes," then continues to talk about the varieties of oils and SPFs Hawaiian Tropic offers. When we get to the woman's face, we see that she is holding a baby, and the voice-over says, "Hawaiian Tropic. Created by one man because . . ." and the woman pictured concludes the sentence, "No one can resist a beautiful babe." This commercial is incredibly insulting, and the use of the baby to justify the word "babe" makes it even more infuriating.

A commercial for Epilady shavers is just as bad. Two women

are walking on a street, talking about how great their legs look. To demonstrate, one woman slides up her skirt and invites her female companion to "feel how smooth." A man overhears their conversation and peers up over his newspaper. "Extremely smooth," he says appreciatively. Oblivious to the fact that they're becoming a public spectacle, the women continue raving about Epilady: no cords, no shaving, removes hair from the root. Leaves their legs smooth for weeks. The commercial ends with another shot of the woman lifting her leg and holding up her skirt. By now a crowd has gathered to check out the results she has gotten with Epilady.

I find it ironic that Epilady, which supposedly liberates women from the nuisance of frequent shaving, still holds onto them as sex objects—little more than a pair of legs. But it's not the only product for legs that's demeaning to women.

A commercial for L'eggs pantyhose also shows a woman baring her legs in public in all kinds of provocative ways, this time to the throbbing beat of the song, "She's got L'eggs. She knows how to use them." She knows how to use them? I'm assuming she knows how to walk. Any other implications are offensive to today's women.

Products that continue to portray women as little more than man-pleasers are flirting with danger. Round the Clock referred to its hosiery as "Pantyhose for men." The heroes of the commercials in this campaign were men. Not women. And not pantyhose. One spot features a man in business clothes, obviously distracted by women's legs as he goes through the motions of his work day. With soft music in the background, we see him distracted while waiting in a hallway, seated at a desk, examining a blueprint. The camera concentrates on his face, and we catch the twinkle in his eye. In the next scene, he is perched on the edge of a bed. He grasps a woman's hand, stares amorously at her legs, then leans back as if he is watching her undress. The commercial ends with the Round the Clock slogan, "Pantyhose for men."

When Round the Clock dropped its catchy but offensive slogan, it came up with a new one even more offensive. A print ad features a leggy model in a mini miniskirt. A giant headline screams like a hawker outside a porno show, "This woman isn't wearing any panties." The fine print below describes Round the Clock's cotton-at-the-top pantyhose, which make it unnecessary to wear panties underneath.

Round the Clock could take a lesson from its competitor, Hanes. Hanes scrapped its "Gentlemen prefer Hanes" (which preceded "Pantyhose for men") tag line in favor of a campaign that focuses on women. The old commercials, which aired for almost twenty years, showed women in a variety of street scenes, dazzling men with their legs. The explanation inevitably was "Gentlemen prefer Hanes." Though more subtle than Round the Clock, the message was the same: Women wear pantyhose not to please themselves but to please their male companions. To its credit, Hanes finally decided that first and foremost, the *lady* should prefer Hanes.

The commercials projecting this new image included one spot at a European fashion show with the designer saying, "A woman's body is merely a framework." After a parade of models in wild, futuristic clothing, the camera pulls back to reveal a woman watching this fashion show on TV while she gets dressed. The scene switches between the fashion show and her apartment, and we notice that she reacts to the designer's forecasts by doing exactly the opposite of what is supposedly in fashion. When the designer says, "You won't see a leg in Paris this year," she slides a sheer black stocking up her leg. At the news that short skirts are dead, she slithers into a mini. Finally, she reaches for the remote control and zaps off the TV as she confidently heads out for the evening. The voice-over announcer—a woman—concludes: "No matter what the gentleman prefers, the lady prefers Hanes."

That's a powerful statement from an advertiser who once used a male-oriented slogan. And the good news is that more and more advertisers, like Hanes, are rethinking their old-fashioned strategies. One of my favorite examples is Maidenform, which in the mid-1980s abandoned its long-running campaign, "The Maidenform woman: you never know where she'll turn up." You remember the ads. They featured women in many different professions who showed up dressed for work with the front of their outfits open so we could see the Maidenform finery underneath their professional garb. The Maidenform woman tried to show that women could be serious professionals and feminine at the same time. But by parading around like a stripper with the front of her costume open, she also perpetuated the myth that women couldn't be taken seriously in public life. Maidenform demeaned the very customer it aimed to attract.

As the 1990s approached, Maidenform was talking a different game: "Women don't wear beautiful lingerie just for men. But thank you anyway" read the headline in a Maidenform ad that showed a close-up shot of a handsome young man. "Lingerie does a lot for a woman. Not to mention what it does for a man" read another similar ad, which described lingerie as one of the secrets women keep from most of the world. Maidenform continued to emphasize the mystery that surrounds women's lingerie. But the new commercials showed an increased respect for the subject. In one, actor Christopher Reeve reminisces about an old girlfriend whose wardrobe seems to consist of six pairs of blue jeans, sneakers, and an old flannel shirt. Underneath she wore beautiful lingerie. Denim and plaid on the outside, she was satin and lace underneath. "I sure do love a woman in an old flannel shirt," he concludes.

Unlike the earlier Maidenform ads, which publicly unclothed the woman, these new ads never even show a woman, or even lingerie. They leave everything to the imagination of the men who feel privileged to share a woman's secrets. As any sex therapist will tell you, the mind is the world's most powerful aphrodisiac. Maidenform's come a long way in learning how to talk to a woman.

When it comes to talking to women, some advertisers are getting smarter—but not all of them. Notice the difference in the way two financial services companies—Prudential-Bache and Merrill Lynch—try to sell their services to women.

Pru-Bache probably thought it would appeal to career women when it chose a spot that features a woman lawyer. But the script of the commercial is bound to have just the opposite effect. Buoyed by a recent courtroom victory, the young lawyer confers with the law firm's elder partner. As two male co-workers lurk in the shadows, speculating that she is about to get a promotion, the senior partner praises her for her work and informs her that she has been made a partner. But he couches the good news in a put-down: Rather than shaking her hand and welcoming her to the partnership, he hands the young lawyer his broker's business card and announces the promotion to her by saying, "Our next junior partner should be getting some good financial counsel. Call my Pru-Bache broker."

After six or more years of toiling to become a partner, the young lawyer would undoubtedly want to celebrate for a moment or two before she dashes to the nearest phone to call Pru-Bache. And what a pompous, paternalistic, self-important chauvinist the old man is. Clearly, he had enough confidence in this woman's intelligence to make her a member of the firm. Yet he apparently thinks she's an imbecile when it comes to financial planning. Would he treat a man the same way?

Contrast the paternalistic Pru-Bache approach to a commercial for Merrill Lynch that has a real-life woman financial consultant selling the company's services to women. Little more than a "talking head," this low-budget spot delivers a sensible pitch for municipal bonds. While the Pru-Bache spot suggests that women, even successful lawyers, are financial airheads and need a man to guide them, the commercial for Merrill Lynch shows a woman delivering sound financial advice to guide both men and women. At a time when women are moving ahead in the executive job market, we should be seeing more commercials like this one that features competent, independent women.

That's why I bristle when I see advertising that portrays women as damsels in distress, like this spot for Honda: Violins play in the background as a woman eats alone in a romantic restaurant. With a twinge of nostalgia, she describes the men in her life whom she met when various cars she'd been driving broke down. Her old clunker died on the highway. Her subcompact stalled at the sight of a cloud. She met Harold on Route 9 and Vinnie on the turnpike. Now that she's driving the more dependable Honda Accord, she's eating alone.

This commercial says great things about the Honda Accord (it's run 85,000 miles without a hitch), but terrible things about women! Is playing the helpless female the only way she can think of to meet a man? And does Honda really mean to say that a woman loses her sex appeal once she becomes more independent?

Maybe this woman would have even more dates if she became an automobile mechanic and came to the aid of helpless men.

Compare the helpless-female message from Honda with the boost of confidence women get from Lady Stetson perfume: A successful woman executive in an impressive big office in the Big Apple contemplates her future and decides to shed her corporate image for a better life. With a spritz of Lady Stetson for courage, she drives across the country and sets up her own business as a charter boat skipper in California. Her boyfriend in New York chucks his career and follows her. At commercial's end, they sail off into the sunset together.

This tribute to independence pays homage to the woman with a pioneering spirit who makes her own way in life. Free-spirited and adventurous, the Lady Stetson woman isn't dreaming about some handsome prince rescuing her from car trouble. And in the course of pursuing her own dream, she winds up with the guy of her dreams while the woman in the Honda commercials ends up eating alone.

Here's another one that talks to independent women: A mother drops her young daughter off at a day-care center, heads to the airport, and catches a United Airlines flight to another city. By the end of that day, she has made an important business presentation, had a business lunch, caught her return flight, and arrived home in time to pick up her child before the center closes.

This wonderful "today" commercial builds confidence in the reliability of the airline and in the self-sufficiency of the woman. She seems to be a single mother who also holds an important job. I'm sure it's not as easy as the commercial suggests, but United has the right idea.

And so do Safeway supermarkets' commercials as they follow hardworking men and women, from executives to firefighters and construction workers, up and down their aisles. Each shopper echoes the Safeway theme, "I work an honest day. I want an honest deal," in spots featuring men as well as in spots centering on women. This is a campaign about Safeway's equitable pricing policy, but it's also a campaign about equality of shopping and equality in the workplace. Understanding that shoppers are not just women and that laborers are not just men, Safeway makes no distinction between the sexes in its commercials. That's a nice way to talk to women—and to men.

———

While we're on the subject of talking to women, lets talk about *who* should do the talking.

The "tried-and-proved" technique of using a male spokesperson to sell a product to women deserves a few words. This "infallible" technique was devised to capitalize on women's feelings of inferiority. The reasoning: Women lack faith in themselves and will therefore lack faith in a product spokeswoman. Sponsors used this comfortable rationale to justify their use of men as the ultimate authority on any subject you could name. It worked every time for years.

This approach is highly questionable today. Women's experience with men as equals has taught them that men are *not* omniscient and that women know a lot more than men about a lot of subjects. One of the ways women are expressing their new-found self-confidence is to protest the use of spokesmen, particularly in ads selling to women. In the coming decade, we should expect to see more women selling more products to both men and women.

I don't mean to imply that today's woman can no longer be convinced by a salesman. On the contrary, in certain product categories women highly value the opinions of men. Certainly Maidenform's adpeople understood that when they drafted Christopher Reeve to sell lingerie. No one will ever be able to sell a woman romance like a man. Sex, I'm glad to report, will be with us for a few more years, at least. It's playing a larger role in advertising than ever before, because sex is freer and more permissive, with fewer social restraints and taboos, than ever before. So men, thank goodness, will not be out of the advertising picture, as spokesmen or anything else.

But advertisers are recognizing that the woman consumer has changed. She has been in the process of changing for more than thirty years, and "we ain't seen nuthin' yet."

The change has had a tremendous effect within the advertising business itself. More women writers and art directors and account executives (as well as product and brand managers on the client side) are already on the scene, making their presence felt. You can feel it in the advertising they're turning out and see it in the results they're getting. Not too long ago, I asked a group of women ad professionals to list the best and the worst recent commercials from the perspective of convincing a woman to buy. Listen to what some of the brightest women in the business have to say about the effect of advertising on other women:

Cappy Capossela:

Here are some classic campaigns I love as a woman:

- *"You deserve a break today"* [*McDonald's*]. Talks as if it really appreciates how hard it is to be a mom and/ or the person who always prepares the meals. Language that sounds like it is talking to real people.
- *"You've come a long way, baby"* [*Virginia Slims*]. Again, language that women could relate to at the time. Gave women credit for having "made it."
- *"I'm worth it"* [*L'Oreal*]. Beautiful but believable women. Women you can like and relate to. Gives the woman permission to treat herself well . . . just because of who she is. Sense of self-esteem, confidence. Not defensive.
- *"You're not getting older, you're getting better"* [*Clairol*]. One of the few advertising campaigns to women that didn't hold up younger, prettier, skinnier (than any of us are) women, but has something positive to say about the benefits of wisdom, experience, and consciousness.
- *"A diamond is forever"* [*deBeers*]. The commercial where the husband and wife are playacting that they don't know each other and that they're on their first date. When they get to their front door, he says, "Happy anniversary" and gives her a diamond. This campaign is romantic without being

cloying and sentimental and implies that a mar-
riage can actually stay alive and have some romance. ("I would have married her all over
again.")

- *"Don't leave home without it"* [*American Express*].
Treats men and women as equals.

- *The Polaroid campaign.* Mariette Hartley and James
Garner. Tongue-in-cheek, clever dialogue. Treats
men and women as different but equal.

- *The Cheer commercial.* A man, dressed as a waiter,
cleans a napkin in a martini shaker, proving that
detergent commercials don't have to treat women
as idiots or even feature women.

Here are some campaigns I hate:

- *"Don't hate me because I'm beautiful"* [*Finesse*]. A
woman who talks like this is a woman to be hated.
She is arrogant, egotistical, and can't be trusted
alone for a minute with your friendship or your
husband.

- *"I can bring home the bacon. Fry it up in a pan. And
never let you forget you're a man. 'Cause I'm an Enjoli
woman"* [*Enjoli cologne*]. This is insulting to a woman's intelligence. It makes fun of the woman who
works, and it also makes fun of the housewife.
This woman has too much to prove, and she's
trying too hard to prove it.

- *"Ring around the collar"* [*Wisk*] and all detergent
commercials that make it seem as if all a woman
has to worry about is getting her family's clothes
white. These commercials play on the guilt that
has kept women in slavery since the Middle Ages.

- *Convenience foods commercials.* I'm revolted by all
the commercials in which women serve frozen pies
and dinners and act like the food is home-cooked.
These commercials imply that women have to lie if

they haven't spent the time to make it from scratch. More of the "Superwoman" complex.

■ *All sanitary napkin, tampon, and douche commercials* that imply that a woman must deodorize all natural feminine odors, that there's something dirty and terrible about having your period.

■ *All liquor and car commercials* that show women as beautiful objects draped around bottles and cars.

Mary Manning:

Deeply conscious that I, too, live in a glass house and probably shouldn't be pitching these stones at fellow advertisers, I have to admit to three pieces of advertising that, as a woman, I find deeply offensive or simply ridiculous:

• The first and most intense dislike is for the Johnny Walker print ad depicting two bikini'd beauties, aerobically taut, jogging on the beach (bodies that any woman I know would die for!). The conversation, "He loves me for my mind [*really!*] and he drinks Johnny Walker," is inane, if not sexist. Now I'm sure women are not the primary target for Johnny Walker, but gentlemen, surely there's no need to turn off the female audience in the bargain!

■ The Finesse ad "Don't hate me because I'm beautiful" provokes a sort of revulsion for someone who could be so self-centered as to say such a thing. It is the antithesis of the wonderful Oil of Olay campaign where a natural beauty claims she doesn't intend to grow old gracefully but fight it all the way. Right on. That's really talking to us maturing women in a spirit with which we can identify.

• The Camel cigarette ad that advises men that the

way to impress a woman at the beach is to throw her bodily into the ocean—"The more she kicks and screams, the better." This sort of advertising is not only in bad taste, but to my mind seems to encourage unacceptable male domination.

Liz Nickles-Murray:

Few things have infuriated me more than the Macintosh commercial I saw when I was eight and a half months pregnant. The spot features a group of businesswomen carrying gifts from an office baby shower to a pregnant co-worker's car. The dialogue reveals that the pregnant woman plans to take three months' maternity leave and simultaneously run her $10 million account from home via computer.

Obviously, there was good intent on the part of the advertiser. What disturbed me was the fact that this spot was (1) sexist and (2) reinforced the worst aspects of the Superwoman Syndrome.

The spot was sexist because no one would ever suggest that a *man* should ever attempt to handle a major personal event involving immense responsibility—say, a child's illness, or indeed, a baby's birth—*and* run a $10 million account from home.

Instead, the spot spoke to a woman's unending absorption of home and work responsibilities—with no end or reinforcements in sight.

Macintosh has run a similar commercial involving a man working in an out-of-office situation.

He was in the Caribbean, on vacation.

On the other hand, American Express has run a commercial showing a couple learning they are expecting twins, then purchasing two layettes together. I found this spot to ring true. I believed it. The couple were jointly involved, and they faced their responsibilities with a combination of wit, reverence, and mutual respect.

If advertising people are smart, you're going to be tuning in to a whole new ball game for the next few years. Maybe advertisers won't like the idea of changing the image of women in their commercials, but they'd better pull out of their spin quickly enough to get to know their new customer. The female consumer of the future will be marching to a different drummer. Advertisers who insist upon playing the same old tunes will be marching alone into oblivion.

The old rules must go. Old formulas won't work. It's a whole new exciting woman we're going to be talking to, and we'll need more new exciting women in our business to talk to her. Nobody understands a woman like another woman.

15

How Not to Talk to the Youth Market

Teenagers are the toughest audience of all to sell. They accept nothing as fact unless you can prove it. They won't listen to you unless they trust you, and they trust almost no one outside their group. Teenagers are different from every other group in our society. No other group is as distrusting, as disdainful, as intolerant of other groups—nor as homogeneous and united in purpose. Their sole purpose in life seems to be to pit their authority against ours. Genghis Khan was a pushover next to a teenager. Teenagers challenge every word you say. They doubt every claim you make. They're defiant and rebellious. They're a challenge to adpeople, and we're not meeting that challenge with our silly little teenage commercials.

Having seen advertising rejected often enough by teenagers over enough years (teenagers may change, but their behavior doesn't), I think I can spot some of the reasons for the rejection. These are some of the biggest no-no's:

1. *Don't try to talk teenagers' jargon.* By the time you become privy to what words and expressions are "in," they're out. Once

teenage language becomes familiar to us, it loses its uniqueness and value to teenagers. Young people prize their own language and resist outsiders invading their turf. You're not one of the gang, and you can't become one by trying to sound like a teenager. More likely, you'll sound like an adult trying to sound like a teenager, and that sounds square.

The airwaves are filled with examples of advertisers trying to talk like teenagers. A spot for Cherry 7-Up describes the soda as "cool," "real," and "a gas." Another spot—for Hostess Choco-Bliss Snacks—is jam-packed with supposed teen hype: "Awesome!" "Hey!" "Yeah!" "Yow!" In a radio commercial for Three Musketeers candy bar, an obviously adult male voice hiply describes the candy bar "experience" as "fffunky" and "total chocolate madness." These spots, which sound like grown-ups trying (too hard) to relate, stand out like nerds at a rock concert, especially on stations or programs with an overwhelmingly teenage audience. They're exactly how *not* to talk to teenagers.

Is there anything you *can* say to this highly critical audience? "Be all you can be," says the U.S. Army to teenagers, in a campaign that could be a lesson to other advertisers. In print, radio, and TV commercials, the army relies on real teenagers to describe the benefits and excitement of joining the military. These young people don't preach or sound fake and don't try to be hip by using a bunch of supposedly hip words. They're the real thing and they don't have to fake it.

2. *Don't try to imitate teenagers' life-style.* Just as important as teenage jargon is the unique teenage life-style. Here too, being different from the old order is something young people cherish. Whether it's layering their clothes, feathering their hair, rocking to a different beat, or listening to music loud enough to puncture an adult's eardrums, they pride themselves on being different. If you try to imitate their life-style, you'd better know every minute detail of it, or your commercial will have a very short life.

Think about how a teenager might react to this spot for McDonald's: A group of young college pledges are lined up in front of a McDonald's as their fraternity leader chants, "Wanna be in my frat, do the McDonald's menu chant!" The first pledge sounds off by reciting the entire McDonald's menu from memory.

That takes the entire thirty seconds of the commercial. I'm sure fraternity pledges have done their share of beer guzzling, mud sliding, and midnight running. But I can't picture them proving their prowess with a catalog of McMuffins, McNuggets, and Big Macs. It's an obvious self-serving rather than teen-serving commercial. Next to reading a telephone directory, I can't think of anything duller than reciting a menu. Here is a surprisingly unrealistic vision of the teenage life-style from a company that is usually so on target with teens. Everyone's entitled to one mistake.

But nobody's entitled to a fiasco—not even one. A mistake can be off by a little. A fiasco is off in left field, and that's where this next commercial is when it comes to understanding the teenage life-style: A teenage boy tells two girls that his tennis partner, who owns a Porsche, is coming over. Both girls frantically scramble to get ready. One is disorganized and can't find her beauty supplies. The other, who has a Caboodles beauty organizer (it looks like a pink, old-fashioned tackle box) locates everything in a flash. While her girlfriend is in a frenzy looking for things and seems to make no progress, our organized heroine calmly puts herself together, applies makeup, and gets to the guy first. She's disappointed to discover that he's a nerd. Serves her right.

Now, I ask you experts out there who have teenagers of your own: How many mistakes can you spot in that commercial? First, how many teenagers do you know who own Porsches? How many boys would be anxious to introduce their girlfriends to a guy with a Porsche—nerd or no nerd? And how many teenage girls do you know who place such a high premium on being organized? This spot has completely lost touch with reality. And with teenagers. It's one big mistake.

While Caboodles loses touch with reality in its effort to portray boy-girl relationships, Swatch phone rings true with a commercial that seems to understand teenagers' social lives. The Swatch phone has two hand sets on a single base station, allowing two people to talk on the same phone in the same place at the same time. So if one Swatch phone calls another Swatch phone, four people can be in on the same conversation. Got it? That's what happens in this spot: A boy calls his girlfriend. He has a shy friend on the other hand set. The girlfriend has a shy friend with her, too. These two shy teenagers have admired each other but never could get up the courage to speak. With their two gregarious friends playing matchmaker and introducing them to one another, the couple finally speak and make a date. This simple commercial speaks volumes for Swatch phone and its sensitivity to teenagers' insecurity in social situations. This phone is presented as an easy way to get in on the social scene. That's a good way to talk to the youth market.

3. *Don't think you know how to talk to teenagers because you're considered hip.* You may be hip within your agency and among your friends, but to a teenager you're not. More likely you're laughable. Trying to be hip is a sure way to lose your audience and your customer. They see right through you. No matter how fat or skinny your tie, how wide or narrow your pants, how faded your jeans, how short or long your skirt or your hair, how patterned your stockings—you ain't a teenager to a teenager and any teenager worth an allowance knows it. You're older, and even a few short years make an enormous difference. You work in an ad agency. You drink wine spritzers. You vacation in Greece and go to Club Med. You ski in New Mexico, buy expensive Italian clothes, dine in fancy French restaurants. Any neophyte teenager knows more about teenagers than you do.

Commercials that try to reach teenagers by being hip just wind up looking forced—like this spot for Nestle Quik chocolate drink mix: Two teenagers wearing Ray-Ban sunglasses hang out in a 1950s convertible parked at the beach. "Yo, what are you guys doing?" asks an off-camera voice. "We're taking a vacation from carbonation," they reply. The commercial ends with a shot of the Quik package wearing Ray-Bans. I bet the kids laughed so hard they spilled their chocolate milk.

Some of the most effective advertising to youth lets teenagers do the talking—in this case, singing. That's what Sprite did with a commercial that opens with a super noting that the spot is produced by students, directed by students, and features students. It goes on to show scenes of students around the high school singing, "I like the Sprite in you." That's a spritely way to talk to the youth market because nothing interests real teenagers like real teenagers (not actors).

4. *Don't think you know teenagers because you were once one yourself.* To a bona fide teenager, we all look like creatures from the

age of the dinosaurs. They can't believe we were ever teenagers. And that goes for people just out of their teens. The teenage years end abruptly on the day your skin clears, the day you pick a major at college, the day you go on your first job interview. From that day on, you're an outsider. But don't fret; it happens to all of us. Even teenagers.

Many commercials aimed at today's teenagers date themselves with references to past fads. In a spot for Teddy Grahams cookie snacks, three adult-sized bears doing Elvis Presley imitations sing the Teddy Grahams theme song, set to the tune of the Elvis hit "Teddy Bear." Does this advertiser really expect to reach the target audience with a hit from their parents' generation?

Another commercial, for Nacho Cheese Doritos, turns back the clock to the copywriter's own teenage years and tries to put after-school detention in modern perspective. With "Dragnet" style music from the fifties in the background, actor Jay Leno goes into the school detention room and asks several teenagers what they're in for. As they meekly reply, Leno sarcastically considers the implications. "Hmph, a future con man!" he remarks to a boy being detained for talking. "A potential inside trader," Leno muses to a girl being punished for passing notes. Finally, Leno passes a boy who was eating in class and who now has his hand in a bag of Doritos. "A future president of the United States," Leno exclaims approvingly.

Aside from the fact that this commercial makes no sense and no point, it has a feeling of the past about it. The look of the classroom. The sound of the music. Even the concept of detention itself, which is not the big deal it was years ago, is borrowed from the past. The spot sounds like it was conceived by a copywriter or an art director reliving his own days in the detention room. Somehow, the whole thing doesn't seem relevant to today's teens.

Another spot, for Burger King restaurants, sounds like the copywriter's boyhood fantasy of "the perfect date." As a matter of fact, the commercial is about a teenage boy's fantasy of his perfect date. He envisions dinner at a crowded Burger King so everyone will see him. He then settles on his fantasy girl—the beautiful blond in his chemistry class. While he orders the best in the house (sans onions, of course), his svelte date has just a chef's salad and then insists upon paying for the meal. The pièce de résistance comes when she drives him home in her car.

This commercial is living in the past—in the days of the goody-goody teenagers on sitcoms like "Leave It to Beaver." To today's modern teenager, it's ludicrous. Having been exposed to X-rated movies and books, *Playboy* and *Penthouse,* and suggestive TV fare, teenagers' fantasies would run a little more toward the exotic; the suggestion of a date at Burger King might strike these kids as little more than a gag.

Speaking of gags, check out this commercial for Pepsi. A teenager walks into a malt shop crowded with young people and places his order: a burger, fries, and a Coke (yes, this is a Pepsi commercial). Suddenly, the music stops and the picture freezes. The teenager's entire meal magically unprepares itself, as if it is unhappy with his choice of soft drink. When he changes his order to Pepsi, the music picks up again, and the meal comes back together.

The super at the end of this commercial reads "Pepsi, the choice of a new generation." But there's nothing "new generation" in this spot. In fact, the creative people seem more focused on their own teenage years than on the new generation. Malt shops, once a popular meeting place for young people, have largely disappeared. The "magic" of unmaking the meal (achieved by running the film backward) is as old as moving pictures.

Contrast the Pepsi commercial, which could just as easily have run twenty-five or thirty years ago, with this spot for Coca-Cola Classic. In a crowded dance club, a disc jockey sees a teenage girl trying to order a Coke from a busy waiter. He "sends" her a Coke via the video monitor.

There's a commercial that speaks to the new generation. The "magic" delivery of the Coke is modern high-tech magic. The spot is video-oriented, like today's teenagers. And it's set in a disco, a more likely hangout than the malt shop of yesteryear. It all adds up to a very appealing spot for today's youth.

5. *Don't think teenagers act the way you think they should act.* They act the way *they* think they should act. I never met a parent who understood his or her teenager. If you think you understand yours, you're either hopelessly naïve or your kid is much older than you think.

Some commercials that target the teenage audience are little more than adult fantasies about how teenagers should behave. In one, for Dr. Pepper, a teenage boy apologizes for missing his little brother's birthday party. The little boy is disappointed, until his older brother surprises him with a new puppy. Warm and wonderful? You bet. Realistic? No way. The only thing big brothers give little brothers is a hard time. Chances are you don't have a teenager like this one but wish you did. This commercial appeals more to parents than to teenagers, though even most parents know it's nonsense.

Here's a commercial that understands the psyche of kids: A young boy looks up admiringly at a tall, beautiful girl standing beside him. He doesn't come up to her waist, and she doesn't waste any of her attention on him. He would give anything to be her size. As he drinks milk over the years, he shoots up until he is taller than she is. At last she notices him. This spot for The Milk Advisory Board understands the desires of youth. They can't wait to grow up and be attractive to the opposite sex—or to the football coach. (Another spot in this wonderful series has a football coach in place of the tall young lady. You know the rest. Other spots feature little girls blossoming into womanhood and being noticed by older boys.) The commercials are wish fulfillment for kids and offer them hope for the future. You can bet they'll drink their milk to grow up fast. The campaign has a sense of humor and appreciation for teenagers' feelings.

6. *Don't insult teenagers' intelligence or talk down to them.* Teenagers, like everyone else, respond to a good, honest, believable selling concept that fills a need—their need. Please don't kill it with an execution that tries to get on the teenage wavelength. Teenagers want to be talked to like teenagers when teenagers do the talking, like adults when adults do the talking. And they know as well as we do that advertisers are adults.

Maybelline had a good selling concept with its Shine Free matching lip and nail colors. But a commercial aimed at teenagers surrounds the concept with a distracting execution. The spot shows a boy and a girl walking on the beach as male and female vocalists sing, "These two were made for each other." It makes an analogy between the boy and girl who were made for each other and the lip and nail colors that were made to match. No doubt the advertiser is trying to create an aura that will appeal to teenagers. But Maybelline spends more time on the aura than on the product. Teenagers would have responded better had Maybelline devoted more time to the message.

Just as advertisers won't win any teenage customers by trying to get onto the teenage wavelength, they won't attract buyers with commercials that insult teenagers' intelligence. Consider this spot for Wyler's drink mixes that features teenage boys playing basketball. Just as one boy goes up for a jumper, everybody freezes except for the boy. He has a drink of Wyler's as he sings: "I want a Wyler's. W-W-Wyler's. Can't wait, tastes great. W-W-Wyler's!" After he drinks the Wyler's, the video resumes and he sinks his shot.

I'm sure the sports setting and production technique are meant to appeal to teenage boys. But the nonsense situation and total lack of substance treat teenagers like idiots and are more likely to alienate them.

Another commercial, for L. A. Gear footwear, is insulting to teenage girls. The spot, which is filled with double entendres (see Chapter 7, "The Seven Deadly Sins of Advertising"), is also filled with insensitivity. A teenage boy eyes a shapely girl and makes a sexually suggestive analogy between girls and cars: "They're responsive, temperamental, and very expensive. And they have great curves."

The sexual innuendo and sexist viewpoint of this commercial might be a turn-on to teenage boys. But it's sure to turn off its share of female buyers, especially those who aren't built like the curvaceous model in the commercial. Most teenagers are already sensitive about their bodies. They don't need this reminder of their insecurities in the middle of prime-time TV.

And speaking of sensitive subjects, how about all the commercials for acne products that sensationalize the reality of acne and make light of a teenager's concerns? Remember the Oxy-10 commercial, discussed in Chapter 7, that treats the battle against acne like a war game and offers unrealistic hopes for a cure? Now compare that insensitive approach with an intelligent message from Stridex medicated pads. This simple commercial features shots of teenagers happily using Stridex pads. The pitch: "Wipe on Stridex and wipe out pimples! Stridex not only fights pimples you have, its keratyltic action removes dirt and oil and opens pores to help stop new pimples from forming."

That sounds like a dream come true for teenagers. Without insulting their intelligence or belittling their concerns, this spot offers a good selling concept that fills a teenage need. It doesn't make the mistake of trying to talk to them like teenagers. It talks to them like adults.

A commercial for Apple Macintosh computers also supplies a good, honest selling concept. The high school principal confronts Greg, a student who has turned in a professional-looking term paper. "When did you start hiring people to do your homework?" the principal asks. "But, sir, I did those myself. On my computer!" Greg replies. "I know that, Greg," says the principal, as Greg grows increasingly nervous. "But what I need to know is . . . what kind of computer?"

This spot, which shows how computers can help with homework, gives teenagers a good reason to buy the product. It doesn't use teenage jargon, pretend to understand their life-style, or try to get on their wavelength. Instead, it addresses an important teenage concern and shows how the product can help students get better grades. I can't think of a better way to talk to the youth market.

7. Don't talk to a teenager the way you talk to everybody else. They're not like anybody else. They know they're different and expect to be addressed differently. Each message has to be tailor-made for teenagers and must create a situation with which young people can identify. It must be sensitive to their special needs, feelings, and vulnerabilities. If the message (product) is good for anybody else, it isn't good enough for teenagers. *Never use anybody (least of all a parent) as an authority to a teenager except another teenager.*

That's exactly the problem with a campaign for Oldsmobile that tries to appeal to the youth market. I'll have more to say about these spots in Chapter 17, which discusses how not to sell a car. From the perspective of reaching a teenage audience, it's a classic example of how to drive teens away. Even as the campaign targets the youth market, it really appeals to the older generation. Olds began with the catchy slogan "This is not your father's Oldsmobile/This is the new generation of Olds." But unfortunately, the commercials directly contradict the message. The spots show celebrities and their young-adult children: Priscilla Presley and her daughter, Lisa Marie; William Shatner and his daughter, Melanie; Scott Carpenter and his son, Jay. Each time, the emphasis is on the famous parent, rather than on the new generation. It would have been a lot smarter to base this campaign on famous teenagers with their nonfamous parents as foils. That would have made a much more effective campaign to teenagers.

Another deadly mistake this campaign makes is that in each spot, the parent loves the car. Anybody who knows anything about young people knows that parental approval is the kiss of death for any product. If their fathers and mothers, those know-nothing old codgers, like the car, it's obviously not for them. I think teenagers come away from this campaign singing, "This *is* my father's Oldsmobile!"

Any ad or commercial that could be aimed at anybody but a teenager, any product that could be used by anybody but a teenager, and any authority other than another teenager will all be rejected by teenagers, whether we're talking about cars or . . .

Massengill douche. One spot opens with a youthful-looking mother and her teenage daughter driving through the pouring rain. Daughter asks Mom's advice (yeah right!) on cleanliness. "Mom, you have that problem, too?" she inquires, as the rain dramatically beats against the windshield. "Every woman on the planet does," Mom replies. "What do you do?" daughter asks. "I use Massengill. That's the one I trust," Mom says confidently.

Give me a break! How many mothers and daughters do you know who talk like that? Mom may be older and more experienced, but few teenagers I know would ask for her advice about anything, let alone douching. They'd be more likely to learn about such intimate subjects from other teenagers, and more likely to believe the advice.

The Massengill commercial overlooks the fact that teenagers rarely respect adult authorities. So does this commercial for Clear by Design acne medicine. Two girls gossip in a school lunchroom. "Ooh, he's so cute," one girl says to her companion, admiring a boy in the school cafeteria. When her friend asks why she doesn't talk to the guy, the teenager self-consciously replies, "My skin's a mess," although there's barely a pimple visible on her face. Her confident, flawlessly complexioned friend offers some friendly advice: "My father's a dermatologist, and he says. . . ." A sudden hush falls over the cafeteria as everyone freezes, straining to hear the advice. The commercial goes on to make a strong claim for Clear by Design—that its formula is preferred by dermatologists three to one and five to one over two leading competitors, which are named. The commercial ends with a voice-over announcer delivering the line, "So, when a dermatologist's daughter talks, you should listen."

Clear by Design had the right idea using a teenager to give advice on an acne product. The blemish in this commercial is that the teenager treats an adult as the authority. Except under the most dire circumstances (or the duress of their parents), teenagers would be unlikely even to go to a dermatologist. To a teenager, a dermatologist is just another adult, and teenagers don't trust adults to begin with. They would be much more impressed if *teenagers*, rather than dermatologists, preferred Clear by Design three to one over other products. Nor are teenagers likely to trust this particular commercial, which is a take-off on the famous— and very adult—campaign for E. F. Hutton. ("When E. F. Hutton talks, people listen.") Any teenager who recognizes the take-off has one more reason *not* to listen. It's another case of the creative team talking to itself, and when adults talk (particularly to themselves), teenagers don't listen.

━━━━━

I've saved for last one of the best examples of how *to* talk to teenagers: a campaign for Levi's 501 jeans that talks their language. This campaign features typical teenagers from various far-flung cities throughout the United States. Each spot features a different city. In Dubuque, Iowa, a group of teenage friends cruise around town in an old convertible, listening to rock music and taking in the sights. A teenage voice-over narrates the tour: "All the friends I have are really good friends [as he passes some friends on the street who wave]. It's Saturday night. Dubuque, Dubuque is the car thing, you know. Everybody, everybody does the car [we're in a traffic jam]. You know you can trust your friends." The commercial ends with someone singing: "Good-night Iowa, wherever you are."

In another spot featuring Lake Charles, Louisiana, we see teenagers enjoying the outdoor life and beautiful scenery of the area with blues guitar music in the background. Again we hear a teenager in a voice-over: "I don't think there's another place in the country like this. Free and great. It's got everything I want" [we see a boat on a beautiful lake at sunset].

Instead of using actors in stereotypical situations, this campaign relies on real teenagers and real teen talk—honest, unrehearsed, totally believable. That's the stuff teenagers want to hear. It reflects their views about friends, places, freedom, life. Unlike so many commercials that try so hard to be hip, these spots don't even try. They just are because they're 100 percent real—using real teenagers, speaking real teen language, saying what teenagers really want to hear. The only question is whether they're good advertising. I think they are. Besides all the teens wearing Levi's 501s in the commercials, the spots establish an aura of authenticity and a feeling that Levi's 501 jeans are the right jeans for America's teenagers. This campaign makes Levi's 501s the teenage authority.

———

Before you attempt to sell anything to teenagers, I suggest you talk to a few. When was the last time you talked to a teenager? It's an experience, and you just might learn something.

16

How Not to Talk to the Mature Audience

Age is a case of mind over matter. If you don't mind, it
doesn't matter.

—Satchel Paige

A man is not old until regrets take the place of dreams.

—John Barrymore

Think of all the labels we apply as people age: senior citizens, old folks, golden-agers, silver foxes, graybeards. Most of these nametags carry negative connotations. And so does most of the advertising featuring older people.

This advertising generally suffers from at least one of the following problems: It stereotypes old people, it pokes fun at them in an effort to appeal to the rest of the population, or it alienates them by showing complete insensitivity to their feelings about growing old.

Some of the common stereotypes about the elderly that appear in advertising are so obvious, I can't believe advertisers could have been oblivious to them.

165

One example is a spot for Toyota Camry that shows four elderly women out for a joyride. Margaret, behind the wheel, confesses that her palms used to sweat when she had to accelerate
onto the highway. As she confidently approaches the entrance
ramp to an expressway filled with giant trucks, she tells her companions what a difference her new Toyota makes. "I just punch
it!" she exclaims, while two backseat drivers cheer her on with
cries of "Yeah, punch it, Margaret!" As the car lurches forward
into the fast lane, the voice-over announcer describes the power
of the Camry. An inside shot of the car shows the women laughing
uproariously, as if they are on an amusement park ride. When
they reach their destination, they get out of the car, raise their
arms triumphantly, and belt out a chorus of "My Toyota, who
could ask for anything more!"

I'll tell you who could ask for something more: America's
older citizens, that's who! They could ask for a little respect and
sensitivity. They could ask not to be portrayed as incompetent
fools. This commercial stereotypes older people as timid drivers
and suggests they will overcome that fear once they hit the road
in a Toyota. It also characterizes them as morons. Whom does
Toyota think it's talking to? If it's young people, the commercial
makes fun of the audiences' parents and grandparents. If the mature market is the target, Toyota has run roughshod over their
feelings. The mature audience is filled with sophisticated consumers. Yet Toyota gives them no compelling reason to buy. Charlie
Skoog, a former colleague of mine who recently retired, observes,
"Any experienced driver, especially one with extra years and miles
on our expressways, is not going to believe any car, no less a Toyota, will solve all the problems of entering and surviving on the
highway. Of all the market segments, the more mature are among
the most difficult to persuade. This growing and affluent market
has often endured pitches that attempted to con them to a new
product or service. Having lived through many such costly and
aggravating seductions, their guard is always up and their suspi-
cions rarely down. On or off the highway, one cannot risk insulting their intelligence. They can spot a phony position a mile
away—particularly when it's so obviously aimed at their vulnerabilities."

Toyota tapped into a lucrative market when it targeted the

over-50 crowd. These consumers hold 50 percent of the discretionary buying power and 77 percent of financial assets, according to the U.S. Bureau of the Census. By the dawn of the next century, they will be an even more significant portion of the consuming public.

But most advertisers haven't taken the time yet to understand this rapidly growing market. By not making that effort, Delta Airlines risked grounding its effort to woo older travelers. One Delta commercial shows an old woman traveling alone on Delta. Once in the terminal, she realizes she's lost her wedding band and panics. The story has a warm, happy ending when a member of the airline clean-up crew finds the ring and returns it to her as she tearfully embraces him. It's a commercial with instant appeal. Our hearts go out to the sweet little old woman, and we feel warm all over for the honest Delta employee who returned the ring. But couldn't a younger person just as easily lose a wedding ring and be just as upset? Or is forgetfulness an exclusive trait of the old? It also makes you wonder how the woman lost the ring. That's not easy to do. It casts doubt on her competence and her level of responsibility. As warm as the commercial is, it can leave older people cold. Why does Delta have to glorify its service by denigrating the competence of the older population?

Another place advertisers' insensitivity shows is in all the commercials for "old folks" products, which portray all older people as helpless, feeble, or incontinent. One spot, for a device called "The Clapper," features a bedridden old woman who turns various electrical devices on and off by clapping her hands. What a turn-off. Despite the fact that this product is not necessarily an "old folks" product, it is portrayed that way. Wouldn't this product be just as appreciated by a yuppie after a hard day on Wall Street, or a mother of two or three at the end of a busy day? But this advertiser chose to position it for old people on their deathbeds. This stereotype of the deteriorating old person completely ignores the fact that most older people today are in pretty good shape.

Another commercial, this one for Lifecall Emergency Medical Response Systems, also plays on the stereotype of feeble elderly people. It opens with the image of a sickly old woman in a hospital bed. The voice-over announcer, who turns out to be the

same woman—now recovered—tells us that when she recently became "deathly ill," she used Lifecall to summon an ambulance, her
next-door neighbor, her family, and a doctor. The video switches
to a more recent picture of the same woman, now smiling like a
Cheshire cat, as she demonstrates how the system works. Holding
up a small square box which she wears like a pendant, the woman
describes how she uses this remote control device to call a twenty-
four-hour emergency medical response service: She merely
presses the button, speaks into the air, and her voice is picked up
by an automatic speakerphone somewhere else in the house.

The commercial includes two additional cases, both of which
feature helpless old people. An elderly man sawing wood in his
home workshop is suddenly gripped by chest pains. An old
woman who has apparently just toppled over lies on the bathroom
floor next to her walker, her head leaning against the tub. In both
cases, the old people summon Lifecall and are politely reassured
that help is on the way. "Protect yourself with Lifecall, and you're
never alone," the voice-over announcer says.

I'm sure Lifecall is a very useful service, but is it useful only
for old people? Don't younger people ever fall, trip, black out,
have a heart attack or an accident? The spot suggests that older
people are always stumbling, falling down, or being stricken by
terrible medical emergencies, that all of them are unsteady on
their feet and in constant danger of falling into a dead faint. One
day this advertiser will wake up and realize that there's a much
bigger market out there for his service and stop scaring older
people.

As much as I hate commercials that scare older people, I'm
even more offended by commercials that poke fun at them.

A commercial for On-Cor frozen entrees features an elderly
man playing the big cheese of a hypothetical imitation cheese
company. Set in a test kitchen, the spot shows the old man sampling various flavors of imitation cheese. As the lab men stand by,
he confuses cheddar with swiss, and swiss with cheddar, growing
increasingly disoriented. Half bemused, half exasperated, his as-
sistants offer to bag the cheddar as swiss. Finally the voice-over
announcer intervenes and tells us that On-Cor Lite uses only real
cheese in its products.

The point of the commercial seems to be that fake cheeses all taste the same, so On-Cor uses only 100 percent real cheese in its frozen entrees. That's not a bad sales message. But unfortunately On-Cor turned it into a joke, making the point at an old man's expense. Maybe young people think this old man is funny, but I'm sure the older people watching this commercial don't. Why use the old man as a clown, emphasizing his forgetfulness and confusion? Helen Hayes once said, "Age is not important unless you're a cheese." And age is not funny, unless you're a fool.

Here's a spot in which Pepperidge Farm made a similar mistake. Dressed in his traditional straw hat and suspenders, the finicky old Pepperidge Farm character prepares for a party he is giving. As he lays out the dessert platter, he unpacks the variety of Pepperidge Farm cookies which he has thoughtfully purchased for each guest: Bordeaux for Karen and Gladys, Milano for Charlie. . . . Having completed the labor, he suddenly realizes the party is not until the following day. "Tragic error," the old man muses, as he helps himself to a cookie.

The tragic error in this commercial was to make fun of the forgetfulness of older people. While older consumers might find Pepperidge Farm cookies more appealing than certain bakery varieties, this absent-minded gent has to be distasteful to them. That's a sure way to make the cookie crumble for the mature market.

Equally insensitive are the commercials that alienate older buyers.

A prime example is the recent campaign for Philips Softone Pastels bulbs. One commercial shows a skinny old man with sunken cheeks and a shrunken body sitting on the sofa as his wife moves around their living room changing light bulbs. "My wife puts Philips all over the house. She says they make everything look more attractive," he says. Just as he interjects, "I don't know about that," his wife turns on the new lights and the old man turns into a handsome young guy in the eyes of his wife, who drools at the sight of him. The commercial ends with the tag line, "It's time to change your bulb."

It's also time for Philips to brighten up. This commercial contrasts the beauty of youth with the ugliness of age. And that's *really* ugly.

Another commercial, for Genesee cream ale, also contrasts

the ugliness and clumsiness of age with the beauty and grace of youth. This one shows a gorgeous, curvaceous young blond, gyrating to rock music. Next to her, a matronly, squat grandmother type, complete with white gloves, a frumpy hat, and a pocketbook slung over one arm, tries to follow the young girl's every movement. Set in limbo, the spot has the two women side by side, with the old woman looking comic, wiggling her hips to the music as the young swinger dances beside her. The awful line is, "This should give you some idea of the difference between beer and Genesee cream ale." And this commercial should give you some idea of the difference between good taste and bad judgment.

The more I think about the commercial, the more I'm horrified by it.

And while I'm not horrified by the Clara Peller "Where's the beef?" commercials for Wendy's, which make older women into silly clowns, I'm not amused by them, either. One of *my* beefs with this campaign, besides my larger criticism of it as confusing (discussed in Chapter 4), is that it uses the comic portrayal of old women as its primary attraction. For instance, in one commercial, Peller enters a hamburger joint (not Wendy's) and inspects the tiny burger as her companion holds up a giant bun with a tiny burger on it. "Where's the beef?" she abrasively inquires, in a line that made Wendy's famous and made Clara Peller a laughingstock. Another spot shows Clara behind the wheel of a truck, giving her girlfriends a rough ride. With tires screeching, she pulls up to a fast-food drive-in window. The attendant sees who's coming and closes the window just as Peller arrives to deliver the punch line "Where's the beef?"

I have to assume Wendy's was targeting an older audience with these commercials, or why would it have chosen a silly, contentious old woman as its spokesperson? A child or teenager or yuppie or middle-aged woman could have been just as funny. If octogenarians were really the target audience, then I think the character of Clara Peller was insulting to them. If the elderly were not the target, then Wendy's used Clara Peller and her equally silly friends as a comical foil for the intended audience to laugh at. In either case, making fun of older people ain't funny to older people.

GMAC used an old man as a pawn in a commercial that tried to contrast its personalized loan service with the depersonalized service of many banks. The spot shows an old man in the bank of the future, struggling to explain his car loan needs to an automatic teller. When he pushes the buttons on a remote control device, a matronly-looking woman appears on the screen. He keeps pushing the buttons, skipping ahead through the prerecorded tape, as she offers him a student loan, a home improvement loan, and finally a car loan. The old man makes a noble effort to comply with the tape's request for information. But over and over again, he is interrupted by a beep and told to begin again. As the machine fouls up, the man grows increasingly frustrated, until he finally asks a bank guard if there is "someone live" he could talk to. The guard, who seems oblivious to the old man's frustration, offers him a calendar. The commercial ends with a pitch for hassle-free GMAC car loans, available from a General Motors dealer.

The obnoxious automatic teller in this commercial would be frustrating to anyone. But the fact that GMAC used an old man as the star is particularly frustrating to older people, who may be sensitive about the challenge of adapting to new technology.

Nor do advertisers score any points by hiring old Hollywood stars to hawk geriatric products, says Don Mix, another former colleague of mine, now retired. Mix and the rest of us who can still remember June Allyson's twinkling smile in rah-rah musicals will be thoroughly depressed by her testimonial for Depend, a diaper for incontinent adults. Mix was equally sobered to see Martha Raye appearing for Polident denture cleaner and Burt Lancaster pitching Humana health insurance. "Great actor though he is, Burt Lancaster doesn't convince me he's an authority on Medicare supplement plans. And don't tell me he goes to Humana doctors instead of his own Beverly Hills specialists," he says.

Mix, who recalls Martha Raye as a vivacious, curvy, slinky singer-comedian, finds it depressing to see his Hollywood idols showing their age. Many of us would rather be left with the memory of these idols intact—the gorgeous, sexy, handsome, swashbuckling heroes of our youth, preserved forever on celluloid. By showing the deterioration of our idols, advertisers are reminding us of our own deterioration. There must be a hundred better ways to talk to older people. And I can suggest a few places to start.

———

Instead of showing old stars deteriorating, for example, advertisers could depict them in the active roles we remember them in. Phillip's Milk of Magnesia set a wonderful tone with a commercial featuring two famous TV mothers: Barbara Billingsley, who played the mother in the TV sitcom "Leave It to Beaver," and Jane Wyatt, the mother in another TV favorite, "Father Knows Best." The commercial, which actually leaves us feeling warm and wonderful about a laxative, shows these moms playing a reassuring role that couldn't help but comfort anybody who isn't feeling up to par. "We're here to gently remind you how much you can depend upon your mom," says Barbara Billingsley at the start of the commercial. And the commercial does just that, even as it delivers plenty of useful information about the virtues of Phillip's Milk of Magnesia. Interspersed with a sales pitch for the product are lines like "Mom knows best!" and "You need your mom!" and "Leave it to mom!" Even the initials for Milk of Magnesia spell the word "mom." The whole approach spells a good commercial.

Here's another tribute to a mother's comforts. Barbara Bel Geddes, who plays a mother on the popular TV drama "Dallas," stands over a hot stove, comparing her homemade vegetable beef soup in one pot with Home Cooking soup from Campbell's in another. As she rhapsodizes about all the vegetables in the delicate broth, she suddenly realizes she can't tell the difference between hers and Campbell's. The message: You can't tell it from homemade.

Unlike the stars in the commercials for Polident and Depend, the mothers in the spots for Campbell's and Phillip's Milk of Magnesia are not portrayed as old people. They are still vibrant, still good mothers, and still look wonderful. Their roles in the commercials are just an extension of the TV roles we remember them for, reinforcing their images instead of destroying them. In the long run, the advertising helps the product by making the message more believable, because it is being delivered by a believable star in a believable role.

And who could be more believable, or smarter, to the 50-plus market than Angela Lansbury, the star of the popular, long-running TV series "Murder, She Wrote." Bufferin wisely chose her as the spokeswoman for their campaign based on the equally wise theme "Bufferin. So you can do the things you want to do." The theme emphasizes that people over 50 can lead full lives despite occasional aches and pains that come with age. Bufferin decided on a spokesperson testimonial campaign after recalling that the campaign that built the brand back in the 1950s had Arthur Godfrey as its spokesman. I've got a feeling history is about to repeat itself. I can't think of a better spokesperson for Bufferin than Angela Lansbury or a better theme for her to talk about to the over-50 crowd.

As these commercials suggest, the best way to advertise to the mature market is to treat its members with respect, as useful contributors to society. McDonald's did just that with a wonderful spot of an elderly retired man's first day of work at the fast-food chain. With soft music in the background, wife kisses her husband goodbye and wishes him luck. Cut to a shot of McDonald's, where two young women speculate about the "new kid" starting work that day. Of course they're surprised when an old man shows up, but they readily offer him training, advice, and encouragement. As the day goes on, they are impressed by the ease with which he handles complicated orders. "Are you sure you never did this before?" one co-worker asks admiringly. At the end of the day, wife greets her husband as he returns home. When she asks how it went, he proudly replies, "I don't know how they ever got along without me."

What a wonderful, respectful portrayal of an old man, one that will undoubtedly appeal to a wide range of audiences. Incidentally, McDonald's has made an active effort to recruit mature workers. And though this spot did not directly support that program, it subtly suggests the idea to potential prospects.

Another gem shows an older black man anxiously awaiting his friends, who seem to have forgotten that they were supposed to meet him at McDonald's. When they arrive, they almost ignore him, and certainly no one lets on that it's his birthday, until a Big

Mac arrives with a candle in it. The scene turns into a warm, happy birthday party among old and dear friends. Here too, the commercial gives a very positive view of mature people and the close relationships they value so much. It not only treats them with respect but shows them doing things that young people do.

Thanks to better nutrition and medical care, older Americans have a brighter future than ever before. They are healthier, wealthier, more active, and better educated than their parents and grandparents were. Advertisers who want to appeal to this generation should picture them not as old has-beens on their last legs, but as vigorous, involved adults looking forward to the future—whether they're buying a new car, starting a new profession, painting a house, or going back to school.

Kodak film got the picture with a commercial that shows an older black woman in a campus setting. Not afraid to be herself, she mingles with younger peers, participates in class, and does her homework on a computer. The spot ends with a graduation ceremony in which the woman's family proudly snaps pictures of her in her cap and gown. She's ambitious, active, full of life, and looking to the future—a very positive image of older people and a very positive reflection on Kodak.

Nike's thinking ran in the same direction when it drafted Walt Stack to do a sneaker commercial. The commercial shows Stack, eighty years old at the time, talking to us while on his daily seventeen-mile run. Not one to stop enjoying life, Stack seems to have lived this long because he takes care of himself. He's an inspiration to people of all ages. How many young people can keep up with Walt Stack?

And how many young people can keep up with the threesome in this commercial for U.S. Healthcare? Fred Knoller (then 91) rides a bicycle in a race, George Bakewell (95 at the time) hits a baseball in a softball game, and Jane Stovall (then 102) flies a plane. Using these older people as inspiration, the commercial sends an important message to the younger generation: "The way to grow old and healthy is to start on a health plan when you're young and healthy. So later in life, instead of just being alive, you can really live." This commercial shows that old people are not all feeble. In fact, thanks to modern medical care, more and more of them are alert, vigorous, robust, and very active.

The best way to talk to the mature audience is to show them happy and having fun, whether they're traveling, participating in sports, or enjoying their families. A spot for Jell-O microwavable pudding shows a grandmother's delight in preparing chocolate pudding for her grandchildren. "Who wants Grandma's pudding?" she asks, as a bunch of grandchildren gather in her old-fashioned kitchen. When they unanimously accept her offer, she shoos them off to play and then whips up Jell-O pudding in the microwave. The children return to the kitchen and gobble it up. "Grandma, your pudding is the best!" one child exclaims. What a wonderful, realistic portrayal of the warm relationship between a grandmother and her grandchildren. And what an accurate portrayal of a modern grandmother who takes advantage of the latest convenience appliances to save herself time.

A commercial for Quaker Oats also shows a grandparent in a nurturing role. Clad in a chef's apron, Wilford Brimley prepares muffins for his granddaughter and then watches with delight as she practically swallows them whole. A wonderful and wise grandfather figure with a warm sense of humor, Brimley has starred in many other Quaker Oats commercials aimed at older people, selling them on the virtues of oatmeal for the reduction of cholesterol. Brimley is such a perfect choice as a spokesman for the product. He's as convincing a grandfather as he is a trusted and believable contemporary. He appeals to the mature audience to whom Quaker targets its message.

Art Carney is also well cast as the fun-loving grandfather in a campaign for Coca-Cola Classic. One spot in this campaign shows Carney comforting his grandson, who has just lost a soccer game. To distract the little boy, Carney offers to buy him a Coke but pretends not to have any change for the soda machine. With grandfatherly magic and to the complete amazement of his awestruck grandson, he pulls two quarters from the little boy's ears, buys a Coke, and then shares it with him. Another wonderful spot features the same pair on the beach, talking "man to man." Grandson tells Grandpa how a little girl just kissed him. Grandpa pretends to be surprised, buys each of them a Coke, and reminisces about a little girl who kissed him many years earlier, during a game of spin-the-bottle. "So what'd you do?" asks the little boy. "I married her!" Grandpa answers. The little boy looks puzzled.

"Does Grandma know?" he inquires. "She's a little suspicious," Grandpa replies.

The irony of the story may be lost on the little boy, but it is not lost on the mature audience. These viewers often perceive themselves as younger than they really are, as some advertisers very perceptively understand. The left-hand page of a two-page spread print campaign for *New Choices* magazine shows a picture of a middle-aged couple with their arms around each other. The headline reads,"At age 59, this is how Irv and Lillian Beck look." On the facing page is a picture of a teenage boy and his sweetheart, necking in an old-fashioned car. The headline, which continues from the opposite page, reads, "But this is how they feel."

Healthier, livelier, and more active than preceding generations, the mature audience has an appetite for romance. We should be seeing more advertising to satisfy that appetite. A recent print ad for Freedent gum shows an older couple dancing cheek-to-cheek. The headline is, "Go ahead, get close." A commercial for Merrill Lynch brokerage includes romantic shots of a retired couple dancing in a gazebo.

———

There's a lot of love, a lot of ambition, a lot of dreams, a lot of plans, a lot of fun—a lot of life left in the mature generation. It's about time advertisers recognize that old people are all of us— a few years down the road.

17

How <u>Not</u> to Sell a Car

Though here's no more competitive business than the automobile business, but for a long time nobody in Detroit advertising circles would admit it. TV advertising treated the car-buying public like a bunch of kids being offered shiny new toys, rather than like the sophisticated consumers they are. During the 1960s—a period that I consider the Dark Ages of automotive advertising—a great plague swept the land, subjecting us to an epidemic of commercials starring that year's blond instead of the previous year's brunette. No sales points were made about the car, no demonstration of the automobile's solid merits distracted our attention from the gimmicks. Plymouth drafted Petula Clark to sing "The Beat Goes On." The folks at Dodge were spreading "Dodge fever." Pontiac was seriously suggesting that "Wide-tracking" would replace boating, fishing, baseball, football, tennis, golf, and possibly sex as a major leisure activity in the country. And Oldsmobile trumpeted apologies for its name by introducing Youngmobiles (blah!) to a new generation.

Looking back on this era, I'm amazed that any of these commercials were actually produced and aired. It seems as if Detroit kept its eyes and ears tightly shut so as not to become contaminated by what was happening in advertising all around them. Those were the days when gaudy, glittering Hollywood techniques were meant to disguise the anemic effort that went into selling American cars. A shrill appeal to eyes and emotions was thought to be more "with it" than a lucid appeal to reason or the mind.

Suddenly, in the early 1970s, something happened to automotive advertising: It got better. Not from any burst of aesthetic integrity, mind you, but solely because of the influx of foreign cars from Germany, France, Italy, Sweden, England, and Japan. Carmakers from these countries brought more than chrome and metal with them. They brought facts and figures so they could talk sense to the American people. We listened so carefully that Detroit began to get frightened. And rightfully so.

Instead of showing fashion models tooling around circular driveways to their multimillion-dollar mansions, the foreign car manufacturers talked about double-disc brakes, overhead cams, safety features, price, gas mileage, and eleven-year life spans. While hundreds of chrome-dipped monsters with childish names revolved on pedestals at the annual orgies we call automobile shows, the foreign car manufacturers used their ads to take potshots at the whole American concept of planned obsolescence, new models annually, and yards of chrome trim.

Commercials for foreign cars were executed in a style to which we were definitely not accustomed. No cast-of-thousands extravaganzas. No cars perched atop mountain peaks. No bathing beauties. No Ringling Brothers special effects. The commercials were simple, direct, inexpensive. The car became the hero in place of the scenario, and the audience bought it. In droves.

Bit by bit, Detroit responded to the transportation wants of the nation by introducing smaller, more economical, and less ostentatious automobiles, but I still wondered if Detroit executives were watching the same TV channels as the rest of us. As their cars became simpler and more economical, their commercials drove hell-for-leather in the opposite direction. Hollywood had come to stay in Detroit. They tried humor in their commercials. They tried jingles. The prospects laughed and sang along with American car commercials, but since these commercials didn't invite them to actually *buy* anything, they didn't. The laughter and singing became giggles and humming and then stopped altogether.

There was a lot of head scratching on Detroit's West Grand Boulevard.

Meanwhile, back at the cash register, the foreign car manufacturers were pitchforking their profits back into more TV commercials, and what beauties they were! The Volkswagen series comes to mind first, of course, because its creators never seemed to run out of fresh ideas. In a nutshell, the genius of VW's advertising was its ability to overcome the unique disadvantage inherent in the look of the car by drawing attention to its many other unique advantages. At the same time, those commercials were turning the distinctive VW look into a reverse-snob-appeal advantage.

The tools were simplicity, believability, honesty, and conviction. One of my favorites was the "Keeping up with the Kremplers" spot, in which a short story unfolds about two next-door neighbors, Mr. Jones and Mr. Krempler. As the scene begins, Mr. Jones is parking his new car in the driveway of his home. Next door, an army of deliverymen carries a refrigerator, a range, a dishwasher, two television sets, a hi-fi, and a whole truckload of other goodies into Mr. Krempler's house. Dumbfounded, Mr. Jones's frustration is complete when Krempler himself pulls up at the rear of the procession driving a spanking new Volkswagen. The point is made that he was able to buy all those things with just the difference in price between his VW and Mr. Jones's new car. It ends on a line that asks how the Joneses will ever be able to keep up with the Kremplers. A great concept, a great execution.

The same kind of superior advertising that built an empire for the small and very ugly little VW produced similar results for Volvo. If any one commercial typified Volvo's consistently good advertising effort, it was the one that opened with a Volvo driving along a highway past abandoned American cars. The audio gives the eleven-year story, a powerful, believable, single-minded point that Volvo had driven home since the beginning of its advertising in the United States. It is simply this: Volvos last an average of eleven years in Sweden where the roads are not paved, so no one knows how long they might last here. Then the announcer delivers the coup de grace: "Other cars may last eleven years [pause], but they're not driving." This, as the Volvo passes scrapped car after scrapped car along the roadside. The commercial ends with these words appearing on the screen: "Volvo lives."

No fun. No games. No jokes. No jingles. Just plain, simple, solid, believable sell. Someone who was about to involuntarily junk a car that had put him into hock for two years could be counted on to feel a definite twinge while watching this commercial. Volvo had a great concept, and the stark, dramatic realism of its execution packed a terrific wallop.

Equally stark, dramatic, competitive spots appeared for Datsun, Mercedes, Mazda, Saab, BMW—almost every car landing on our shores. Foreign-auto executives licked their lips at the delicious prospect of taking a bite out of the huge American automobile market.

How did spots like these go over in Detroit? For one thing, the head scratching stopped. For another, the eyes were opened. And finally, the gears started turning. Slowly, but they were turning. Before long, American cars—not all of them, but enough to be encouraging—were being sold via effective, no-nonsense commercials, too.

The first sign of a breakthrough was Ford's "quiet ride" campaign, an approach that succeeded for several reasons. First, its positioning was unique—nobody else was talking about a quiet ride. Second, the "quiet factor" is an important element in a car-buying decision, particularly for Ford, because of Ford's old but not forgotten reputation for producing rattle-ridden tin lizzies. Third, a "quiet ride" is demonstrable, and the commercials demonstrated it well.

Ford hit the believability jackpot when it produced a commercial that stars an audiometer measuring the sound level inside its car (sixty-five decibels) as it rides along a smooth-surfaced road. Suddenly, the car is subjected to a shake/torture test so strenuous that the gas tank must be removed and the shocks cooled to avoid overheating. That was the windup; now comes the pitch.

Pretorture test conditions are duplicated—the smooth road, the steady speed—and the audiometer is put to work again to see if any of the parts have become loose and noisy. They haven't. The audiometer registers the same sixty-five decibels after the torture drive as before, and Ford proves that it builds automobiles that stay tight and quiet under stress.

Even better than the "quiet ride" was a commercial that struck me as one of the simplest, most unusual, most effective commercials of that era. It never showed a car, and it didn't talk about features. It didn't even try to sell me anything. But, oh, what a selling job it did for Ford!

Quite simply, the commercial posed three true-or-false questions to potential car buyers. They all sounded true to me, but then an announcer informed me that they were all false. "Today," he continued, "you have to know more about cars before you buy one, so please write in for a free Ford booklet called *Car Buying Made Easier*. The first part of the booklet is completely devoted to automotive facts, and the last part is prejudiced—it's all about Ford products."

This was one of the hardest-selling commercials Ford ran in those days. If you were in the market for a new car—any car— you felt you had to write away for that booklet. It was a refreshing, honest, and provocative low-key commercial, and I got the nice feeling from it that Ford really cared.

———

As the automotive market grew more competitive in the 1980s, so did American automotive advertising, and it became better than ever before. One of Detroit's answers to foreign competition was an appeal to patriotism and national pride. Chevrolet, Buick, and Chrysler have all set the message to music. Chevrolet invites us to "Listen to the heartbeat of America." Buick tells us "The great American road belongs to Buick." And Chrysler recalls the government's help during a financial crisis: "Here's to you, America, here's to the red, white, and blue/You were there for Chrysler, now Chrysler's here for you."

Most of the show business is gone from automotive advertising. In place of the glitz, car manufacturers offer more informative commercials to show consumers why they should buy their particular car instead of the competition. Although there are no breakthrough campaigns quite like the VW and Volvo campaigns of the 1970s, overall there's a lot more good automotive advertising on TV today because there's a lot more competition.

One sign of the new competitive spirit is the large number of comparative commercials. Ford Escort compares itself, feature by feature, with three imports: Nissan, Toyota, and Honda. The Oldsmobile Cutlass Supreme wins a slalom race against Thunderbird and Cougar. And look at the advertising war between Ford and Chevrolet over the expanding market for pickup trucks. For many years Ford was the leader in that market, but in 1988 Chevy took out the heavy artillery in its bid for first place. The resulting campaign includes a Ford truck bursting into flames because it lacks the pickup to escape a runaway dynamite car that a Chevy outruns easily. Another spot shows a Chevy truck bursting out of a ditch that immobilizes a struggling Ford. Commercials like these pulled Chevy truck sales out of a hole.

I loved the macho demonstrations comparing the sheer power of the trucks. But I seem to have been in the minority. The campaign sparked a professional outcry against negative advertising that ultimately led both companies to turn down the volume. What resulted were kinder, gentler commercials, but the comparisons continued. Ford, which several months earlier had shown a Ford towing a Chevy, substituted a spot in which a good samaritan Ford owner helps a Chevy out of a rut. A commercial for Chevy compares the acceleration of the two pickups as they pull identical trailers.

These comparative commercials suggest that automotive advertising has come full circle to the strategy used in one of the first competitive car ads: the famous "Look at all three" print ad for Plymouth during the 1930s. The campaign put Plymouth, then in business for only three years, on the map by inviting people to compare the car's features with those of long-established Ford and Chevy—the leaders at that time. Now, after an unfortunate detour during the 1960s and 1970s, automotive advertising seems to have returned to the competitive spirit of the old Plymouth campaign.

With the American auto market becoming more and more fractionalized, with more and more car manufacturers competing for it, comparative advertising isn't confined only to Detroit or only to performance. It also gets into price. Watch:

Joe Isuzu, the company's notorious sleaze (more about him later in this chapter), goes into a Toyota dealership. After a friendly exchange, he asks, "What's the real difference between your Corolla and my I-Mark?" All the Corolla salesman can think of is that the Corolla costs about $1,000 more. Then nervously he asks, "You're not going to use that in a commercial, are you?" The commercial ends with a shot of an Isuzu and a super noting that, with incentives, Isuzu costs up to $2,000 less than a Corolla.

In a scene that reminds us of a first-grade arithmetic lesson, another car spot compares the cost of a Peugeot 405 with the cost of a comparable Mercedes or Volvo. The commercial shows a businessman standing behind stacks of money representing the cost of the Mercedes 190. A super over the stacks reads, "The Mercedes 190, $31,590." With music in the background, the businessman moves away one stack of bills. Now the super reads, "The Volvo 740, $20,685." The music continues as the businessman removes yet another stack. This time, the super reads, "The Peugeot 405, $14,500." After a brief glimpse at the car, a voice-over announcer asks, "Which one will it be?" obviously choosing the Peugeot. The video shifts back to three stacks of bills. The announcer says: "Oh yeah—here's your change," revealing, in stacks of bills, the difference in price between the Peugeot and the Mercedes. I can't think of a more explicit or memorable way to show that Peugeot costs much less than Mercedes and BMW.

Here's another Peugeot price commercial I like even better: The Peugeot speeds along a superhighway, as we hear about the awards it recently won. We can spot the emblems of the cars it passes: the interlinked rings of the Audi, the star of the Mercedes, the leaping Jaguar. This commercial doesn't name names, but we can clearly identify the targets. With starting prices under $15,000, Peugeot has left behind "some very pricey competition."

While Peugeot competes with more expensive cars by appealing to economics, Lincoln goes after the Cadillac market with commercials that appeal to image. A rookie valet at a swank hotel is told by two older and wiser co-workers to park only the Lincoln Town cars. That means he must park almost every car, since so many patrons of this ritzy establishment own Lincolns. As we watch the overworked valet scurrying around, the commercial adds one competitive fact: In the past three years, more than 91,000 Cadillac owners have switched to Lincoln. Even without giving a single reason why, that's a pretty convincing argument for Lincoln.

As the Lincoln commercial suggests, for many people a car is not only a means of physical transportation; it signifies psychological transportation as well. A car stands for recognition, pride, and status. Thanks to lenient auto financing terms (in some cases 0 percent), it is one of the few things available to people through which they can compete for status with their more affluent neighbors. It fortifies our personal image, and its purchase is never taken lightly. Image has always been important in automobile advertising. But it is even more important in today's hotly competitive market.

Sterling, a relative newcomer with English bloodlines, seemed to recognize the importance of image in positioning a car that is virtually unknown. Unfortunately, after the advertising, the car is still virtually unknown. The advertising tried to portray the Sterling as the choice of dapper, dashing, daring English adventurers by using Patrick Macnee of "The Avengers" as spokesman and James Bond music in the background of a chase scene. But in their great desire to give the car an image, they forgot to give the consumer a reason to buy it.

While the Sterling commercial tells me absolutely nothing about the car or its image, a commercial for Jaguar leaves no room for guesswork. With classical music in the background, the spot opens with a wide-angle view of a stately British mansion. The announcer (of course he has a British accent) tells us about the Jaguar tradition: The car is swift, sure-footed, quick to respond, and able to stop on a dime. Its interior—of polished wood and rich leather—is as elegant as a 400-year-old manor house. And the execution leaves absolutely no doubt of the heritage of this magnificent auto as we follow it on its swift journey through the beautiful English countryside, until it comes to rest in the circular gravel driveway of the English manor. This commercial says a lot about the car's British image and a lot about its performance.

On the subject of image, one of my favorite commercials is a dealer spot for the Honda Prelude, made for the New York/New Jersey/Connecticut area. This one, called "a true story," shows a tough-talking cop sitting on a desk in a dimly lit police station. He talks about a recent case in which a woman calls up to report that her new Honda Prelude has been stolen. But the story has an interesting twist: The thief has apparently pulled up in his old Prelude and switched it for the brand new one. Now the woman is left with the old Prelude, the thief has the new one, and the cops are looking for a guy who likes Hondas. The cop ends his monologue by assuring us "You can't make this stuff up." What a terrific (and low-budget) commercial. With a twist of irony, Honda lets us know that the new Prelude is so good, a thief would be willing to risk stealing to update his image.

Some carmakers spend years trying to change an image. Oldsmobile, stuck with a fuddy-duddy name, has always battled its image as a car for old people. Remember the corny "Youngmobile" campaign of the 1960s we mentioned earlier? Well, Oldsmobile is still at it. You'd think that if it hasn't worked in all this time, Olds would give up and try something else. Instead, Olds introduced the slogan "This is not your father's Oldsmobile/This is the new generation of Olds." The campaign features famous people and their adult children, and each spot tries to play up the car's appeal to the new generation. By the time these commercials convince the kids that Oldsmobile is young, the kids will be old. Just telling kids the car is young doesn't make the car seem young to the kids. The best way to convince them is to prove it through the product. The worst possible way to do it is through their parent. Any parent knows that. Any kid knows that. So how come Olds doesn't know it?

In one spot, Lisa Marie Presley is walking on the beach, reminiscing about her mother, Priscilla Presley. "You know what moms are like," she recalls. "You bring home a new guy, they put their foot down. Come home a little late, they put their foot down." When Lisa Marie got a new Olds, the same thing happened: Priscilla Presley got in the car and put her foot down (this time on the accelerator). As the commercial closes, the car is speeding along a beach with Priscilla Presley at the wheel. If "this is a new generation of Olds," why is Priscilla Presley, the mother, driving? And why is she using the disapproving expression, "I put my foot down!"—a saying she has used in the past to discipline her daughter? Not only does this ridiculous commercial tell me nothing about the car, it gives the impression that Oldsmobile still belongs to the older generation.

Two other commercials in the same campaign get so bogged down in special effects that again we miss the message. One features William Shatner, who played the lead in "Star Trek." The announcer tells us that the Olds is powered by a fuel-injected engine and monitored by an on-board computer. Shatner's daughter Melanie, who is at the wheel, remarks, "I guess some things were just meant for the next generation." So far, so good—at least the commercial has told me something about the car, and at least the daughter is driving. But I could skip the science fiction that follows. William Shatner appears in the seat next to his daughter. "Ready, Dad?" she asks. The camera moves behind them, and we get a view of the dashboard, which vaguely resembles the cockpit of the Starship U.S.S. Enterprise. Suddenly the car flies off into space. So does the commercial.

The same goes for a spot featuring astronaut Scott Carpenter and his son, Jay. In this one, Jay talks about his father's training as an astronaut and what Scott Carpenter was willing to go through "to get his hands on his dream machine." Jay has found his own "dream machine"—the Cutlass Supreme. When he takes his father for a ride, the car turns into a vertical position and lifts off into space. Again, the commercial pays more attention to the parent than to the son, who is supposed to represent the new generation of Olds buyers.

Here's the best one in a campaign destined for failure: "Let's Make a Deal" host Monty Hall tries unsuccessfully to borrow a new Oldsmobile from each of his three kids. He offers to fill up the car with gas if his son Richard will let him borrow it. Richard declines, since Olds has already given him a premium of a year's supply of free gas. Monty ups the ante: He offers his daughter Marilyn $50 if she will let him use her new Toronado. Marilyn says no: She got $1,500 cash back from Olds when she bought the car. Growing increasingly desperate, the great dealmaker goes to his daughter Sharon and offers to help finance her Cutlass Calais. But Sharon doesn't need his help: She already got 4.9 percent financing from Oldsmobile. This time Olds gets a message across. Unfortunately, it's about its deals, not its cars. And the deals don't make the cars any younger. Unfortunately, too, the star of the commercial is famous Dad, not the kids. And Dad doesn't make the cars any younger, either.

In fact, this campaign did nothing to boost Oldsmobile sales. In the first year the commercials ran, Oldsmobile's car sales fell 8.3 percent to 543,459 cars, down from 592,401 a year earlier. The second year, sales dropped an additional 15 percent, and Oldsmobile dropped the campaign.

Several manufacturers are competing for a slightly older buyer than Oldsmobile is after, as they pitch family-oriented cars to the "thirtysomething" crowd. But a surrealistic commercial for Nissan looks as if it's shooting for a thirtysomething Martian crowd: A small girl plays alone on a wind-swept hill as the announcer says, "Some car makers wouldn't put kids and fun in the same sentence. We think they belong in the same car." This 15-second spot ends with a shot of the Nissan Access, set off by clouds. What an awful commercial! If Nissan wanted to convince me that it was family-minded, it totally lost my vote when it started the commercial with a negative comment about kids. To make matters worse, there's no link between the little girl and the car and no mention of why the Nissan Access might be a good car for families with kids.

Saab made a similar blunder with an equally negative commercial. This one shows a family driving in a car. The husband and wife are in the front seat, and the kids are in back. It looks like everybody is having a wonderful time. Then the camera pulls back to reveal that the scene is really a movie set. The people are actors, the car a prop. The voice-over announcer says: "This isn't a real family. No real family ever got along this well in a car. It's just the way car companies want you to imagine your family in their cars." The commercial ends with a warning: "Don't buy the wrong car. Don't leave anything to your imagination." Again, I'm offended by the suggestion that families don't get along in cars. Even if it's true for some families, this unpleasant reminder doesn't make me want to rush out and buy a Saab. And, though the commercial warns me not to buy the wrong car for my family, it tells me nothing about what makes Saab the right one.

Unlike the Nissan and Saab commercials, which don't say anything about the cars' features, the following commercial for Mazda's MPV tells us everything about a family car. A mother is happily driving a car filled with children. The terms used to describe the car are "unique," "special," and "friendly." Already I feel upbeat. Next, the commercial discusses the car's features: It carries seven like a wagon, is as versatile as a van, and has a high-performance Mazda engine. Now that's a commercial that makes me think "family transportation" and tells me a lot about what I should buy and why I should buy it.

For my money, feature-oriented commercials are among the most effective automobile advertising around. As you may recall from Chapter 4, Jackie Mason's hilarious skit for Honda Prelude was a total distraction from the car's four-wheel steering—the feature that Honda was trying to promote. But compare that commercial, in which the execution destroyed the concept, with another, much simpler commercial for the same Prelude where the execution *was* the concept. Picture a horizontal split-screen with two cars being digitally timed as they race through a slalom. As the cars screech through the turns, the announcer reads a letter to the editor of *Road and Track* magazine, written by a Honda Prelude owner who seems to be a car enthusiast. The letter refers to the fact that the Prelude, with its four-wheel steering, can travel through the slalom faster than any other production car in the world, including the Porsche 944. The cars finish with the Honda Prelude beating the Porsche. Part demonstration, part testimonial, all convincing, this simple commercial leaves Jackie Mason's comedy routine far behind. While Mason just confuses, this commercial convinces me what a car with four-wheel steering can do. The reader's letter and Porsche comparison make the feature more believable, more understandable, and more desirable.

If only Porsche had done as well. One recent commercial shows a Porsche speeding along with rock music in the background. The announcer says, "School's out forever! School's out for summer! What could be more exciting than two days of high-performance racing school?" The commercial ends with an offer of two days of racing school for buyers of the Porsche 944. I'm not quite sure whom they're talking to, and I don't think they are either. Kids? How many of them can afford a Porsche? Adults? You mean they can't drive the car until they go to racing school? Aspiring racing drivers? You can't sell a lot of cars to them. Maybe Porsche's adpeople should go to advertising school instead.

Here's a speed commercial done well. An American businessman and his German host talk shop as they speed along the Autobahn in a chauffeured Mercedes. The German turns to the visitor and tells him they will be arriving in twenty minutes. When the American sounds surprised, his host explains that they are traveling at 125 miles per hour. The fact that the car can be travelling so fast, so effortlessly, so comfortably that the passenger is completely unaware of the speed says a lot about the power, the stability, the aerodynamics of the car. Now that's a commercial about speed.

By now you've probably guessed I have a preference for car commercials that tell me something about the car. And that's just one of the reasons I see stars when I watch nine out of ten spots for Isuzu. After several years on the air, Joe Isuzu, who has exploited his reputation as a liar, may well be the most recognizable character in TV advertising since Charmin's Mr. Whipple. But that's not enough to sell cars. Would you part with $11,000—or more—after watching Joe Isuzu impersonate Frankenstein? In the spot I'm referring to, Joe Isuzu, in the character of Dr. Isuzustein, has crossed a sports car with a truck to create the Isuzu Amigo. When his assistants, El and Moe, ask if the car is safe, Isuzustein answers, "Trust me." (Why should I trust a man who has billed himself as a liar?) The mad doctor flips a switch, and the Amigo emerges. But it seems Isuzustein has inadvertently combined his assistants as well. Is that supposed to be funny? More importantly, is that supposed to sell a car?

And how about this unfortunate perversion of a classic Aesop's fable? Joe Isuzu, dressed in lederhosen, is in the Austrian woods with an Isuzu Trooper. Twice he calls for help—first because his Trooper is stuck in the mud, and later because he can't fit all his firewood into it. Both times the townfolk come running, only to find that Isuzu has cried "wolf." But next thing he knows, Joe Isuzu and the Trooper are being attacked by real live wolves. This time Isuzu cries "wolf," and nobody comes. The commercial ends with a wolf burping. And me vomiting.

Maybe the creative revolution in advertising has gotten out of control. Jack Trout and Al Reis, fathers of the "positioning" strategy in advertising, recently observed, "As more and more ad agencies tried to be 'creative,' they redefined the word to mean 'being different.' And as ad campaigns became more and more different, they started to lose touch with reality. Technique became the focus." The Isuzu campaign is a perfect example. Although it has been one of the most awarded campaigns in recent years, these kudos are not reflected in car sales. Reports indicate Isuzu is selling very few cars in the United States compared to other Japanese imports, despite a huge advertising budget. And even worse, company sales are declining each year. Despite the fact that Joe Isuzu is a smash, Isuzu's efforts to sell cars have bombed. It couldn't have happened to a funnier guy.

Contrast Isuzu's emphasis on entertainment with the no-nonsense approach Honda used to introduce the Acura. Back in 1986 everybody knew you couldn't sell a $30,000 Japanese luxury car in America. Everybody but American Honda. The manufacturer was well aware that for decades, European automobiles had been smugly satisfied with the notion that they had a permanent lock on the American luxury performance car market. And why not? American and Japanese automakers hadn't ever tried to market an automobile that could compete with the revered nameplates from the lands of storybook castles. But American Honda saw an opportunity: By the early 1990s, the fastest growing area in the automobile market would be the luxury and sports car segments. And much of the increase would come from a population that was growing out of the Japanese import cars of their youth, one that was ripe for a new choice in luxury performance automobiles.

For the engineers of Honda, designing the cars that would become the Acura line was not out of their reach. Honda's technical prowess is proven regularly on the world's Formula One circuits, winning back-to-back championships against the likes of Porsche, Ferrari, and BMW.

But the luxury performance car market is not driven purely by product. Buyers are heavily influenced by prestigious images, word-of-mouth reputations, and emotional associations that can't be built in a day.

How would Honda, with an upstart entry, compete with the lofty perceptions of automakers having up to one hundred years' experience?

They had two choices. They could have gone the line extension route (when a manufacturer introduces a new product under an existing brand name) and simply introduced a luxury Honda.

Or they could introduce a brand-new car, with a brand-new name, through a brand-new dealer network. Honda and its agency very astutely chose to start from scratch and introduce a brand-new luxury automobile, which they called Acura, and started building it an instant image. They began capitalizing on Honda's existing reputation for reliable, well-designed automobiles, while adding a prestigious twist to appeal to the upscale target market. The position: "A new dimension in performance automobiles from a new division of American Honda," backed by the simple, descriptive theme line "Precision crafted automobiles." The execution, both TV and print, reflected the crisp, precise, serious nature of the product and the message. No funny spokesmen. No jokes. No comedy. No distractions. All serious. All car. All features. All sell. And did it sell! Within twenty months, Acura had outsold the top five European automakers. In the year 1988, almost 130,000 Acuras were sold in the United States—more than any other luxury import by far, including Mercedes-Benz, BMW, Jaguar, or any of the others. That's got to be one of the marketing miracles of the decade. So while Isuzu was busy winning all the awards (Acura won none), Acura was busy winning all the sales. Now, *that's* funny. Ha! Ha!

━━━━━━

And in the last analysis, that's the only thing that counts: selling cars. When it's honest like the Acura campaign, simple like the Mazda commercial, real like the Honda Prelude spot, pointed like the Mercedes demo, or strong like Chevy and Ford trucks, the commercial sells the car. Or rather, the commercial lets the car sell itself. That's what Detroit forgot until the straight-talking imports taught them a new lesson in competition.

18

How Not to Introduce a Product

In a word, don't introduce the introduction.

Oh, it's tempting. Think of all the fun the Getty Oil people must have had years ago when they put together their "Bridge on the River Kwai" commercial to introduce a new campaign. But does "fun"—or manufactured, irrelevant excitement—transmit enough sales information to sell the product? This bit of staging didn't. All it did was to subject us to that relentless, whistling theme from the movie while scores of marching gas attendants and rolling vehicles passed in review over a bridge. It was only after the umpteenth airing that I began to discern a sales point amidst the fanfare: Getty gives you more miles for your money because Getty sells only premium quality gasoline at regular prices. Could have fooled me. I thought they were selling a brand-new sport: marching.

The irrelevant, nonfunctional, obtrusive execution actually obscured a perfectly valid sales message. The product was forgotten while the commercial marched on and on. In the interest of putting together an exciting introductory commercial, advertisers can lose their heads.

192

And I can lose my temper. When I see hype used in the introduction of a new product, I can't help but get the empty feeling that the agency and the client have no faith in the product they're introducing. They feel they have to resort to borrowed excitement, since there's no excitement in the product itself. I can almost understand and forgive that. But I see red and count to ten when hype completely overshadows an exciting new product which has a legitimate reason for being, a meaningful Unique Advantage, and a benefit significantly superior to anything being delivered by any other product at that time.

As you can see from the Getty example, when advertisers introduce the introduction, they use a device to hype the excitement of a new product. These commercials usually either overpower the product's reason for being or ignore it altogether. The sales message tends to hide behind show biz glitz and bravado or is placed in exaggerated historical perspective as one of the great discoveries in the history of the world. Both are equally deadly. Here are examples of the two most common devices advertisers use to introduce the introduction:

1. *Hollywood-style introductions.* In these commercials, advertisers obscure the sales message with a variety of distractions, from marching bands to musical comedies to Hollywood stars. The introductory commercial for the new $30,000 Sterling automobile, mentioned in the preceding chapter, actually featured one celebrity and referred to another. With James Bond theme music prominently playing in the background, a Sterling speeds along a winding road, hotly pursued by a mystery man on a motorcycle. After eluding the motorcycle, the car comes to a stop and its driver gets out. It is Patrick Macnee, star of "The Avengers," the popular TV spy show from England. "I suppose you were expecting someone else," says Macnee, implying that I should have expected Roger Moore. You're damn right I was expecting someone else. I was expecting someone who would tell me a thing or two about the car, something which this commercial neglects to do. The commercial is so caught up with celebrities (in this case, the idea of mistaking one celebrity for another) that it never gives me a reason to buy a Sterling. I know no more about the Sterling

after having seen this commercial dozens of times than I did before I saw it for the first time. I don't call that an introduction, I
call it an insult—to both the product and to advertising.

When you introduce a new product in any market—especially one as hotly competitive as the automobile business (as discussed in the preceding chapter)—you better damn well tell
people why you brought out the product in the first place, why it's
better than what's out there now, and why they should consider
buying it. If you haven't done that, you've done a great disservice
to your client. A quick look at the Sterling sales figures compared
to Acura (two very similar cars introduced at about the same time)
will show just how much of a disservice this advertising did to
Sterling.

Sundance Sparklers—a mixture of natural fruit juices and
sparkling water—lost potential customers by introducing its introduction with a gimmick. The commercial shows two different
scenes of people opening a Sundance Sparkler. In one scene, a
man and woman sit down for a romantic interlude. In another, a
little boy rests on a porch step after what we imagine was a vigorous bike ride. Just as the people in each scene remove the bottle
cap, they are suddenly bathed in a blinding light emanating from
the bottle. The announcer says, "When you open a Sundance
Sparkler, something refreshingly different happens. . . . It puts
refreshment in a whole new light."

What a perfectly rotten way to introduce a new product! Although Sundance tells us what the product is, the commercials do
nothing to give us a reason for trying the product or to differentiate it from other fruit-flavored soda waters. A late entrant in that
already crowded market, Sundance seems to be searching desper-
ately for a way to look different from other products in the category. But by relying on a corny gimmick, the introductory
commercials introduced the introduction, not the product. The
gimmick is centered around the word "light" (shades of Bud
Light)—as in "perspective." It has nothing to do with a feature,
benefit, or Unique Advantage of the product. You remember the
light but nothing about the Sundance Sparkler. I'm afraid I don't
see the light.

Polaroid got off to a good start with an introduction for its
Impulse camera but ruined what might have been a good com-

mercial by adding a musical comedy routine. The spot begins by
telling us about something new from Polaroid. The product has a
catchy name: the Impulse camera—a Polaroid camera so small
you can carry it with you and take pictures on impulse. So far, so
good. But after that the music kicks in, and show business takes
over the introduction. The announcer urges us to "go where it
takes you," a vocalist picks up the beat, chanting, "Go with your
impulse," and we're off following a young woman on an all-night
soiree through the mean streets, into a pool hall, a disco, and as-
sorted other night spots. When the sun comes up, we follow our
heroine into a corporate boardroom filled with stern-looking executives seated around a conference table. One turns to her and
says, "Your meeting. You nervous?" She replies jokingly, "I didn't
sleep a wink," as the Polaroid pictures of the night before spill out
of her bag onto the table.

What a distraction from the product! Like most typical prospects, I can't relate to the woman, her nocturnal binge, her life-
style, or her use for the camera. Most people would probably use
it for pictures of friends, relatives, babies, vacations, birthday parties, the usual. I just can't picture this commercial convincing anyone that he or she needs this camera. And, come to think of it,
what *is* so special about the Impulse camera anyway? I could go
with my impulse using any small camera—it doesn't have to be a
Polaroid. Aren't all small cameras impulse cameras? And many
are smaller than this one. The only thing this one does that's special is give me pictures right away, but Polaroid makes no big mention of that feature in the commercial. The commercial is
introducing the introduction, not the camera. Get the picture?

2. *Documentary-style introductions.* Sometimes advertisers use
history or their own heritage to give importance to a new introduction.

That's just what Reynolds did in introducing Reynolds plastic
wrap. The commercial shows a sampling of kitchen gadgets from
the 1960s and 1970s that are obsolete today—an egg slicer, a
hand-operated egg beater, and a special dish that holds one ear
of corn. Although these old gadgets have been updated, the commercial tells us, Reynolds aluminum foil has never been improved
upon. Instead, Reynolds is coming out with another product to

supplement its aluminum foil . . . Reynolds plastic wrap, billed as a new product. The problem is that while the product is new for Reynolds, it is not new to the audience, which has relied on other brands of plastic wrap for years. Reynolds uses the obsolete kitchen tools not to introduce its new product, but to tell us how great its old product is. Although the commercial does show several uses for the new product, I never find out why I should switch to Reynolds plastic wrap, rather than stay with the brand I already use. Is Reynolds a better product? Or should I switch to Reynolds plastic wrap just because of this "great" event in the history of a company that pioneered aluminum foil? By introducing a product which is not new, Reynolds resorts to introducing the introduction, and no one is fooled except the advertiser.

So, all documentary-style historical introductions are wrong, right?

Wrong! In the right hands, for the right product, they can be among the most powerful of introductory techniques. Advil was the right product in the right hands, and it revolutionized the analgesic category with its introduction in 1984.

Both Advil and Datril bought the right to introduce an over-the-counter ibuprofen painkiller at the same time. (Until that time, ibuprofen was available only by prescription.) The race was on, and Advil left Datril at the starting gate with a superb introductory commercial. The spot begins with a giant aspirin rolling across the screen. We're informed that its date of introduction was 1899. Behind the aspirin we see Tylenol, introduced in 1955. And, finally, in 1984, there's Advil with ibuprofen, a major development in nonprescription pain relief. We're also told it contains the same medicine that's in the prescription drug Motrin and that one Advil is just as effective as two regular aspirin, yet gentler to the stomach. The commercial ends with the theme line "Advanced medicine for pain."

The history of the pain reliever category using the other products was key to the introduction of Advil. It symbolized the march of medicine and instantly positioned Advil as the latest advance in painkillers. That opening visual has been used in every Advil commercial since—and in every print ad. In an instant, it says everything you'd want to say about the product: it's new, it's different, it's better, it's the latest scientific advance, it's a breakthrough—you need it! That's what a great introductory commercial should do. Advil does it all.

While the Advil introduction showed the history of other products, a recent commercial for Ben-Gay Warming Ice shows how the company's original product gave birth to a new item. But the commercial is cluttered with irrelevant historical footnotes: Since the turn of the century, there have been sixteen presidents, 580 Nobel Prize winners, and twelve men who've walked on the moon. During all this time, there's been one original Ben-Gay. I feel like I'm playing a game of Trivial Pursuit. What do presidents, Nobel Prize winners, and men on the moon have to do with Warming Ice? Absolutely nothing. The product, we ultimately learn, is a new and different Ben-Gay formula which goes on cold but warms as its scent disappears. Though the commercial tells us that Ben-Gay Warming Ice can be used for relief of minor arthritis pain, that's all we learn from this spot. I wish that instead of spending all that time introducing the introduction, Ben-Gay had told me more about the product. Why is it better than/different from regular Ben-Gay? Does it have any other uses? And finally, why should I buy the product? So what does the commercial leave us with? The last frame, which should summarize the product's unique benefit, says visually and in audio, "A once in a lifetime introduction." And that about sums up the problem with this commercial. I hate to rub it in, but it sells the introduction and not the product.

———

So much for the most popular formats used in introductory advertising. I'm sure you get the point.

No matter what format is chosen for the introduction, it all goes for naught if the *timing* is off.

It's no crime to be the second (or even third or fourth) to introduce a new breakthrough product idea, particularly if you can improve on it. But it is criminal to try to introduce it as though the number one product didn't exist. You fool no one but yourself. I've already discussed Sundance Sparklers and Reynolds plastic wrap earlier in this chapter. Some years back, Brim thought we were all asleep when it introduced its decaffeinated coffee. It opened with a wife at the breakfast table, forbidding her husband to have another cup of coffee and sadistically rationing his share to half a cup. This, so he can sleep at night. (I'd lose sleep, too, if I had a wife like that.)

In the next scene, we find her crowing over her new discovery: Brim, tasting as good as his favorite brand, but decaffeinated to let him sleep.

Where had we heard that strategy before? In every other decaffeinated coffee commercial on the air. Sanka had done the same thing for years, only better, with its "hidden camera" approach. So why shouldn't I stick with Sanka? Give me one reason, Brim—any reason—to switch.

As an introductory commercial, this one left something to be desired. Like excitement, news, and believability.

It's tough to be second with a new product intro, but it can sometimes be much tougher and much more expensive to be first. If your product is too far ahead of its time, it can be an absolute disaster. Gablinger's, the first low-carbohydrate (light) beer, discussed in Chapters 2 and 5, was such an absolute disaster. Quite apart from the problem of its taste, Gablinger's hit the market just a few years too soon. Produced by the makers of Rheingold beer, once the number one brand in New York, Gablinger's contributed to the demise of the Rheingold Brewery in the early 1970s. Gablinger's, named for the scientist who developed the process for removing the carbohydrates, was not only mistimed, it was also misnamed. It could have been called Rheingold Light because, in reality, it was the first light beer. But America wasn't ready for light beer yet. If it had been introduced just a few years later, Americans could be calling for Rheingold Light instead of Bud Light. No use crying over spilled suds.

Though timing is important, the content of the advertising is also critical to the introduction. A good introduction should make four important points. It should let us know the product is new, describe the product, give us a reason to try it, and tell us the maker of the product.

Why can't there be more introductory commercials like the one that told the world about Alka-Seltzer cold tablets? It began with a standard announcer's pitch for the new product. Then, suddenly, an off-screen voice began lobbing questions at the announcer. Both the questions and the answers covered everything we need to know before we'd buy the product. The commercial ended with the voice asking if this is a real, live commercial.

Yes, it's a real, live commercial—and a good introductory one at that. Four important points were made (the introduction, the nature of the product, why we need it, and the maker of the product) in a refreshingly irreverent way that didn't distract us from the concept.

Here's another introduction that's picture-perfect. This one, for Kodak Ektar film, is aimed at the professional photographer. It shows quick cuts of high-quality photo images (a speeding race car, a windsurfer, the beak of a bird), interspersed with copy that's seen on screen as it is heard and practically screams out everything we want to know. The content of this commercial could be used as a model of the perfect introductory spot: "It is from Kodak" (parenthood, so I know it's film); "For the advanced photographer" (target audience); "It delivers the highest resolution. Superior image structure" (two reasons why the film is better); "It is called Ektar" (the name). The spot ends with a shot of the film package, so I know what to look for when I go to the store.

That's what an introduction should do.

Unless advertisers draw attention to the product itself and its Unique Advantage, their efforts are doomed to only partial (at best) success.

Save the fanfare. Save the gimmicks. Save the documentary. Sell the product, not the introduction.

19

Marketing Quiz

Two products are about to compete for the same market. If either one of them can gain more than a 50 percent share, the rewards will be enormous. It will probably become the most famous, most talked-about, and most successful product in the world. So famous that it might even change the course of the life of every American, and possibly every single person on earth.

The market these products are competing for is now wide open for a new brand in the category, and potential buyers include every male and female citizen of the United States over the age of 18. Everyone is a potential customer—rich and poor, young and old, industrialist and laborer, farmer, big-city dweller, Easterner, Westerner, Northerner, Southerner.

The category? An essential product, a basic staple that everyone will buy in one of the two brands within the next couple of months.

It can't be stressed enough that, due to special circumstances, there is room for only one product to be marketed successfully in this category. Initial purchase is the essential objective. The surviving product can thrive very profitably on initial purchases for at least four years without the need for repeat orders.

Most important of all is the fact that the result of this marketing battle may well be determined by the products' exposure on TV.

Now then. If I give you some basic facts about each of the two brands and their histories, can you predict the outcome of the marketing battle?

BRAND A: This is an old product that's been on the national scene for more than twenty years. It reached its peak in popularity eight years ago, waned, then hit another peak four years later before again falling back. This is the second brand of a successful company whose number one brand achieved record popularity and has dominated the category. One of the peculiarities of the category is that even the most popular brands are marketed for only a short period of time. Some fade from the scene after only four years, others last as long as eight. No brand, with one exception, has ever remained in distribution for more than eight years. This requires the constant introduction of new brands. Brand A, a line extension of the leader, has been selected, after a series of successful test market battles against other entries of the same company, to replace the leading brand. Brand A is being promoted as a new and improved product. Distribution, inherited from the leading brand, is excellent. Best of all, the brand has a good, professional marketing machine behind it and a seemingly inexhaustible budget with which it plans to concentrate on suburbanites, special-interest groups, executives, business leaders, professionals, and persons upscale in age and socioeconomic standing.

Special problems: Extremely well-known nationally but with a questionable reputation for efficacy. Image is one of a good but very bland, very weak, middle-of-the-road product with no distinctive character. Now must follow in the footsteps of extremely popular, extremely strong, extremely distinctive brand. Instead of benefiting from the rub-off of the leading product with which it is closely associated, it suffers by comparison. Although Brand A has been around for many years, it has never captured the imagination of the American public. The product is weak in large cities and with all minority groups, especially blacks. Nor is it particularly strong with working people anywhere. Brand A has a reputation for always being a bridesmaid but never a bride—an adequate substitute product but never first choice. The problems might stem from its packaging, which doesn't come across well on TV. Recently repackaged, it is meeting with mixed success, and improvement is not readily apparent.

BRAND B: This is a new product from an old company that hasn't had a winner for almost a decade. Historically, it's been generally successful, but always on a local level. It has been test-marketed in selected states and has made a surprising, if not spectacular, showing against other test brands. On the basis of these tests, Brand B is now being marketed nationally for the first time.

Distribution channels are excellent nationally, with particular strength in the big-city markets. Stronger in urban areas and with people younger in age and lower on the socioeconomic ladder than those who choose Brand A, this product can count on blue-collar support in northern and eastern markets. It is also highly preferred by ethnic consumers.

Brand B has access to a large advertising budget, which nevertheless still falls short of Brand A's resources.

Special problems: Brand B has no national recognition and is virtually unknown to the American public. It has a funny, hard-to-pronounce, and even harder-to-remember name that sounds foreign. Packaging is bad—the product appears small, ungraceful, and user-unfriendly compared to Brand A. Little is known about Brand B's efficacy, ingredients, features, benefits, past successes, or claims. Even more important, the American public is completely unaware of Brand B's unique advantage, if it even has one, or why they should buy it over better-known Brand A. In addition, Brand B has a local marketing staff, inexperienced in national campaigns. The effort seems disjointed, with several famous consultants working independently from the regular marketing staff. No strong leadership or direction is visible.

———

All right, folks, those are the facts. Now, can you guess the outcome of this marketing battle? Which brand do you think won the larger-than-50-percent share of market?

If you guessed Brand A, you guessed correctly.

And I'm sure you guessed something else, too. The examples cited above pertain to the biggest marketing battle of them all: the national presidential election. I chose the 1988 campaign because, in my opinion, it was the one presidential election whose outcome was most determined by advertising—both good and bad. Good for Brand A (George Bush). Horrid for Brand B (Michael Dukakis) because the Dukakis advertising team committed the single biggest political advertising blunder in my memory: *They forgot to introduce their candidate.* And of course, Brand A's popular predecessor needed no introduction. He was Ronald Reagan.

The objective of the Bush campaign had to be to build an image of a leader with presidential stature. At the same time, the campaign had to make the image of this new leader believable by building on the foundation of Mr. Bush's existing image. It accomplished both tasks admirably. The wonderful five-minute image commercials depicted George Bush as an All-American hero: in war as a Navy fighter pilot and in peace as a dedicated public servant. The commercial then juxtaposed this heroic George Bush with the private George Bush, a sensitive, warm, human, loving father, father-in-law, grandfather. The spots were made to order for the George Bush persona and his theme of "A kinder, gentler America." These kind and gentle pro-George Bush commercials were rotated with unkind and anything-but-gentle anti-Michael Dukakis spots with deadly effect. George Bush was the star of the image commercials but, cleverly, never appeared in the competitive ones. These cutting spots ripped Dukakis for everything from his war record to his record of accomplishment as governor of his home state. They were devastatingly effective. So effective, in fact, that a confused, befuddled, badly-slipping Michael Dukakis panicked under the pressure and replaced his chief advertising strategist (shades of Coca-Cola). The new ad maven immediately launched a new campaign knocking George Bush— a pretty dumb thing to do, particularly that late in the campaign. The result was predictable. George Bush was swept into office with a huge plurality, while Mike Dukakis took only ten states.

After the humbling defeat, many political and advertising experts, including those who had been on the Dukakis staff as consultants and whose work never saw the light of day, criticized the strategy of the Dukakis campaign for never having responded to the Bush competitive jabs. Several of these experts had their expensive commercials actually produced and paid for with campaign funds, only to be scrapped. The confusion and waste within the Dukakis inner circle were so acute that dozens of creative superstars volunteered their services and created advertising with no direction, no strategy, no common theme. Some of these frustrated creatives later leaked their unused commercials to the ad trade press, convinced that if their commercials had run, Dukakis would now be president of the United States.

Of course, every adman and adwoman in the country is convinced that he or she could have done a campaign that would have made Mike Dukakis a winner. I am no exception. The Dukakis campaign was wrong. The campaigns I saw that were done by his frustrated consultants and which never ran were wrong, too.

Should Dukakis have ignored Bush's charges or should he have responded to them, as most political analysts had later suggested? He should have done neither. He should have been oblivious to them. He should have had his own campaign strategy for victory mapped out well in advance and stayed the course. The day you let your opponent's strategy dictate your own is the day you've lost the campaign.

What should Dukakis's strategy have been? The answer is, or should be, taught in every first-year advertising course because it's so basic: **THE PRODUCT IS THE HERO! THE PRODUCT IS THE HERO!** Doubly so if it's a new product. The first objective in advertising a new and unknown product must be to get it known, to get its package recognized, to explain its reason for being, and to clarify why it's different and better than its competition. People must get to know a product, particularly a political candidate, before they can feel comfortable with him or her. People don't vote for candidates they feel uncomfortable about or don't know. They have to get to know everything they can about the candidate—personal and political. The more they know, the more comfortable they are, the more likely they are to vote for the person. And that's the job of advertising. It's that elementary.

I would have recommended a campaign to introduce Michael Dukakis to the American people, and I would have stuck with it no matter what George did or said. Guess who would have been the star of my commercials? Right! Michael Dukakis himself, in person, warts and all. Yes, I know he isn't exactly Mr. Charisma, but he is what he is and it was good enough to get him elected lieutenant governor and then governor twice in the state of Massachusetts. It was good enough to win primary after primary against half a dozen to a dozen tough, prominent, charismatic, smart, Democrat Party opponents. Dukakis was accustomed to facing an audience or a camera and coming off well enough to persuade people to vote for him. He was capable of learning to compensate for the natural polish and smoothness he lacked. If Ike, Richard Nixon, Jerry Ford, Jimmy Carter, and, yes, George Bush could be taught, so could Mike Dukakis. At the beginning of the campaign I would have had Dukakis introduce himself as a person to the American electorate: his ancestry (a wonderful, warm immigrant story—the stuff America is made of, the stuff George Bush can't match); his family (parents, wife, children); his schooling (every bit as prestigious as Bush's); his academic accomplishments (he was a professor at Harvard); his political accomplishments (in contrast to Bush, who had never won an elected office). I would have continued this personal phase of the campaign until research verified that the American people knew who Mike Dukakis was and felt pretty good about him as a human being. Then I would have launched Phase II of the campaign and had the candidate tell America why he wanted to be president, what he could do for the country and its citizens, what his plans were, and how they differed from those of George Bush. Most important, I would have told them why it was so important for them to vote for Mike Dukakis. All that information should have been delivered personally, sincerely, face to face, without rancor.

I wouldn't have paid a bit of attention to what George Bush was doing. As a matter of fact, in contrast to this proposed warm, personal campaign, Bush would have come off as the heavy with his competitive spots. They would have boomeranged on him. And I would have stayed with the campaign come hell or high water or venomous George Bush commercials.

This simple, honest, product-is-hero campaign would have introduced Michael Dukakis to America as a human being and as a future president. Or rather, the campaign would have had Michael Dukakis introduce himself. Executionally, the spots would have been the opposite of Bush-slick. They would have looked almost like a friend's home movies. And they would have cost very little more. The commercials that Dukakis ran, and those done by his consultants that never ran, were all more interested in the advertising than in the product being advertised. They were gems of expensive production. None of them featured the candidate. Both camps seemed to be ashamed of him and walked away from what they considered to be the liability of an inferior product. Inexcusable!

If they had a new packaged-goods product to introduce, wouldn't they show it? Wouldn't they talk about its Unique Advantage? Wouldn't they try to convince me of its superiority? And wouldn't they show the package? How could so-called advertising experts forget or ignore the basics? If they had remembered, who knows, maybe we'd have President Dukakis. With no comment as to whether that would have been good or bad or whether the better man won, I feel that each candidate is entitled to his or her best shot. Dukakis didn't get the best advertising. As a matter of fact, he got lousy advertising. But, then again, he's got nobody to blame but himself. And maybe that's why he didn't deserve to be president.

———

As to the more philosophical question of whether candidates should be sold like soap or toothpaste (a fact my marketing quiz attempted to satirize), with the help of marketing specialists and advertising agencies, my answer is a resounding "No!" How the candidate looks, how he comes across on TV, even the way he does his hair may have more bearing on his electability than his experience, his competence, or his qualifications.

And I don't think it should.

Do you really want a president whose rough spots have been so smoothed and virtues so glamorized that you don't know what you're "buying" when you vote?

Can you be absolutely certain that your vote wasn't influenced in this (or any) election by the "image" you saw on TV?

Indeed, did we elect a carefully orchestrated series of "images" to the White House, or a living, breathing man whom we knew well at the time we elected him?

I really don't think candidates should be allowed to advertise. First, because the candidate with the largest budget has the greatest advantage. Second, because one may be more charismatic or more "advertisable" than the other, and charisma is hardly the same thing as leadership. Third, it's always possible that one candidate may hire a better advertising agency than the other. Which would get him or her elected because a "better" public image was projected. Which brings us full circle back to why I don't think candidates should be allowed to advertise at all.

I say no, because none of the above-named factors, which could determine the outcome of a very close race, have any bearing upon a candidate's qualifications for office.

I'm confirmed in this conviction when I consider the consequences of unlimited peddling of political images. I don't mind making a mistake when I buy a bar of soap or a shaving cream or a meatball. As long as they're not harmful, how much have I lost by buying them one time? But making a mistake when spending my vote—that's something else again. I can't return the "purchase" or obtain a better substitute within ten days. And the "product" bought may turn out to be harmful after all. Very, *very* harmful.

Nor would I, as an advertising man, mind making a mistake when selling that bar of soap or shaving cream. Mistakes happen. Advertising agencies often find that the public doesn't like the product as much as the agency did. So the product is quietly withdrawn from the market, and the agency chalks it up to experience. An adperson can't afford that luxury when helping to foist an underqualified candidate upon the public. When you're selling the president, the stakes are too high to allow a margin for error. And that's why I think no one should sell the president at all.

Candidates should sell themselves.

This is not to say that the miracle of mass communication should be ignored; its potential for good is just too great. I do think, though, that all media should be required to donate equal space or time as a public service to all of the candidates, allowing them to deliver their messages (live or taped in the studio) as well as to confront each other publicly on the issues. The networks would also run an equal number of taped spots supplied by the candidates. The only restriction would be that the spots must feature the candidate delivering his or her own message, with no gimmicks to interfere or unduly influence the electorate. For these commercials, the networks would be paid for the time just as they are today. Imperfect as this solution would be (a dynamic personality and glib delivery will always sway voters), it would at least be a step in the right direction. And some would argue—rightly so, I think—that a dynamic personality and glib delivery are almost prerequisites for the job of president, anyhow.

In any case, it would be a whole lot fairer. Then advertising could get back to its real vocation: selling products and services, instead of people.

20

David Does Goliath's Job

Once upon a time, when everyone was rich and airtime was less expensive, big-budget advertisers lavished fistfuls of money upon their agencies for 60-second commercials. Today, the cost of both production and airtime for a 60-second commercial is so prohibitive that these "long" commercials are used almost exclusively for institutional or corporate-type messages by huge companies sponsoring documentary TV specials.

When the 60-second commercial nearly went the way of the vacuum tube, the 30-second spot became king. And today we see increasing numbers of 15-second commercials, which are now as popular as 30-second spots. More than just "reminder" commercials, these 15-second spots often carry the full message. Advertisers have discovered that fifteen seconds can really pack a wallop.

The more 15-second spots I see, the more I believe that there's no point that can't be made in fifteen seconds if you know what you want to say. Whenever I see a 30-second commercial followed by a 15-second version of the same spot, I invariably like the 15-second spot better. The shorter commercials are usually lighter, punchier, and more single-minded.

But, you may ask, do the 15-second spots get squeezed to death between the longer, 30-second commercials? Are they long enough to register a company name? To create an image? To do

a demonstration? Can you use 15-second commercials to sell multiple uses for a product, to sell multiple products (harder yet), or
to get a conceptual point across? Can these little spots be used to
introduce a new product? To instill trust or confidence in a product or service? Can you emphasize the Unique Advantage of a
product in fifteen seconds? Can you stir emotion? Sell quality?

A good short spot can do any one of these things—and more.
I'll prove it:

1. *Register a company name.* I began to formulate my opinions
about the power of short commercials the first time I saw this one
for the Oppenheimer Fund, some years back. This commercial
registered a new company, a new name, and a new corporate symbol in only ten short seconds. All it took was enough time for four
hands to grasp one another at the wrist, forming the new logo.
The name flashes upon the screen below the completed logo, and
wham-o! A visual image of the fund that's hard to forget is established. Can you imagine what Oppenheimer could have done with
the luxury of fifteen seconds?

2. *Create an image.* To make the point that its products are for
serious athletes only, Avia footwear created a series of 15-second
spots that work as well independently as they do back-to-back.
Each of these Lilliputian-sized commercials contrasts a nonath-
letic, nonsweat, sedentary, sometimes unhealthy "activity" with a
vigorous physical, healthful one. One, which shows a smoldering
cigarette in an ashtray, carries the message, "If this is the only
workout you give your lungs, Avia doesn't want you to buy their
aerobic shoes." Cut to a group of slim, attractive women, pound-
ing their feet to the beat in a strenuous aerobics class. Another
spot, which runs back-to-back with this one, shows the rim of a
cocktail glass with swizzle stick. "If this is what an afternoon of
mixed doubles means to you, Avia doesn't want you to buy their
tennis shoes," the announcer says. The camera shifts to a tennis
court, with a tough, hard-fought game in progress.

Other 15-second spots in the same campaign feature basketball stars. One shows a TV viewer switching channels between
sporting events, finally settling on a basketball game in progress.

"If this is the only way you participate in different sports, Avia doesn't want you buying their cross trainers," says football star Brian Bosworth. Next we see Bosworth cross-training on a basketball court in Avia Cross Trainers. Another spot features basketball star Clyde Drexler playing video basketball. Drexler's message: "If this is the only kind of basketball you want to play, Avia doesn't want you buying their shoes." Then we see Drexler playing an actual game of basketball in Avia shoes.

With bold copy and even bolder imagery, Avia lets us know that its products are not for armchair athletes. The simplicity and power of the message fits the 15-second spot perfectly. To do these spots in thirty seconds would be overkill.

3. *Do a demonstration.* Can a short spot demonstrate a product's features? Remember the Tinactin commercial discussed in Chapters 4 and 5? A woman in a locker room after a workout watches her foot catch on fire as she complains about the burning of athlete's foot. She sprays Tinactin on the foot, and the flame goes out. Would you believe it took only fifteen seconds? Yes, there was a 30-second version of the spot. But the demo is equally hard-hitting and effective in fifteen seconds. Maybe more so.

And how about this wonderful 15-second demonstration for Fuji film? Three swimmers line up, poised to dive into a swimming pool. Can you tell which one is a blown-up Fuji photo? Two divers take the plunge. The third one, who remains stationary, is the photograph. In fifteen seconds, Fuji demonstrates that its pictures are so alive, they practically breathe.

Krazy Glue took the 15-second demonstration even farther. As you may recall from Chapter 8, Krazy Glue demonstrated the strength of its product by suspending a construction worker in midair by gluing his hard hat with him in it to a steel girder. But this wonderful 15-second demonstration does even more, which brings us to the next purpose a 15-second spot can accomplish.

4. *Sell multiple uses for a product.* Once it has convinced us that Krazy Glue is strong enough to hold the burly construction worker in this precarious position, the 15-second spot goes on to accomplish its next mission. Crammed into the rest of the spot are quick cuts and/or audio mentions of eleven—count 'em—eleven

household items Krazy Glue can bond—everything from a metal brooch to a cycle grip. Nice. Neat. Simple. All of that and more. And all of that in just fifteen seconds.

5. *Sell multiple products.* If I ever had any doubts about how much information a 15-second commercial can deliver, they would have evaporated when I saw a recent spot for Acutrim diet pills, in which three different Acutrim products for three different types of users were put across in one spot—beautifully. Since dieters have different needs, Acutrim developed three different formulas: maximum strength, for people with insatiable appetites; late-day strength, for people who get hungry late in the day; and sixteen-hour steady control, for those who need an all-day appetite suppressant. This 15-second spot not only identifies the three types of users and the right pill for each but never even seems rushed. In fact, when I saw the 30-second version of the same spot after seeing the 15-second one, I thought it dragged a little.

6. *Make a conceptual point.* Can a short spot do something more than straightforward advertising? The Partnership for a Drug-Free America used a very effective 15-second commercial to show the effect of drugs on the brain. As you may recall from Chapter 9, the commercial is a simulation and shows a man in a kitchen preparing to fry an egg. Holding up the uncracked egg, he tells us it represents the brain. Next, he points to the skillet heating on the stove. "This is drugs," he says, as the pan begins to smoke. He breaks the fragile shell, dumps the egg into the sizzling pan and, as it crackles and expands, boldly concludes, "This is your brain on drugs. Any questions?"

After you've watched this commercial, is there any question that fifteen seconds is time enough to make a conceptual point if you know the point you want to make and how to make it dramatically? Little David's slingshot strikes again.

7. *Introduce a new product.* Picture an extreme close-up of the top of a Sara Lee chocolate cake that fills your entire TV screen. "There's nothing more dangerous than being alone with an entire Sara Lee chocolate cake," the announcer says, as we eye this giant mound of temptation scattered with chocolate chips. Slowly the

camera pulls back, and the picture of the cake grows smaller and smaller until we see just a tiny little cake sitting beside a large mug of coffee. A hand reaches out to grab it, and we notice the cake is smaller than the hand. To reduce the "danger" of eating the entire cake, Sara Lee has introduced snack-sized cakes. This commercial does everything a good introduction should do. It tells us what the product is (the same Sara Lee cakes we already know, but in snack size). It tells us why we need it (being alone with an entire cake is too dangerous). And it is excitingly introductory. How can you do all those things in fifteen seconds? For Sara Lee it was a piece of cake.

8. *Instill confidence or trust in a product or service.* Look at what a 15-second commercial did for Eye Lab stores. Many people think stores that sell glasses are so concerned about sending you home with new frames, they don't pay much attention to what's in them. So Eye Lab set out to change that vision with a short, sensible commercial that does the job. It shows a woman trying on several different pairs of frames. An offscreen voice interrupts her selection: "Before you try on any of our thousands of frames, we'd like you to try on these." The camera shifts to the woman's face covered with a phoropter—the outer space-like device that eye doctors use to determine a patient's prescription. The point is obvious: Eye Lab is just as concerned about good vision as it is about selling you frames. That does a lot to build confidence in the efficacy of Eye Lab stores. And it only takes fifteen seconds to make you see the light.

9. *Emphasize a Unique Advantage.* The Unique Advantage of Mitchum anti-perspirant has always been its strength—it's so strong, you don't sweat. Mitchum turned that Unique Advantage into an understandable unique benefit in a 15-second spot of a yuppie couple frolicking in bed one early morning. The message: Mitchum is so strong and effective, it even works the next morning. In fifteen seconds Mitchum emphasized the Unique Advantage of its product with a believable, effective scenario. No sweat!

And how about this one? A young man chomps at a baseball bat as if he were eating an ear of corn. As he nibbles, the film accelerates until he has devoured the entire bat. The product?

WFAN—New York's all-sports radio. The message: WFAN satisfies "New York's insatiable appetite for sports." In short (as it were), the Unique Advantage of the station in fifteen seconds.

10. *Stir emotion.* Fifteen seconds is more than enough time to sell emotion. Lifesavers candy proved that with a spot that shows a father and son fishing. With crickets chirping in the background, Dad and his little boy sit on a dock, their lines cast expectantly in the water. All we see is their legs—the long lanky legs of the father, and the much shorter pair belonging to his son. "Dad, I never catch anything," the little boy whines in a moment of discouragement. "Here, have a Lifesaver," the father offers reassuringly. Suddenly the son perks up: "Can we do this again tomorrow?" What a sweet, warm commercial. And it took only fifteen seconds to make me feel warm all over.

11. *Sell quality.* Sometimes you don't even need as much as fifteen seconds to get your message across. Beck's introduced its premium beer into this country with 10-second spots exclusively. Beck's succeeded by making only one simple point over the years: that Germany is the fatherland of quality beer and that Beck's is the favorite quality beer in Germany. Marvel at the simplicity of this early commercial: "To be the best-selling premium beer in any country is something. To be Germany's best-selling premium beer is really something." With dramatic commercials like this, Beck's won a following among American beer drinkers and became the number one imported German beer. And then Beck's could run commercials like this one: "You've probably tried the premium German beer that sells best in America. Now try the premium German beer that sells best in Germany." Still sticking with 10-second spots, Beck's updated the message: "The best beer in the world comes from Germany, and the best German beer in America is Beck's. So drink the best of the best. Beck's. The number one imported German beer." Here's another: "The best beer still comes from Germany, and the best German beer in America is Beck's." In other variations on the theme, Beck's ran ' pots in a variety of cities, playing up local features and referring to the fact that Beck's is the number one imported German beer in each particular city. Beck's proved that 10-second commercials can be used to introduce a quality product at a premium price and to make

the product a leader. I raise my stein to Beck's. And to the big power of short commercials when you know how to use them.

———

I guess what all this is leading up to is a solid, unqualified endorsement of short commercials. It's good to know that if you can't outspend your competition, you can still outsmart them. Even today.

You should know, though, that short commercials pose a tremendous challenge to creative people. They challenge them to crystallize the single most important point they think should be made for a product. And that's good discipline for any creative person, even one with all the time in the world.

Short commercials are tough. You can't fake them. Any creative person who tries a 10- or 15-second commercial for the first time begins to understand at last the meaning of the old quip, "If I had more time, I'd write a shorter letter."

21

Untested Theories About TV Testing

Adpeople, it's a fact of life: Someday every commercial we put on the air will have been subjected to some sort of test before, during, or after it appears on TV.

We'd better learn to live with this fact. Even if it makes us feel like jurors who have been told that a verdict was reached while we were out to lunch. Ad agencies will have to learn to live with it, too. Because with commercial production costs going up and up and the cost of airtime rising, an increasing number of advertisers are demanding proof that their commercials are any good before they put a wad of money behind them.

The problem is finding the TV testing technique we can all live with best. To me, the only really acceptable test is the one at the cash register. We've all (eventually) got to accept that one. The closest we can come to that is an in-market test in which the client spends the money to produce the commercial, selects a test market where distribution is good, buys time to run the commercial, and watches to see how it pays off in the stores. Such a test, to my way of thinking, is the only really valid one.

But it's prohibitively expensive.

So what now? As a second choice, I could learn to live with any testing method that approximates an in-store situation involving an exchange of money. It sure beats the old pencil-and-paper type of research. What people say they'll do on a written questionnaire or to an interviewer can differ markedly from what they'll actually do in a store. People tend, for example, to react favorably to happy, entertaining commercials, even though those commercials may be selling them nothing but a belly laugh. By the same token, they may react negatively to commercials that bring up unpleasant subjects but that do a heck of a job of selling at the same time.

Not so long ago I had the experience of watching one of the commercials I did turn in a so-so performance in group interviews and questionnaire testing—and then go on to break the bank on an in-store test. And I've had just the opposite happen, too. Which forces me to conclude that when it comes to actually spending their hard-earned money, consumers have no compunction about behaving in a manner totally opposite to the one they indicated on a pencil-and-paper survey.

I don't care at all about how people say they'll act, think they'll act, or would like me to believe they'll act in a buying situation. I only care about how they *do* act in the cash register line.

I don't believe in pencil-and-paper research; I believe only in dollar-and-cents research.

Theater testing is a popular technique in which selected consumers are gathered in a theaterlike auditorium to watch commercials, either exclusively or mixed in with television pilot shows. They fail to produce valid statistics as far as I'm concerned, precisely because they are unreal situations. First of all, the audience is captive, and secondly, the audience associates the theater with entertainment and therefore responds better to entertaining commercials.

Nor do I trust "Star Wars" devices. I've seen people turned into guinea pigs for TV testing, with their blood pressure, eye movements, perspiration, skin impulses, pupil dilation, brain waves, and even their dreams plotted and checked. I've seen people—sometimes through one-way mirrors—wired, cajoled, goaded, and psychoanalyzed. I've seen lie-detector tests. I've watched group therapy sessions on closed-circuit television conducted by Ph.D.s. I know all about bathroom flushometer tests (how many home toilets are flushed during commercial interruptions). And there's even a testing method involving foot pedals.

All this in an attempt to find out whether people, consciously or subconsciously, like and respond to a given commercial. Now I'm not qualified to criticize any of these methods on scientific grounds. I don't necessarily like them or dislike them. In fact, I don't give a damn about any of them. All I care about is whether the commercial makes a buyer react favorably toward the product in a store. That's all. I don't care about people's subconscious feelings or if these feelings are better clues than conscious reactions to the ways in which consumers will act at the check-out counter.

When discussing consumer reactions, the name of the game is not *how*, it's *whether*.

With that in mind, it's pretty hard for me to give much credence to any but on-air tests. There's no substitute for the privacy of the viewer's own living room, because there the viewer is king. He or she may not even *watch* the commercial, whereas in a test situation the participant is forced to watch. In all testing methods except on-air, the testers take for granted this most important of all factors for the success of a commercial: Will it attract the attention of the viewer in the first place, so the person will actually watch it to the end?

Let me tell you some of the theories I've developed after years of warfare against certain kinds of TV testing. The first theory begins with a strong hunch that most outstanding commercials will test poorly initially. People have a tendency to reject the unconventional, the unpredictable, the unknown, the daring, the challenging situations that make them feel uncomfortable. The challenge frightens them, so their reaction to it may be negative on a test, even though the commercial may be selling them without their even knowing it.

Conversely, a benign and relatively harmless commercial will generally test well. If it's entertaining, all the better. Viewers will feel comfortable with it. Its predictability will invite recognition, and recognition invites a feeling of security. Familiar, logical, and nice to have around as an old friend, a commercial like this is guaranteed not to grate or challenge or get anybody mad. It won't even make the viewer do any unpleasant work, like thinking. Soothing as a good sitz bath, your unimaginative, entertaining commercial is bound to command a favorable reaction under test conditions.

I'm willing to bet two bits that many of the commercial concepts we consider successful today—both professionally and in dollars and cents—tested poorly at first. If agencies and advertisers had been gutless or had been shackled to testing evaluations, some of the era's best campaigns would have never seen the light of day.

And who knows how many never did?

Theory number two: Take those successful TV campaigns that tested so poorly the first time around. Test them again via the same method after they've been running on TV awhile, say about six months, and see what happens to the scores. By this time the shock of unfamiliarity has worn off. The audience knows what to expect. They know the commercial. Feel comfortable with it. Accept it. And suddenly it leaves the pedestrian commercial that tested so well behind in the dust. Get the picture?

So where does that leave advertisers who are about to spend thousands producing a commercial and millions running it? Aren't they entitled to know if the commercial is any good or not? Of course they are! And shouldn't they have the right to test the commercial? Of course they should! And won't some of the results of this test be helpful to the agency when it comes time to make another, stronger commercial? Of course they will!

All I'm saying is that an advertiser should take the results of any test as a guide, not as an absolute verdict. And finally, the commercial should be subjected to the most crucial test (and often it's the most reliable test) of all: the test of *human intuition*—the advertiser's own and the agency's.

I have one theory left, and this is it: The people who succeed in advertising are the ones who know that making a sale rather than a high test score is the purpose of a commercial. The easiest thing a creative person can do is to construct a commercial that will score high using any given testing method. I can do it. So can any other creative person with half a brain. I've done it for a lark. Unfortunately, too many do it for a living.

In the end, even with our vast knowledge of how and why the human mind works, we just can't predict the behavior of others. For all the scientific gadgetry at our disposal, the most sensitive instrument for predicting the behavior of human beings is still the intuition of other human beings.

Thank goodness.

22

The Regulation of TV Advertising

Let me come right to the point.

The day is fast approaching when the only thing an advertiser will be able to say about a product on TV is its name, its function, and where it can be bought.

Mind you, I understand the reason for the existence of network self-regulatory bodies. I even agree with the purpose they're supposed to serve. But when the creative directors of agencies complain that their best commercials are being turned down or watered down by the TV stations, it's time to take another look at these regulatory bodies.

First of all, which ad agencies are complaining? Is it the charlatans, hucksters, wheeler-dealers, and marginal operators of the business? It is not. I'm talking here about the most respected and admired agencies, the most reputable advertisers.

Ed McCabe, one of the most highly respected creative people in the history of advertising and an honored member of the prestigious Advertising Hall of Fame, had this to say to *The New York Times Magazine* years ago regarding a commercial his agency had made for a client: "The networks are our biggest problem. . . .

221

You've got to document every goddamn comma. All you need is a confrontation with the networks to send you screaming to the booby hatch." A management supervisor at the same agency complained in the same article, "You get a different response from each network. One accepted it [the commercial], one said you've got a problem, and one said you're commercializing God—that's a no-no. [Hebrew National hot dogs was the client.] They set standards for taste and morality in the ads, and they destroy those standards in their programming." Since then, the situation has gotten even worse.

What do agencies mean when they claim their ads have been "watered down"? Generally speaking, they feel that the regulatory bodies have a tendency to lean over backwards in the direction of playing it safe. That's understandable, if not especially desirable. But agencies are also saying that these regulatory bodies are becoming more and more arbitrary in their interpretation of their own regulations. No matter how sound those regulations are by themselves, that's bad. In many cases, what you can do on television is separated from what you can't do by such a thin line as to challenge credibility. What's worse, the line has been known to waver. Agencies are saying that some of the decisions they're being handed are downright silly, and finally, that standards vary from regulatory body to regulatory body. And that's the worst of all.

An agency with a drug or health account is not going to screech about close scrutiny when it's applied to the claims it makes for the product. The agency knows as well as anyone that the direct effect the product is likely to have upon the public's well-being makes such scrutiny necessary.

I'm talking about products that do not affect the public health in such an immediate way, about the use of claims that do not involve out-and-out lies, exaggerations, weasels, or impossible-to-substantiate statements.

I'm talking about truths that can be proved.

Truth and honesty in advertising are desirable goals. So desirable that I'm campaigning for more truth. The full truth. If a product has a provable advantage over a competitor's, I feel advertising for that product should be entitled to tell that truth, even if someone else's product is hurt by it.

Someone is always hurt by the truth. That's how it should be.

I'm vigorously opposed to any attempt by regulating bodies to remove all trace of competitiveness from commercials. That would be a shame. It's removing the guts from advertising. The challenge. The bite. And much of the results. And, more important, it's depriving the public of all the facts it is entitled to know.

To me, the whole objective of advertising is to prove to the public that your product is better than your competitor's. The most effective commercial I can imagine is one that says, "Here is my product, here's my competitor's product; now let me show you why mine is better." To a limited degree, we have commercials that do just that running right now. I think we'll see more of them as advertisers realize that if what they say is true and able to be proved to the satisfaction of a regulatory board, they should have the right and should exercise that right to make and run this type of commercial.

What do the regulatory bodies say about the use of direct comparison in TV commercials? The TV Code Review Board "urges advertising to offer products or services on their positive merits, and to refrain from discrediting, disparaging, or unfairly attacking competitors, competing products, other industries, professions, or institutions." The American Association of Advertising Agencies, as quoted by the National Association of Broadcasters, says that "although it believes in competition in advertising . . . it does not believe in advertising which untruthfully or unfairly depicts or disparages competitive products or services." Agreed.

But I would hope that both of these august bodies would defend to their dying breaths the kind of advertising that truthfully and fairly depicts a difference between products. If advertisers allow advertising to be stripped of its most potent weapon—the demonstration of a product's advantage over competitive products—they will have only themselves to blame when they'll be permitted to give only the name, rank, and serial number of their clients' products on television. And then there will no longer be the kind of advertising we all believe in, the kind that built brands and giant companies from nothing, the kind that permits a new company with a better product to take on the giants and beat them. In fact, it won't be advertising at all. And this will no longer be the business I want to be in.

We—not just advertising people, but all of us in a free society—have an obligation to fight unfair competition wherever it crops up. But we have an equal obligation to defend vigorously fair competition and to protect the medium in which it can flourish. That brings me to the point I think some of our regulatory bodies are missing: In the final analysis, the public has the right to know the true and complete facts before it chooses between products. Doesn't it? Advertisers have the right to benefit from their ingenuity in developing better products, don't they? And adpeople have the right to decide when, where, and how they will tell the public about the product in the strongest possible way, don't they?

Or do they?

When cigarette commercials were banned from the airwaves, I spoke out to castigate the government for that decision because it usurped the advertiser's right to select where to advertise. I also said that the public, not the government, should be the judge of a product's merits and that the decision to remove cigarette advertising from TV showed a complete lack of faith in the intelligence of the American people. I still think so. If cigarettes are as harmful as researchers say, and the government is so concerned with the health of its citizens, then why didn't it have the guts to go all the way and prohibit the manufacture of cigarettes altogether? I would have respected it for that. Instead, the government continues to accept, with no trace of reluctance, the taxes derived from cigarettes and eases its conscience by banning cigarette advertising from the often violence-racked TV tube.

Be honest: Did the censorship imposed by the Federal Communications Commission actually stop people from smoking? Or, more important, did it stop youngsters from starting? Not on your life! Does the absence of hard liquor advertising on TV stop alcoholism? And marijuana, heroin, cocaine, and crack have all done quite well without TV advertising, thank you.

The simple fact is that the "Big Daddy must protect us from ourselves" philosophy is not only alien to us, it's also ineffective. It doesn't really discourage the use of the forbidden product. And where will it end? If a restriction is placed on one product, other products are endangered. Putting it another way, if a government agency can ban the advertising of a legal product in a particular medium, what is to stop the government from banning advertising of other legal products? (And why such advertising should be banned in one medium and not in another I'll never know. Do they think that kids and cigarette smokers don't see newspapers, magazines, and posters? Maybe the government thinks they can't read.) After all, some detergents are pollutants. They could be next. Or deodorant or mouthwash or beer or anything for any number of reasons!

In today's marketing, television advertising can spell the difference between life or death for a product. Which regulatory body has the right to play God?

I'm certain that all the regulatory boards, both governmental and industry-related, would disclaim any desire to play God, insisting instead that they're only doing a job that advertising agencies should be doing for themselves: putting concern for public welfare before concern for one's pocketbook in choosing the advertisers whose messages will reach millions via TV advertising. The clear implication in sermons like these is that if we advertising agencies were less greedy, the need for such regulatory bodies would not exist.

Bull!

Let me point out that a couple of agencies publicly refused to handle cigarette accounts well before the product was banned from TV. So much for the greedy theory.

However, what some of these agencies lack in greed they make up for in hypocrisy. I hasten to point out that while these same pious defenders of the American consumer were curling their corporate lips at cigarettes, they thought nothing of handling automobiles with known safety defects that have the potential to kill and maim a helluva lot more of our citizens than cigarettes will.

These same agencies see nothing wrong with preparing advertising for toothpaste when all dental authorities tell us that brushing with water is just as effective. They sell soft drinks so full of sugar as to rock our metabolic systems. They sell milk and cream and bacon, all of which play havoc with our cholesterol counts. They advertise franks as "all meat" when they're mostly fat. And they help move products of all descriptions with profit margins that are unconscionable.

Look, I'm not condemning these agencies for handling accounts like these. I just condemn their hypocrisy. Years ago, for example, a large agency resigned a cigarette account because it was just placing the advertising in media and not being paid to create it. The story the agency put out to cover itself was that it no longer felt comfortable with a cigarette account. Doing the creative work, it is assumed, would have made it feel so much more at ease. This is what I mean by hypocrisy.

Would I handle a cigarette account? Absolutely, even though I gave up smoking many years ago. Our citizens have been bombarded since 1970 with information about the hazards of cigarette smoking. It's been in all the newspapers, in all the magazines, on all the radio and TV stations of the nation in the single greatest campaign ever launched against anything. A warning appears prominently on every print ad of every cigarette brand in America. And just in case anyone missed the message, it's stated again on the cigarette package every smoker picks up at least twenty times. If, in the face of the evidence, certain adults, knowing full well the hazards associated with cigarette smoking, nevertheless make the decision to smoke, who has the right to tell them they can't? And, so long as people are going to smoke, I want them to smoke my brand.

———

So what does that mean to the regulatory bodies?

It means that the time is ripe for them to rethink the whole concept of free enterprise. That "truth in advertising" means the whole truth, not just that portion of it that doesn't embarrass anyone else. It means that forbidding a legal product access to an advertising medium amounts to outright censorship and constitutes an infringement upon that advertiser's rights as well as the public's right to choose.

And lately a lower form of censorship has raised its ugly head. It's not really censorship; it's something much worse. It's intimidation—no, that's too mild a word—it's outright blackmail!

I'm referring to the organized letter-writing campaigns by various special-interest groups, particularly religious conservatives who object to certain programs on network TV. They would like to force their moral code of what's right and what's wrong on all of us. They're trying to accomplish their goals with a barrage of "black" mail sent to heads of advertising agencies (I get about three letters a day, some of which are semiliterate), threatening to boycott the products of any of the agency's clients who sponsor shows they consider to be violent, sexy, or sacrilegious. The shows involved include some of the nation's favorites like "The Golden Girls," as well as scholarly documentaries on subjects like abortion. Of course, they are the sole judge and jury of what's wholesome and what's lascivious, what Americans can watch and what they shouldn't be allowed to see.

These people have a perfect right to make these decisions for themselves. They have every right not to watch anything they find offensive. But what right do they have to prevent others from making the same free choices? Including advertisers and ad agencies, who have the right to sponsor whatever shows they determine will deliver the right audience for their product at the most efficient cost. Sponsorship of a program does not necessarily constitute an endorsement of the show's content. It is only an endorsement of the show's audience. For advertisers or their advertising agencies to submit to these threats is a larger threat to our basic American freedoms.

Big Brother, go home and take your scary family with you.

23

Advertising Awards: The Envelope, Please

Each year I brace myself for the umpteenth annual showing of the Cannes Commercials Film Festival finalists at Lincoln Center. It's the only advertising awards show I attend. And, it's the worst of them all.

Every year I promise myself I'll never go again, and every year I break my promise. Why? For three reasons. First and most important, because I know, like, and admire the people who started this event as a fund-raiser for a very worthy cause, and I've supported them right from the beginning. Second, because the dinner party after the screening is the most creative, most innovative, most spectacular event of the year, and each year my wife and I look forward to it. And third, because it's so bad that it constantly reminds me how silly all awards shows are.

Each year at the festival I see examples of the worst advertising created around the world—and mind you, I see only the finalists. In a lucky year I see five commercials out of the fifty or so screened that I consider advertising, even by the most liberal standards.

The winner—the one commercial voted the best in the world

228

by a panel of judges who may be the most unqualified and most prejudiced in the world—is usually the most entertaining production that money can buy. But then again, almost all the commercials are entertaining and funny and triumphs of execution over content. And they're applauded and acclaimed by the cream of New York's young advertising crop, who are guided through this magical maze of advertising mayhem by a couple of wise and witty ad biggies. Every year I slide lower in my seat and cringe. And I'm ashamed.

Is this what advertising is all about?

No, dammit, it's not!

If you've gathered that I don't agree with the idea of competition for advertising awards, you're right. I think the awards are nonsense and that they reduce the credibility of the business to the level of Hollywood.

The advertising business is a profession practiced (I hope) by professionals. At least we'd like to think of ourselves as professionals. If doctors and lawyers manage to survive without awards and competitions, why can't we? Can you imagine doctors giving awards for Best Appendectomy of the Year, or lawyers for Best Landlord-and-Tenant Litigation of the Year?

Doctors don't publicly announce the acquisition and loss of patients. Lawyers are less discreet about their business than they once were, but they still generally don't publicize their clients with great fanfare, as we do. We allow gossip sheets and gossip advertising columnists to exist, feeding them news of our conquests and courting their favor. Is that professional?

And how about the Hall of Fame? We now have a Hall of Fame not only for copy and art but also a general Hall of Fame, to which clients as well as agency people have been elected.

We've got to be kidding! What egomaniacs we are, so obsessed with our own self-importance! Let's put what we do in perspective. We're not engaged in the fight against cancer. We don't alleviate human suffering. We don't pursue great humanitarian causes. None of us will ever win a Nobel Peace Prize, or even beat Hank Aaron's home run record. I'm not belittling what we do. I'm proud of what we do. But in the context of mankind, let's stop getting carried away with ourselves and forget this Hall of Fame nonsense. If we must have our little pats on the head, let's do it right by holding one big award competition in which the winners are picked seriously, not by laugh meter.

The forced gag is almost a prerequisite to winning an award. As a result, you can hardly watch a TV commercial or listen to a radio commercial anywhere that isn't based on a gag, a joke, a pun, a comedy routine, a capsulized situation comedy, a skit, or, at the very least, a closing yak. Creative people know humor is the shortcut to awards. So they keep turning out humorous commercials.

Surely laughter can't be the only way to attract people, to stir them, to move them to action. There must be other ways, like honesty, simplicity, believability, conviction. Is humor the bribe we offer our prospects so they'll buy our products?

I am certainly not against humor in advertising, or even against humor winning awards, with these restrictions:

1. It must not get in the way of the message.
2. It must be functional to the sale of the product.
3. It must help to make sales points, not obscure them.
4. It must be compatible with the nature of the product.

Humor can be a great and valuable tool of advertising. It can also be a dangerous weapon in unskilled hands. There's nothing worse than something that's a little funny. Sadly, most of the humor in advertising is a little funny.

The day has finally arrived when advertisers are looking at the numbers and finding that the smiles don't add up. That there is not necessarily a direct correlation between smiles and sales, between the laugh register and the cash register. That selling a funny commercial to a client may be easier than selling a serious product to a prospect.

After all, you know why so many "funny" commercials reach the air, don't you? For two reasons: Funny commercials win awards, and funny commercials represent the easy way out. A skit is easy to sell to a client because when the agency presents it to the ad manager, the ad manager smiles; and when the ad manager presents it to the president, the president smiles; and when the president presents it to the chairman, he smiles; and when the chairman presents it to his wife, she smiles; and when neighbors and fellow country club members compliment the company's officers on their entertaining commercials, the whole world smiles.

But people don't buy products because they find the commercial *amusing*. They buy products because they find the commercial *convincing*.

And I find very few award-winning commercials to be convincing. So let's stop creating commercials to please awards committees and keep in mind what a commercial is supposed to do: It's got to convince someone who is not using your product to try it once, for a believable reason. If the people who create commercials would think of themselves as consumers and ask themselves, "If I am using a competitor's product, would this commercial convince me to try this other product?"—we'd see more and better reasons for trying the products advertised on TV.

If all advertising people were *completely* honest with themselves, I wonder how many of the award-winning commercials would have been run in the form in which we saw them? I can't believe the creators of the Joe Isuzu campaign would themselves buy an Isuzu because they were influenced by the lying, obnoxious, untrustworthy Joe Isuzu. Nor would anyone from the agency that created the zillion-dollar Federal Express campaign trust their valuable package to Federal Express because of what they learned from some motor-mouthed, fast-talking salesman.

And nobody, not even the president of Wendy's own agency, is going to stop off at the fast-food chain for a burger because a contentious little old lady with a big bass voice set the country asking, "Where's the beef?"

No, if we're going to go on giving ourselves awards, we are obliged to give awards to the very best we can turn out. To the kind of commercials that sell. To the execution that crystallizes the concept best. To the copy that gives us the best switching idea.

To insure this, we must pick the most qualified people to judge and the best method of judging. I've seen too many of these judging sessions turn into a good time for all. I've seen too many popularity polls, too much jealousy, too much bitchiness, too many deals. And too many biased juries and jurors who all think the same way.

No system for judging commercials is foolproof, but certainly the way we're doing it today can't be right.

Nor can this overproliferation of ceremonies and award-granting organizations be right, either.

Some shows give so many awards for so many things to so many people that almost everyone wins something. (The more winners, of course, the more tickets sold.) Besides the winning commercial, there are four or five runners-up, plus four or five more "recognitions" in every category from Apparel to Utilities. As if that weren't enough, there are further awards that get almost as silly as best performance by a male schnauzer in a 30-second beer commercial. And these awards are judged by a jury of thousands nobody's ever heard of, most of whom, by my standards, are not qualified to judge anything more serious than a beauty contest. The latest wrinkle in awards is actual cash prizes instead of medals or statuettes. How mercenary can they get?

———

On the positive side, I'd like to compliment the American Marketing Association on its Effie award, which seems to have more sense to it than most. This association demands that each entry be accompanied by a marketing strategy, objective, and documented proof of its success before it can be considered for an award. That makes good sense, because it's really awfully silly to give an award for advertising excellence to an ad that failed to sell the product. Some of the most decorated campaigns of the last few years have been the most disappointing failures in the marketplace. Not only have they failed to do anything for the product, but in some cases the agency winning the award lost the client because of poor results.

Unfortunately, the Effie awards are not as popular as some of the others. I'm not sure why, unless it's because all those show biz whizzes never heard of a marketing strategy. Maybe they couldn't figure out the objective of some of their nonobjective creations. Or maybe, just maybe, they had a hard time documenting the success of some of the stuff that's been collecting the fancy hardware at all those Hollywood orgies run by the other awards shows.

Agencies pay through the nose for these shows: entry fees, hanging fees, and tables for themselves and their clients at all the awful luncheons and dinners where the food is terrible and the service worse. Nobody really enjoys them, but everybody's afraid to miss them. (I miss them all except the Cannes festival for reasons I've already explained.)

If advertising creative people are so childish and insecure as to require the security blanket of awards, at least let's cut the awards shows down to one—one good one with a qualified jury and proof that the advertising was an unqualified success. That would be bearable, and awards might take on meaning again.

Or best of all, let's lionize the advertising person's only real award: the knowledge that his or her ad sold the product. I think Al Hampel, ex-creative director of the agency once known as Benton & Bowles, said it best in his now-famous line: "It's not creative unless it sells."

In the last analysis, that's the only award that really counts.

24

The Spectrum Analysis®: The Three Most Important Questions in Advertising

Whenever I see lousy advertising, I try to analyze why I think it's lousy. Over the years, this exercise has helped me become aware of not only what makes advertising bad but, more important, how to make it good. It all comes down to three questions. The failure to ask them guarantees bad advertising. And while answering all three questions doesn't guarantee great advertising, it at least assures reasonably good advertising. The three questions are the simplest, most basic, most obvious questions you can think of. Maybe that's why so many adpeople don't think of them. The questions must be asked in order because the answer to each influences the answer to the next one. And they must be asked before any copywriter puts down a word or any art director picks up a magic marker. The questions?

The first one is *who*—who are you talking to? Any creative person who doesn't demand the answer to this question from the account or research people is masochistic. If they don't have the answer for you, don't have the creative for them. And don't settle

The Spectrum Analysis® is a Registered Service Mark of Hank Seiden.

for a general answer—demand a very detailed description of the demographics and psychographics of the target audience. The better you know your customers, the better you can sell them.

The second question is *what*—what do you say to them? What *one* thing? When you say more than one thing, you say nothing. You're looking for that one salient appeal that will make the *who* identified in the first question want to try your product. You can't possibly know what you want to say if you don't know to whom you're saying it. Choose carefully because if you're wrong, you've wasted your client's money. How do you know you're right? You don't. Only the *who* people know for sure, so go ask them. Good research leads to good advertising.

The third question is the first question everyone jumps to answer because it's the fun and games, the show biz of the ad game. And that's just the problem—answering the third question first is the single biggest reason for third-rate advertising. First-rate advertising requires that it be answered third. The question is *how*—how do you say it? Execution can make or break the advertising. It will break it—I guarantee it—if you haven't already answered the first two questions. *How* a message is communicated depends upon the message to be communicated. The objective of the *how* question is to determine how best to communicate the *what* to the *who*. You should test various executions of the same concept to the target audience.

These three questions hold the answer to good advertising: *the right execution of the right appeal to the right audience.* It's as easy as *who, what, how!*

I have developed an easy way to answer these three simple questions. A way that also assures me that I don't go off half-cocked and answer these crucial questions before I've considered all the possibilities. I call it The Spectrum Analysis. The Spectrum Analysis is a methodology for arriving at the *who, what, how* for any product or service at any point in time. At my agency, we do a Spectrum Analysis for every client at least once a year, more often if the competitive environment changes. If the competition changes its position, its budget, its distribution, its claim, its pricing, its promotion, its product, or if its share changes, or a new competitor comes into the category, we do another Spectrum Analysis to review our strategy. It has never failed to give me new insights into old or new problems. At its best, it has opened my eyes and my mind and enabled me to view things in new ways and has led to innovative, breakthrough, unique solutions that I would never have come upon without The Spectrum Analysis.

Here's how it works:

"**WHO ARE WE TALKING TO?**" must be the first question asked. It leads to the first spectrum of The Spectrum Analysis, called:

THE TARGET AUDIENCE SPECTRUM

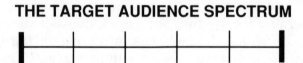

Since no advertiser, not even the largest, has enough money to reach everyone in the prospect universe, *the objective of this first spectrum is to select the most likely prospects for the product* from among all the possible target audience segments.

The outer parameters of this spectrum and the criteria to be considered will vary with the product and its competitive situation at the time. Existing research, new research, a combination of both, and/or intuitive feeling may and should be fed into the spectrum. Eventually, a single segment on the spectrum is selected as the primary target audience, with possible secondary audiences identified as well.

"**WHAT DO WE WANT TO SAY TO THEM?**" is the next question, and it leads to the second spectrum of The Spectrum Analysis, called:

THE APPEALS SPECTRUM

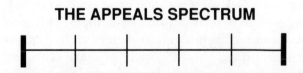

The objective of The Appeals Spectrum is to determine the one single appeal that will most likely influence the target audience (as identified in the preceding spectrum) *to buy that product.* Since all good advertising is single-minded, The Appeals Spectrum forces the selection of a single salient appeal after due consideration of all other possible appeals. It is a search for the product's "Unique Advantage" over competition, be it an inherent advantage, a preemptive advantage, a perceived advantage, or even a unique "disadvantage."

By and large, intuition, creativity, and gut feel play a larger role in plotting The Appeals Spectrum (which is more subjective) than in plotting the previous Target Audience Spectrum (which should be objective). Three appeals are usually selected for concept testing among a sample of the target audience to determine the single strongest appeal. (In the event that only one appeal seems viable, that appeal is tested monadically against a control.)

"HOW DO WE SAY IT?" is the third and last question. It leads to the final spectrum of The Spectrum Analysis, called:

THE EXECUTION SPECTRUM

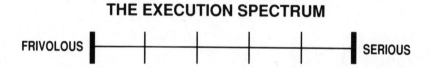

FRIVOLOUS   SERIOUS

The objective of The Execution Spectrum is to determine how best to communicate the selected appeal to the selected target audience (as already determined by the preceding two spectrums). Which executional technique is best for any particular product depends upon the appeal to be used to sell that product. *How* a message is communicated depends upon the message to be communicated. The *how* must always be compatible with the *what.* Serious appeals for serious products should be communicated seriously, or credibility will suffer. Fun appeals for fun products should be communicated with fun executions, or credibility of the fun will suffer.

Unlike the two previous spectrums, the outer parameters of The Execution Spectrum generally remain the same for all products and all situations, as do the points on the spectrum. The techniques of execution are finite. There are only a limited number of ways to execute any commercial or print ad. I have narrowed it to twenty-four techniques which loosely cover all the advertising I've ever dealt with.

Several execution techniques (three is ideal) are selected for testing. Rough ads or storyboards combining the winning appeal with each of the three selected executions are then tested among the target audience, and the strongest executional technique is determined.

The winning ad or commercial is the final result of The Spectrum Analysis, since it combines the right appeal with the right execution to the right target audience.

———

That's it. It's a lot simpler to do than to explain. To prove it, here are three examples from my files. They cover three different products (one is a service), three different problems, and three different solutions. The only thing they have in common is The Spectrum Analysis. (Sorry, I can't reveal the names of the products, but you're free to guess.)

Problem 1:
How Do You Mass Market an Italian Wine to an American Public Uncomfortable With Wine?

Who?

See Figure 1. Note that we decided the most important criterion to look at in the selection of a target audience was present drink preference. We knew that our wine had to replace some other drink for share of belly. We eliminated all the audience segments on the right side of the spectrum (class) for reasons of incompatibility with our product (a naturally effervescent, inexpensive, semi-dry wine) and/or inability to provide a mass audience, which was a key goal. The two audience segments most compatible with both product characteristics and the possibility of mass sales were soft drink and beer drinkers. We then identified everything we knew demographically and psychographically

Figure 1

THE TARGET AUDIENCE SPECTRUM
BY DRINK PREFERENCE

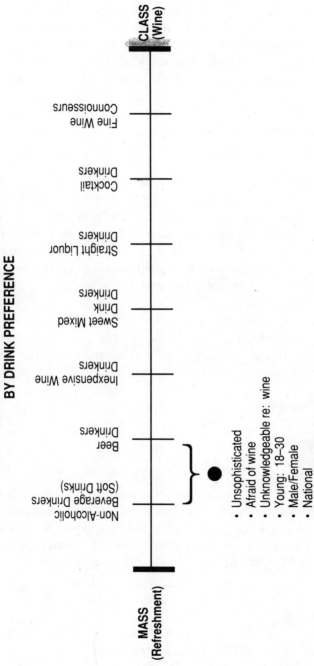

MASS
(Refreshment)

CLASS
(Wine)

Non-Alcoholic Beverage Drinkers (Soft Drinks)

Beer Drinkers

Inexpensive Wine Drinkers

Sweet Mixed Drink Drinkers

Straight Liquor Drinkers

Cocktail Drinkers

Fine Wine Connoisseurs

- Unsophisticated
- Afraid of wine
- Unknowledgeable re: wine
- Young: 18–30
- Male/Female
- National
- Hot dog & burger crowd
- Like slight effervescence
- Like ice-cold refreshment

about soft drink and beer drinkers, particularly as it related to their feelings about wine. Understanding these traits would be crucial to communicating our message to them.

Another critical point was made absolutely clear by this spectrum: *We were not competing in the wine category. We were a refreshment.*

What?

See Figure 2. We knew from our positioning as a beverage that we had to eliminate all appeals competitive with wine. All four beverage appeals on the left of the spectrum were strategically correct, but the two most competitive against soft drinks and beer were the most focused. These appeals would equate our wine with the target audience's soft drinks and beer (refreshing, ice-cold, casual, picnics, hot dogs and burgers, fun), making them comfortable with it.

And, very important, by equating our wine with soft drinks and beer, we weren't asking the target audience to change its life-style (very difficult to do) to accommodate wine. We were only asking it to change its drink within its present life-style (much easier).

How?

Since we were appealing to soft drink/beer drinkers, trying to convince them that our wine could serve as a substitute, the execution should look and sound as much like soft drink/beer commercials as possible. The executional techniques most associated with those commercials are musicals, jingles, contemporary situations, settings, young people having fun (see Figure 3).

Summary

Who? Soft drink and beer drinkers.
What? Substitute our wine for soft drink/beer. Same serv-

Figure 2

THE APPEALS SPECTRUM

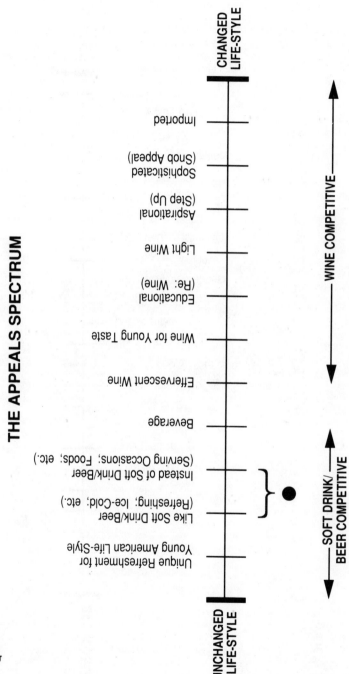

CHANGED LIFE-STYLE

Imported

Sophisticated (Snob Appeal)

Aspirational (Step Up)

Light Wine

Educational (Re: Wine)

Wine for Young Taste

Effervescent Wine

Beverage

Instead of Soft Drink/Beer (Serving Occasions; Foods; etc.)

Like Soft Drink/Beer (Refreshing; Ice-Cold; etc.)

Unique Refreshment for Young American Life-Style

UNCHANGED LIFE-STYLE

WINE COMPETITIVE

SOFT DRINK/ BEER COMPETITIVE

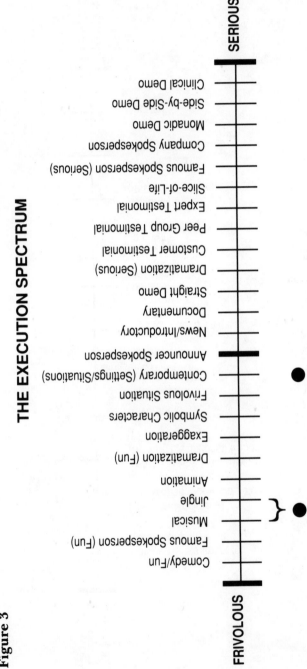

Figure 3

THE EXECUTION SPECTRUM

FRIVOLOUS

Comedy/Fun
Famous Spokesperson (Fun)
Musical
Jingle
Animation
Dramatization (Fun)
Exaggeration
Symbolic Characters
Frivolous Situation
Contemporary (Settings/Situations)
Announcer Spokesperson
News/Introductory
Documentary
Straight Demo
Dramatization (Serious)
Customer Testimonial
Peer Group Testimonial
Expert Testimonial
Slice-of-Life
Famous Spokesperson (Serious)
Company Spokesperson
Monadic Demo
Side-by-Side Demo
Clinical Demo

SERIOUS

ing occasions, same food, same fun, same ice-cold refreshment.

How?   Mimic soft drink/beer executions (musicals, jingles, contemporary).

Addendum: This was the first time a wine was positioned as a refreshment/beverage; the first time an imported wine was successfully sold to a mass market; the first time it was suggested a wine be served ice-cold. This wine almost immediately outsold all other imported wines combined—as much as twelve times more than its nearest competition.

Problem 2:
How Does a Fitness Center Distinguish Itself From All Others Making the Same Promises?

Who?

See Figure 4a, and note that we eliminated those who already belonged to other health/fitness clubs because, first, they didn't represent immediate sales since they were not likely to switch until their memberships expired and, second, because most of them would be unhappy with the serious nature of our club and its emphasis on cardiovascular fitness. Most joined their present clubs for the social atmosphere and their emphasis on the body beautiful. They would find our facilities lacking—with no pools, no body-building equipment, no snack bars, and mandatory, unglamourous, standard uniforms.

We also eliminated independent exercisers because they were a tough sell—basically loners, nonjoiners, already in good shape, and too small a market.

The sedentary group represented by far the largest potential market, if we could find a new reason, more motivating than any ever given before by any of the other fitness clubs, for them to join.

Figure 4a

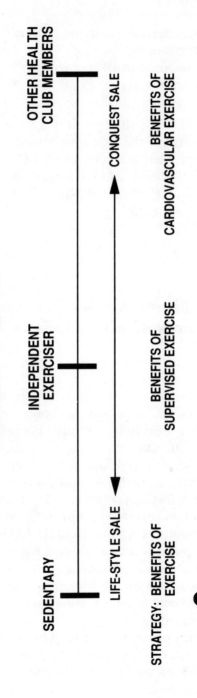

THE TARGET AUDIENCE SPECTRUM
A. BY EXERCISE LIFE-STYLE

SEDENTARY

INDEPENDENT EXERCISER

OTHER HEALTH CLUB MEMBERS

LIFE-STYLE SALE

CONQUEST SALE

STRATEGY: BENEFITS OF EXERCISE

BENEFITS OF SUPERVISED EXERCISE

BENEFITS OF CARDIOVASCULAR EXERCISE

As highlighted in Figure 4b, career status was an important criterion because all of our locations were situated in business districts and all present members were white-collar executives. Because junior executives were still in good physical shape, too young to be concerned about their health and not earning enough to afford our relatively high membership fee, we eliminated them from our target audience.

Middle managers, however, had reached the age when they knew they were quickly falling out of shape, were beginning to feel their age and vulnerability to younger rivals, and were earning enough to be able to manage the high fee. They were a secondary market for us.

We chose top management executives as the primary prospects because they generally knew they were out of condition, worked too hard, were losing energy, feeling tired, and had seen many of their contemporaries forced out or into retirement. We assumed that many had also been advised by their doctors to get more exercise. And, of course, money was no object. From another point of view, they were doubly attractive because they could recommend and influence a profitable corporate membership.

Thus, the target audience for our fitness club was a sedentary top-level executive, aged 45 to 65, with an office close to one of our centers.

What?

See Figure 5. Health and vanity appeals were traditional in the industry. Some clubs stressed health more, others, vanity. Our client, over many years, had explored every aspect of the health appeal and had possibly already attracted every health-vulnerable prospect in the area. The club's membership roster had been on a plateau for several years. In order to broaden our appeal to sedentary top executives who had never responded to either health or vanity and to distinguish us from all others, a new appeal was needed. Considering our target audience, the career appeal, never proposed by any club before, seemed relevant. Within the overall career appeal, the specific benefit of "Energy for Success" seemed very motivating for our audience. An important sec-

(*Text continues on page 248.*)

Figure 4b

THE TARGET AUDIENCE SPECTRUM
B. BY AGE AND CAREER STATUS

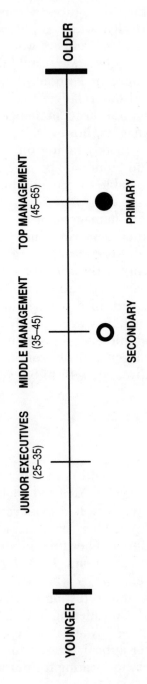

Figure 5

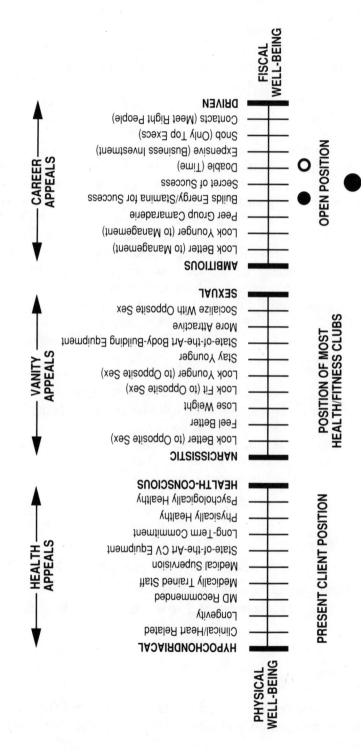

THE APPEALS SPECTRUM

ondary appeal was the assurance that each workout session would require only an hour of the member's valuable time.

How?

As noted in Figure 6, we selected customer testimonials as the appropriate executional technique for our selected target audience and appeal. Our upper management prospects would respond favorably and believably to other top-level executives like themselves who were members and who assured them that this exercise program gave them the added energy they needed for success in their business and personal lives. Better still, the executives we selected all looked lean and vigorous, and all had recently been in the news with announcements of major promotions or other accomplishments.

Summary

Who?   Sedentary upper management executives.

What?   Our fitness club will give you the energy for continued business success.

How?   Testimonials from other upper management executives who attributed their success to the energy they got from our fitness club.

Problem 3:
How Do You Make an Old Antacid, With an Old Name, an Old Form, Old Generic Claims, Selling Fifth in Its Category, New and Exciting Again?

Who?

See Figure 7a. Everyone who ever suffered from heartburn, gas, or indigestion and used an over-the-counter remedy for re-

Figure 6

THE EXECUTION SPECTRUM

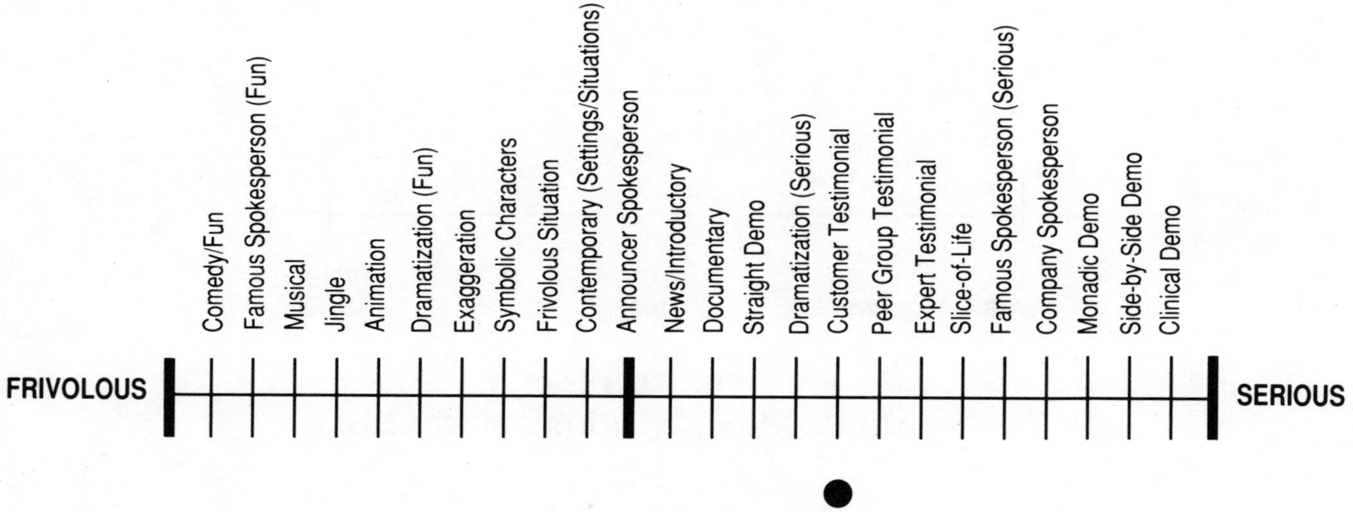

SERIOUS

- Clinical Demo
- Side-by-Side Demo
- Monadic Demo
- Company Spokesperson
- Famous Spokesperson (Serious)
- Slice-of-Life
- Expert Testimonial
- Peer Group Testimonial
- Customer Testimonial
- Dramatization (Serious)
- Straight Demo
- Documentary
- News/Introductory
- Announcer Spokesperson
- Contemporary (Settings/Situations)
- Frivolous Situation
- Symbolic Characters
- Exaggeration
- Dramatization (Fun)
- Animation
- Jingle
- Musical
- Famous Spokesperson (Fun)
- Comedy/Fun

FRIVOLOUS

Figure 7a

THE TARGET AUDIENCE SPECTRUM
A. BY BRAND USAGE

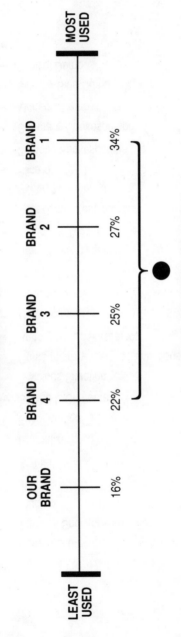

LEAST
USED

OUR
BRAND
16%

BRAND
4
22%

BRAND
3
25%

BRAND
2
27%

BRAND
1
34%

MOST
USED

USERS OF COMPETITIVE BRANDS:
CONQUEST SALE

lief was in our target audience. The overwhelming majority of them used one or more of the four leading brands. This was a classic conquest sale strategy.

———

Since we were the smallest advertiser in the category, we advised concentration of funds against the heavy users in the target audience (see Figure 7b). Those 31 to 40 percent of the target audience accounted for 75 to 80 percent of total usage.

What?

See Figure 8. Heartburn, gas, and indigestion are the price paid by all our prospects for eating the forbidden foods they love. Antacids are taken to relieve the pain. The ultimate promise to people in our target audience would be to enjoy all their favorite foods without fear of pain or discomfort. It is possible if the antacid is taken as a preventive either before eating or right after eating but before pain begins. We would position ourselves as the first antacid pain *preventer*, rather than as a pain *reliever*, as all antacids, including ours, are currently positioned.

How?

See Figure 9. Serious claims for serious products deserve serious executions. Competitive claims against competitive products deserve competitive executions. There's nothing more serious or more competitive than a good competitive side-by-side demonstration. There is no better way to prove something than to show it. Secondarily, this new claim deserved to be treated as big, exciting, breakthrough news because it was big, exciting, breakthrough news to our target audience. The execution recommended was a convincing, competitive demo within a newsy format.

Summary

Who?   Frequent antacid users who treat with competitive products.

(*Text continues on page 255.*)

Figure 7b

THE TARGET AUDIENCE SPECTRUM
B. BY FREQUENCY OF USAGE

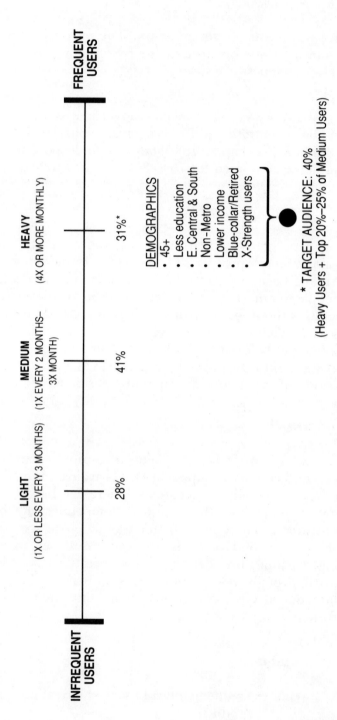

LIGHT
(1X OR LESS EVERY 3 MONTHS)

MEDIUM
(1X EVERY 2 MONTHS–
3X MONTH)

HEAVY
(4X OR MORE MONTHLY)

FREQUENT
USERS

INFREQUENT
USERS

28%

41%

31%*

DEMOGRAPHICS
• 45+
• Less education
• E. Central & South
• Non-Metro
• Lower income
• Blue-collar/Retired
• X-Strength users

* TARGET AUDIENCE: 40%
(Heavy Users + Top 20%–25% of Medium Users)

Figure 8

THE APPEALS SPECTRUM

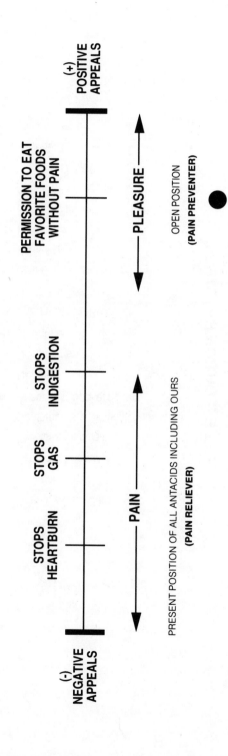

Figure 9

THE EXECUTION SPECTRUM

FRIVOLOUS

Comedy/Fun
Famous Spokesperson (Fun)
Musical
Jingle
Animation
Dramatization (Fun)
Exaggeration
Symbolic Characters
Frivolous Situation
Contemporary (Settings/Situations)
Announcer Spokesperson
News/Introductory
Documentary
Straight Demo
Dramatization (Serious)
Customer Testimonial
Peer Group Testimonial
Expert Testimonial
Slice-of-Life
Famous Spokesperson (Serious)
Company Spokesperson
Monadic Demo
Side-by-Side Demo
Clinical Demo

SERIOUS

What? Now you can eat your favorite foods without pain.

How? Side-by-side scenarios of our user enjoying favorite foods versus competitive user avoiding them, presented as a news story.

―――――

The Spectrum Analysis. It works for me.

Since advertising is not a science, there are no infallible formulas or adpeople. As a matter of fact, the longer I'm in this business, the more I realize how fallible I am. But since advertising is not an art either, there must be some things we know for sure (almost), some body of knowledge accumulated by others throughout the history of advertising, some principles that we know from our own experience work better than others.

We're professionals. We're expected to have a higher batting average of advertising successes than a layman would have. That's what we're paid for. And generally we earn our money because our experience has taught us what usually works and what usually doesn't. The Spectrum Analysis with its three questions is the most important thing I've learned in all my many years in the business.

Index

257